GMAT

Vocabulary Classified 词汇

词以类记

■ 张红岩 编著

群言出版社
QUNYAN PRESS

· 北 京 ·

图书在版编目(CIP)数据

词以类记. GMAT词汇 / 张红岩编著. —北京：群
言出版社，2013（2017.12重印）
ISBN 978-7-80256-436-7

Ⅰ. ①词… Ⅱ. ①张… Ⅲ. ①英语—词汇—研究生—
入学考试—自学参考资料 Ⅳ. ①H313

中国版本图书馆CIP数据核字（2013）第063786号

责任编辑：陈　佳
封面设计：大愚设计

出版发行：群言出版社
地　　址：北京市东城区东厂胡同北巷1号（100006）
网　　址：www.qypublish.com（官网书城）
电子信箱：dywh@xdf.cn　qunyancbs@126.com
联系电话：010-62418641　65267783　65263836
经　　销：全国新华书店

印　　刷：北京鑫海达印刷有限公司
版　　次：2013年5月第1版　2017年12月第11次印刷
开　　本：880mm×1230mm　1/32
印　　张：13
字　　数：240千字
书　　号：ISBN 978-7-80256-436-7
定　　价：35.00元

作者自介

余自幼随知青父母拓荒于大兴安岭，长于辽西古镇兴城，求学乃率性而为，先后修习英语、计算机和工商管理，奉行"Live and learn"，现于北京大学教育学院就读教育经济与管理博士课程。曾于新东方早期挥汗于三尺讲坛，五年间学生超二十万众。受益于新东方讲坛对讲师心智与技能多方面的磨炼，后于留学法国期间以五分钟英语演讲，在学生会竞选中获得来自全球四十二国的、两百多名中高层经理人同学百分之七十的支持，当选法国高商（HEC）MBA学生会主席。乃有机会深入了解所谓欧洲精英阶层，深悟外语在国际交流中的重要，反思我国留学教育中的积弊，现主张将应试教育与应用能力二者尽可能和谐推进，本书便以备考 GMAT 和 MBA 应用为双重目的，方法上沿用"词以类记"这一已证实的有效途径，选词上遍寻最新资料提炼出最全词集，期冀读者多听勤记，尽早超越词汇瓶颈，并应用于考场、课堂和未来管理工作当中。

　　八年前，在新东方教过了二十万学生并见证其中三分之一的学子出国留学后，我也加入了留学生的队伍。和本书的大部分读者一样，我参加了GMAT 考试。我按照国际一流商学院的要求将 GMAT 考到 700 分以上，并于2002~2004 年就读法国高商(HEC)。这所全球最早的商业专科学校以法国人特有的浪漫和专业精神深深地陶冶了我，使我即便今日写此书时也带着不只是希望让大家获得高分这样一个简单的目的，因为在编著此书的过程中，我脑海中时常浮现出下面这个场景：

　　2003 年春天的一个下午，我漫步于诺曼底的海滩，天气十分晴朗，新鲜潮湿的和煦海风吹得人心旷神怡，一个古铜肤色的老人守着一副钓竿，凝望着大西洋，一只老狗蹿前蹿后，不时躺卧在装鱼的水桶边，这幅经典的"老人与海"的画面吸引我轻轻地靠近，却不愿出一言打破这持续已久的宁静。我好奇地向那鱼桶中望去，想看看老人的成果，却只见清水不见鱼。半晌，终于看到老人起竿，从拉线的力度和钓竿的弧度看应该不是一条小鱼，果然一条约40 厘米长的鱼出水了，老人稳健地抄起网，抓到鱼，娴熟地卸下鱼钩，最后走近海水，很自然地将那条鱼放生了。

　　钓鱼是为了放鱼，记单词是为了不用记单词。

　　GMAT(MBA) 词汇到底是什么？我以一个编著了还算为大家所喜欢的GRE / TOEFL / IELTS 词汇书的作者的身份来做个简要介绍：GRE 词汇不是为了在工作学习中用的(绝大多数词汇只在今生今世考此试时才有用，我曾经在留学期间使用 GRE 词汇使老外当场"死机")；TOEFL 和 IELTS 词汇更像是广谱抗菌药，有普适性而无针对性；对于一个立志接受 MBA 教育的学习者来说，无论是在国内读还是国外读，由于其核心课程的理念均源自现代西方经济学、管理学、市场学、金融学、统计学等学科，所需的英语词汇量基本上是相同的，本书的 GMAT 与 MBA 词汇是为了那些以高分通过GMAT 考试并在学习与工作中需要掌握 MBA 必备词汇的读者而设计的，具有应对考试的针对性和现实应用的实用性。

考试针对性：

借助词频分析软件对迄今可获得的 GMAT 资料加以分析，从中得到的有效词条大约有 12 万条，去除不需记忆的专有名词、同词异形、动词不同时态，和过于简单的基础词汇，得到约 3900 个词条，再经过筛选合并得到本书给出的 3000 GMAT 核心词汇，这个结果以词频分析数据为支撑，选词超过目前市场上已有 GMAT 词汇书 1000 多词的标准（目前多为 2000 以下）。这使得那些未经过 TOEFL、IELTS 词汇记忆过程的考生，也能直接接触 GMAT 核心词汇。那些目标只是攻读管理类专业硕士和博士的考生也不必再去背诵 GRE 的超大词汇库，也不必担心以往的 TOEFL 或 IELTS 无法满足 GMAT 考试的需要，直接命中 GMAT 核心词汇。

现实应用性：

在拿到 OFFER 就读 MBA 之前，我曾经有一段时间踌躇满志，希望弥补一下自己在各方面知识上的不足。我认真地看统计学、微积分、经济学等学科的教材，却总是不得要领，觉得如同在海洋中漂泊一样，舀哪瓢水都不踏实。如今读 MBA 对我来说早已成为过去时了，当年教授们常用的词汇和从事管理工作的实践证实，其实所谓"最佳的 MBA 前准备"就是把教授们常说的各类术语搞清楚记下来就好了，而这些概念其实也是 MBA 毕业后要在工作中经常使用的。结合个人体验和众多 MBA 学生的论坛经验，我总结出 200 个 MBA 必备词汇作为本书最后一部分，把握那些词及其意义是读书前最佳的准备，同时也是外行进入 MBA 圈子的捷径。

如何高效率地掌握本书的词汇

GMAT（MBA）核心词汇数目并不算少，在短期内掌握确实需要很好的战略。这里推荐有三：听觉与视觉结合；练习与记诵结合；考试与复查结合。

听觉与视觉结合：

通过听单词来辅助记忆是我对单词记忆最坚定的主张，利用本书配套的音频边听边记具有非常重要的意义，列举其三：

1. 尽管 GMAT 不考核听力，但考虑到这些词汇未来会成为你在 MBA 学习和之后工作中的积极词汇，听熟它们是应对未来必需性应用的关键。

2. 听单词有助于增强记忆效果，建议每天将学过的单词通过听来复习，可以利用乘地铁时、车上、路途中、睡前等机会，这对加深记忆非常见效。

3. 有助于克服惰性，快速复习。词汇书一般要在考前背诵过或复习过 10 遍左右，很多人达到 15 遍。这不是说每一遍都像最初那样要一两个月认真记诵才能完成，未来有很多遍可以通过听单词来快速复习，边听边回想，记得住就不翻书，记不住的就停下来翻书去查证。

练习与记诵结合：

背过单词后通过做练习题来检验记忆效果是最有效的记忆方法之一，而这些练习最好不选用真题。否则在未来练习到一些真题时会有自欺之感，不能客观地进行自我评价。本书的练习没有选真题，而是设置了一个个最适合各个词汇的小语境。

考试与复查结合：

在你备考 GMAT 的过程中一定有过多次模考，这是检查词汇是否记牢的最佳机会。每次考试后记住查证其中影响你理解文章的单词，以进一步加深对这些词的记忆。

最后我给大家的建议是：当你成功地获得 GMAT 高分后，也不要丢弃本书，帮助你通过考试只是本书帮你钓到的第一条鱼，在你未来的 MBA 学习和之后的工作中你都会发现本书是个很好的工具，这本渗透着你汗水的词汇书也许将一直陪伴着你。

感谢好友新东方前副总裁铁岭先生的建议，他帮我坚定了无论如何该为这个很重要的小众考生群体做些事情的决心；非常感谢郝米娜、方芳两位女士在编辑工作中付出的努力。

祝每个读者都能通过本书这个钓竿得到你想要的鱼！

张红岩

目录一

目录二

❖ 属性 ❖

❖ 状态变化 ❖

❖ 物体行为 ❖

❖ 自身行为 ❖

❖ 涉他行为 ❖

❖ 正向评价 ❖

❖ 负向评价 ❖

❖ 负向行为 ❖

❖ 人及相关动作 ❖

❖ 语言 ❖

❖ 其他 ❖

❖ 词组 ❖ / 365

❖ MBA 词汇 ❖ / 371

GMAT 按学科分类 Subjects

Word List 1

数 学(一)

数学(一)

abscissa	[æbˈsɪsə] *n.* 横坐标
	【派】ordinate(*n.* 纵坐标)
absolute value	绝对值
acute angle	锐角
	【派】obtuse angle(钝角)
addition	[əˈdɪʃən] *n.* 加法
adjacent angle	邻角
algebra	[ˈældʒɪbrə] *n.* 代数
algorithm	[ˈælgərɪðəm] *n.* 运算法则
angle bisector	角平分线
angular	[ˈæŋgjələr] *adj.* 有角的，用角度量的；骨瘦如柴的；棱角分明的
	【例】He has a more *angular* figure than his father.
arc	[ɑːrk] *n.* 弧线，弧形物
area	[ˈeriə] *n.* 面积
arithmetic	[əˈrɪθmətɪk] *n.* 算术，计算
arithmetic mean	算术平均数(总和除以个数)
arithmetic progression	等差级数
arm	[ɑːrm] *n.* 直角三角形的股
average	[ˈævərɪdʒ] *n.* 平均数
average out	达到平均数；最终得到平衡
bisect	[baɪˈsekt] *v.* 把…一分为二（to divide into two equal parts）*n.* 二等分
	【例】The new road will *bisect* the town.
	【派】bisection(*n.* 一分为二，对分)
bracket	[ˈbrækɪt] *n.* 括弧；臂架 *vt.* 把…括在括弧内；把…归为一类
	【例】Don't *bracket* me with him just because we work for the same company.
breadth	[bredθ] *n.* 宽度；宽容
	【例】My wife is a woman of great *breadth* of mind.
calculator	[ˈkælkjuleɪtər] *n.* 计算机
	【派】calculate(*v.* 计算；估计) calculation(*n.* 计算)

连线题

denominator	运算法则	midpoint	偶数
arithmetic	弧线	integer	中位线
breadth	算术	even number	不变量
calculus	宽度	geometry	中点
arc	微积分	isosceles triangle	整数
formula	系数	hypotenuse	分数
digit	小数	invariant	等式
dividend	分母	equation	直径
decimal	对角线	fraction	横坐标
algorithm	数字	diameter	代数
coefficient	被除数	abscissa	几何学
diagonal	除数	algebra	弦，斜边
divisor	公式	median	等腰三角形

选词填空

angular	bisect	calculate	dimension	concentric
indices	minus	divisible	length	millimeter

1. I am trying to _____ how much money we need.

2. We need to know the exact _____ of the room.

3. The street plan of the city has evolved as a series of _____ rings.

4. There are 1,000 _____ in one meter.

5. A long road _____ the town from east to west.

6. Twelve is _____ by four.

7. He is a tall, thin boy with _____ face.

8. These are valuable _____ for weight management in obese children.

9. Two _____ two leaves nothing.

10. The hotel pool is 15 meters in _____ .

练习题答案

连线题答案

denominator	分母	midpoint	中点
arithmetic	算术	integer	整数
breadth	宽度	even number	偶数
calculus	微积分	geometry	几何学
arc	弧线	isosceles triangle	等腰三角形
formula	公式	hypotenuse	弦，斜边
digit	数字	invariant	不变量
dividend	被除数	equation	等式
decimal	小数	fraction	分数
algorithm	运算法则	diameter	直径
coefficient	系数	abscissa	横坐标
diagonal	对角线	algebra	代数
divisor	除数	median	中位线

选词填空答案

angular	bisect	calculate	dimension	concentric
indices	minus	divisible	length	millimeter

1. I am trying to (calculate) how much money we need.
2. We need to know the exact (dimensions) of the room.
3. The street plan of the city has evolved as a series of (concentric) rings.
4. There are 1,000 (millimeters) in one meter.
5. A long road (bisects) the town from east to west.
6. Twelve is (divisible) by four.
7. He is a tall, thin boy with (angular) face.
8. These are valuable (indices) for weight management in obese children.
9. Two (minus) two leaves nothing.
10. The hotel pool is 15 meters in (length).

Word List 2

音频

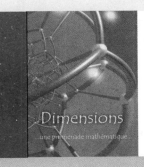

数 学(二)

数学(二)

multiple ['mʌltɪpl] *n.* 倍数 (a number that contains a smaller number, an exact number of times)

【例】20 is a *multiple* of 5.

multiply ['mʌltɪplaɪ] *v.* 乘；增加 (to increase by a large amount)

【例】Children will learn to *multiply* in the second grade.

【派】multiplier(*n.* 乘数)

natural number 自然数

negative number 负数

number ['nʌmbər] *vt.* 达，总计

【例】The population of the town *numbered* about 5,000.

number lines 数轴

numerator ['njuːməreɪtər] *n.* （分数的）分子 (the number above the line in a fraction)

【例】5 is the *numerator* in 5/6.

numerical [njuː'merɪkl] *adj.* 数字的，用数字表示的，数值的 (expressed or considered in numbers)

【例】Make sure the files are organized in *numerical* order.

【派】numerically(*adv.* 数字上)

obtuse angle 钝角

octagon ['ɑːktəgɑːn] *n.* 八边形，八角形

odd number 奇数

ordinate ['ɔːrdɪnət] *n.* 纵坐标

parallel lines 平行线

parallelogram [ˌpærə'leləgræm] *n.* 平行四边形

parameter [pə'ræmɪtər] *n.* 参数；【物】参量

pentagon ['pentəgɑːn] *n.* 五边形；五角大楼(美国国防部)

perimeter [pə'rɪmɪtər] *n.* 周长 (the whole length of the border around an area or shape)；周边，边缘

permutation [ˌpɜːrmju'teɪʃn] *n.* 排列，序列 (one of the different ways in which a number of things can be arranged)；互换

【例】a sandwich shop that sells every possible *permutation* of meat and bread

perpendicular	[ˌpɜːrpən ˈdɪkjələr] *adj.* 垂直的(vertical)，成直角的；直立的
	【例】a road *perpendicular* to the highway
	【派】perpendicularly(*adv.* 直立地)
plane	[pleɪn] *n.* 平面
plus	[plʌs] *n.* 加号 *adj.* 正的 *prep.* (运算中)加(add)
	【例】Three *plus* six equals nine.
polygon	[ˈpɑːlɪgɑːn] *n.* 多边形，多角形 (a flat shape with three or more sides)
	【派】polygonal(*adj.* 多边形的)
positive number	正数
power	[ˈpaʊər] *n.* 次方，乘方
	【例】How much is the sixth *power* of nine?
prime factor	质因数
prime number	质数
product	[ˈprɑːdʌkt] *n.* 乘积
proper fraction	真分数
pyramid	[ˈpɪrəmɪd] *n.* 棱锥，角锥；金字塔
quadrant	[ˈkwɑːdrənt] *n.* 象限，四分体
quadratic	[kwɑːˈdrætɪk] *adj.* 二次的 *n.* 二次方程式
quadrilateral	[ˌkwɑːdrɪ ˈlætərəl] *adj.* 四边(形)的 *n.* 四边形
quadruple	[kwɑːˈdruːpl] *adj.* 四倍的，四边组成的 *n.* 四倍数 *v.* (使)成四倍 (to increase and become four times)
	【例】The company has *quadrupled* its profits in just three years.
quotient	[ˈkwoʊʃnt] *n.* 商，商数
radial	[ˈreɪdiəl] *adj.* 光线的；半径的；沿半径转动的
	【例】*radial* roads leading out of the city center
radius	[ˈreɪdiəs] *n.* 半径(距离)(the distance from the center to the edge of a circle)
ratio	[ˈreɪʃioʊ] *n.* 比例，比率
	【例】The *ratio* of nursing staff to doctors is 2:1.
rectangle	[ˈrektæŋgl] *n.* 长方形，矩形
rectangular prism	矩形棱柱体
regular polygon	正多边形
remainder	[rɪ ˈmeɪndər] *n.* 差数，余数；剩余物

rhombus	['rɑːmbəs] *n.* 菱形
right angle	直角
right triangle	直角三角形
salient	['seɪliənt] *n.* 凸角 *adj.* 显著的，主要的（most important or noticeable）
	【例】the *salient* points of the report
	【派】salience(*n.* 突出；特点)
scalene triangle	不等边三角形
semicircular	['semi'sɜːrkjələr] *adj.* 半圆的
side	[saɪd] *n.* 侧面，边(one of the flat surfaces or edges of a shape)
	【例】A cube has six *sides*.
spatial	['speɪʃl] *adj.* 三维空间的
	【例】This part of brain judges the *spatial* relationship between objects.
	【派】spatially(*adv.* 空间地)
square	[skwer] *n.* 平方数
square root	平方根
straight angle	平角
subset	['sʌbset] *n.* 子集
	【例】a small *subset* of the city's immigrant population
subtract	[səb'trækt] *vt.* 减去(deduct)
	【例】If you *subtract* 2 from 6, you get 4.
	【派】subtraction(*n.* 减，减法)
sum	[sʌm] *n.* 和；总数 *v.* 合计(summarize)；概括
	【例】Gerald will open the debate and I will *sum* up.
	【派】summing(*adj.* 求和的)
surface area	表面积
tangent	['tændʒənt] *n.* 正切，切线 *adj.* 正切的，相切的
	【派】tangency(*n.* 接触；相切)
theorem	['θiːərəm] *n.* 原理；定理，命题(statement in mathematics)
times	[taɪmz] *n.* 倍(数)；年代 *prep.* 乘，乘以(multiplied by)
	【例】Two *times* two equals four.
total	['toʊtl] *n.* 总数，合计
trapezium	[trə'piːziəm] *n.* 梯形
triangle	['traɪæŋgl] *n.* 三角形
triple	['trɪpl] *v.* 三倍于(increase by three times as much)
	【例】The company has *tripled* in size.

variable	['veəriəbl] *n.* 变量 *adj.* 可变的，变化无常的 (likely to change)
	【例】Expect *variable* cloudiness and fog tomorrow.
	【派】variably(*adv.* 易变地) variability(*n.* 变化性，易变)
variance	['veriəns] *n.* 【统】方差；差异，不一致 (difference)
	【例】Tradition and culture are often at *variance* with the needs of modern living.
vector	['vektər] *n.* 矢量，向量
vertex	['vɜːrteks] *n.* （三角形、圆锥体等与底相对的）顶，（三角形、多边形等的）角的顶点
vertex angle	顶角
vertical	['vɜːr tɪkl] *adj.* 垂直的 (perpendicular, upright)
	【例】*vertical* window blinds
	【派】vertically(*adv.* 垂直地)
vertical angle	对顶角
whole number	整数
width	[wɪdθ] *n.* 宽 (breadth)
	【例】What's the *width* of the desk?

Man errs so long as he strives.
人只要奋斗就会犯错误。

——德国诗人、剧作家 歌德
(*Johann Wolfgang Goethe, German poet and dramatist*)

练 习 题

连线题

permutation	负数	subset	半圆的
pyramid	分子	variable	子集
pentagon	平行线	remainder	梯形
numerator	参量	semicircular	三角形
positive number	五边形	theorem	变量
quotient	排列, 序列	trapezium	正切, 切线
negative number	平面	tangent	差数, 余数
radius	正数	surface area	比例, 比率
rectangle	多边形	triangle	菱形
parallel lines	棱锥	variance	平方根
plane	商, 商数	ratio	表面积
polygon	半径	square root	定理, 命题
parameter	长方形	rhombus	方差, 差异

选词填空

multiply	vertical	spatial	width	vertex
plus	perimeter	parallel	sum	subtract

1. The railway is _____ with the canal.

2. The origin in a polar coordinate system: the _____ of a polar angle.

3. The cliff is almost _____.

4. The little girl has begun to learn to add and _____.

5. You will have to pay the _____ of the two sets of costs.

6. What is the _____ of this polygon?

7. John is doing a research on the _____distribution of Chinese culture.

8. Five _____ two equals seven.

9. We then _____ the total by 10.

10.That is a road of great _____.

连线题答案

permutation	排列，序列	subset	子集
pyramid	棱锥	variable	变量
pentagon	五边形	remainder	差数，余数
numerator	分子	semicircular	半圆的
positive number	正数	theorem	定理，命题
quotient	商，商数	trapezium	梯形
negative number	负数	tangent	正切，切线
radius	半径	surface area	表面积
rectangle	长方形	triangle	三角形
parallel lines	平行线	variance	方差，差异
plane	平面	ratio	比例，比率
polygon	多边形	square root	平方根
parameter	参量	rhombus	菱形

选词填空答案

multiply	vertical	spatial	width	vertex
plus	perimeter	parallel	sum	subtract

1. The railway is（parallel）with the canal.
2. The origin in a polar coordinate system: the（vertex）of a polar angle.
3. The cliff is almost（vertical）.
4. The little girl has begun to learn to add and（subtract）.
5. You will have to pay the（sum）of the two sets of costs.
6. What is the（perimeter）of this polygon?
7. John is doing a research on the（spatial）distribution of Chinese culture.
8. Five（plus）two equals seven.
9. We then（multiply）the total by 10.
10.That is a road of great（width）.

Word List 3

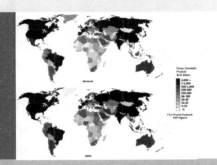

经　济

经 济

accountant	[əˈkaʊntənt] *n.* 会计师
	【派】accounting(*n.* 会计，会计学) accountancy(*n.* 会计工作)
agent	[ˈeɪdʒənt] *n.* 代理商，经纪人(representative)；【化】作用剂
	【派】agency(*n.* 代理行，经销处)
antitrust law	反托拉斯法
audit	[ˈɔːdɪt] *n./v.* 审计
	【例】The *audit* of the man's estate revealed unpaid taxes.
	【派】auditor(*n.* 审计员)
bankrupt	[ˈbæŋkrʌpt] *adj.* 破产的，倒闭的 *n.* 破产者
	【记】bank(银行) + rupt(断) → 破产的
	【例】The firm went *bankrupt* before the building work was completed.
	【派】bankruptcy(*n.* 破产)
borrowing	[ˈbɒːroʊɪŋ] *n.* 借款
brokerage	[ˈbroʊkərɪdʒ] *n.* 经纪业；佣金，经纪费
	【派】broker(*n.* 经纪人)
budget	[ˈbʌdʒɪt] *n.* 预算，经费
capitalistic	[ˌkæpɪtəˈlɪstɪk] *adj.* 资本主义的，资本家的
	【派】capital(*n.* 资本；首府，首都) capitalism(*n.* 资本主义) capitalist(*n.* 资本家 *adj.* 资本家的，资本主义的)
commercial	[kəˈmɜːrʃl] *adj.* 商业的，商务的(relating to commerce)
	【例】He failed to see the *commercial* value of his discovery.
compound interest	复利
consortium	[kənˈsɔːrtiəm] *n.* (数家公司或银行联合组成的)财团；联营企业
coupon	[ˈkuːpɑːn] *n.* 赠券；配给券
currency	[ˈkɜːrənsi] *n.* 通货，货币(money)
deficit	[ˈdefɪsɪt] *n.* 赤字
	【例】The government tried to avoid a budget *deficit*.
economic	[ˌiːkəˈnɑːmɪk] *adj.* 经济学的，经济的
	【派】economics(*n.* 经济学)
economical	[ˌiːkəˈnɑːmɪkl] *adj.* 节省的，节约的
	【例】My new car is *economical* of fuel.
economy	[ɪˈkɑːnəmi] *n.* 经济；节省，经济实惠
financial crash	金融危机

fiscal	[ˈfɪskl] *adj.* 政府财政的 (related to government finances)
	【例】The increase of taxation is an important *fiscal* policy.
free market	自由竞争的市场
GNP	Gross National Products 的缩写, 国民生产总值
import relief	进口援助 (设置壁垒以保护民族工业)
inflation	[ɪnˈfleɪʃn] *n.* 通货膨胀 (a continuing increase in prices)
	【例】*Inflation* is now running at over 16%.
interest rate	利率
inventory	[ˈɪnvəntɔːri] *n.* 物品清单; 库存品
	【例】We made an *inventory* of everything in the apartment.
investment	[ɪnˈvestmənt] *n.* 投资, 投资额; (时间、精力的) 投入
	【例】A Certificate of Deposit remains one of the safest *investments*.
invigorate	[ɪnˈvɪɡəreɪt] *vt.* 鼓舞, 激励 (if something invigorates you, it makes you feel healthier, stronger and have more energy)
	【例】He felt *invigorated* after a day in the country.
keynesian	[ˈkeɪnziən] *adj.* (英国资产阶级经济学家) 凯恩斯的; 凯恩斯主义的
laissez-faire capitalism	放任自由式资本主义; 自由资本主义
list price	标价
managerial	[ˌmænəˈdʒɪriəl] *adj.* 经理的 (relating to the job of a manager); 管理上的
	【例】*managerial* skills
margin	[ˈmɑːrdʒən] *n.* 成本与售价的差额, 赚头 (the difference between what it costs a business to buy something and what they sell it for); 保证金
	【例】*Margins* are low and many companies are struggling.
mark up	涨价
mark down	降价
mercantilist	[mɜːrˈkæntɪlɪst] *n.* 重商主义者
merchandise	[ˈmɜːrtʃəndaɪz] *n.* 商品 (commodities, goods) *vt.* 买卖, 经营 (market)
	【例】If the product is properly *merchandised*, it should sell very well.
	【派】merchant (*n.* 商人)
monetary	[ˈmʌnɪteri] *adj.* 货币的, 钱的 (relating to money, especially all the money in a particular country)
	【例】the government's tight *monetary* policy

mortgage	['mɔːrgɪdʒ] *n.* 抵押借款 *vt.* 抵押

【例】We *mortgaged* our house to start Paul's business.

nickel	['nɪkl] *n.* 镍，镍币
outlet	['aʊtlet] *n.* (河流等)出口，通风口；发泄(感情或精力)的方法；销路
output	['aʊtpʊt] *n.* 产出，产量(the amount of goods or work produced by a factory, etc.)；输出
pension	['penʃn] *n.* 养老金，退休金

【例】At what age can you start drawing your *pension*?

per capita	[pər 'kæpɪtə] *adj.* 照人数分配的，人均的(of or for each person)

【例】*Per capita* incomes rose sharply last year.

premium	['priːmiəm] *n.* 保险金(the cost of insurance)
privatize	['praɪvətaɪz]*vt.* 使私有化

【例】The government *privatized* a state-owned corporation.

【派】privatization(*n.* 私有化)

proceeds	['proʊsiːdz] *n.* [*pl.*] 收入(款项)
produce	['prɑːduːs] *n.* 农产品(food produced on a farm)
productivity	[ˌproʊdʌk'tɪvəti] *n.* 生产力，生产率(the rate at which goods are produced, and the amount produced)

【例】high *productivity* levels in manufacturing

profit	['prɑːfɪt] *n.* 利润(money gained after costs paid)
profitable	['prɑːfɪtəbl] *adj.* 有利可图的，可获利的(producing a profit or a useful result)

【例】The advertising campaign proved very *profitable*.

【派】profitably(*adv.* 有利地) profitability(*n.* 盈利性)

purchasing price	买价
quota	['kwoʊtə] *n.* 限额，定额(portion, share)
rate	[reɪt] *n.* 费率；比率

【例】Australia's unemployment *rate* rose to 6.5% in February.

rating	['reɪtɪŋ] *n.* 级别；等级，军阶；(商人、商店等)信用程度
real estate	不动产，房地产
receipt	[rɪ'siːt] *n.* 收到；收据(a piece of paper showing that you have paid for something)；收入

recession [rɪ'seʃn] *n.* 经济衰退（a difficult time when there is less trade etc.）; 后退

【例】There is deep *recession* in the U.K.

recurrent [rɪ'kɜːrənt] *adj.* 经常发生的，周期性的（happening or appearing several times）

【例】Political revolution is a *recurrent* theme in Riley's books.

【派】recurrently（*adv.* 反复地）

revenue ['revənuː] *n.* 收入（income, returns, earnings）

sale price 卖价

simple interest 单利

sluggish economy 萧条的经济

statistic [stə'tɪstɪk] *n.* 统计数据

【派】statistics（*n.* 统计学，统计表）statistical（*adj.* 统计的）statistically（*adv.* 统计上地）

stipend ['staɪpend] *n.* 薪水（salary）; 养老金（pension）

stock [stɑːk] *n.* 股票；家畜；储备（storage）
adj. 普通的，惯用的（usual）

【例】*stock* item

【派】stockholder（*n.* 股票持有者，股东）

subcontract [ˌsʌb'kɑːntrækt] *n.* 转包合同，分包合同
vt. 转包

【例】Some of the work will be *subcontracted* to another company.

subsidize ['sʌbsɪdaɪz] *vt.* 资助，补助（pay costs）

【例】Farming is heavily *subsidized*.

【派】subsidized（*adj.* 资助的）subsidization（*n.* 资助）

subsidy ['sʌbsədi] *n.* 补贴；津贴（allowance）

surplus ['sɜːrpləs] *n.* 过剩，剩余（物资）*adj.* 过剩的（extra, excess）

【例】The farmer's *surplus* grain was stored in silos.

tariff ['tærɪf] *n.* 关税，关税表

transaction [træn'zækʃn] *n.* 交易（business, trade, deal）

【记】trans（交换）+ action（活动）→ 交易

treasury ['treʒəri] *n.* 宝库，宝藏；国库，国库券

【例】*Treasury* Bill

turnaround ['tɜːrnəraʊnd] *n.* 周转期；起色；彻底转变（a complete change）

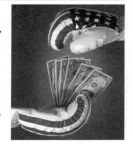

【例】The average *turnaround* for a passport application is six working days.

turnover ['tɜːrnoʊvər] *n.* 营业额，销售比率（the amount of business）

【例】The illicit drugs industry has an annual *turnover* of some £200 billion.

unemployment [ˌʌnɪm'plɔɪmənt] *n.* 失业（joblessness），失业人数，失业率

property ['prɑːpəti] *n.* 财产（possession）；性质

【例】Some of the stolen *property* was found in Mason's house.

proxy ['prɑːksi] *n.* 代理人（deputy）

【例】I'm acting as a *proxy* for the president while he's on vacation.

collateral [kə'lætərəl] *n.* 抵押品

consume [kən'suːm] *vt.* 消费，消耗（spend）

【记】con + sum（结束）+ e → 全部结束 → 消耗

【例】Americans *consume* a huge amount of sugar each year.

【派】consumer（*n.* 顾客）consumption（*n.* 消费，消耗）

takeover ['teɪkoʊvər] *n.* 收购；接收；控制

【例】Thornbury has announced a *takeover* bid of a regional TV company.

default [dɪ'fɔːlt] *n.* 不履行责任（nonfulfilment）*v.* 不履行；拖欠债务

【记】de（犯）+ fault（错误）→ 拖欠债务

【例】If they can't raise the money to pay the debt, they will have to *default*.

Ordinary people merely think how they shall spend their time; a man of talent tries to use it.

普通人只想到如何度过时间，有才能的人设法利用时间。

——德国哲学家 叔本华

（*Arthur Schopenhauer, German philosopher*）

练 习 题

连线题

financial crash	会计师	tariff	房地产
deficit	预算	transaction	收据
list price	资本家的	property	收入
accountant	保险金	collateral	关税
capitalistic	金融危机	receipt	有利可图的
mortgage	库存品	output	自由竞争的市场
currency	标价	statistic	交易
pension	通货膨胀	real estate	产出，产量
inventory	通货，货币	profitable	财产
premium	抵押借款	free market	抵押品
inflation	限额	revenue	周转期
quota	赤字	turnover	统计数据
budget	养老金	turnaround	营业额

选词填空

bankrupt	consume	invigorate	productivity	recession
subsidy	unemployment	commercial	surplus	privatize

1. The government wants to _____ some state-owned enterprises.
2. Our top priorities must be profit and _____ growth.
3. A rapid rise in price soon leads to mass _____.
4. At my age, a walk into the town is enough to _____ me.
5. Computers have greatly increased _____ in business offices.
6. America's textile industry had been badly hit by the worldwide economic _____.
7. Food _____ are necessary for keeping down the price of dairy products and bread.
8. The fire soon _____ the wooden buildings.
9. The firm went _____ before the building work was completed.
10. The manufacturers in some countries dumped their _____ commodities abroad.

练习题答案

连线题答案

financial crash	金融危机	tariff	关税
deficit	赤字	transaction	交易
list price	标价	property	财产
accountant	会计师	collateral	抵押品
capitalistic	资本家的	receipt	收据
mortgage	抵押借款	output	产出，产量
currency	通货，货币	statistic	统计数据
pension	养老金	real estate	房地产
inventory	库存品	profitable	有利可图的
premium	保险金	free market	自由竞争的市场
inflation	通货膨胀	revenue	收入
quota	限额	turnover	营业额
budget	预算	turnaround	周转期

选词填空答案

bankrupt	consume	invigorate	productivity	recession
subsidy	unemployment	commercial	surplus	privatize

1. The government wants to（privatize）some state-owned enterprises.

2. Our top priorities must be profit and（commercial）growth.

3. A rapid rise in price soon leads to mass（unemployment）.

4. At my age, a walk into the town is enough to（invigorate）me.

5. Computers have greatly increased（productivity）in business offices.

6. America's textile industry had been badly hit by the worldwide economic（recession）.

7. Food（subsidies）are necessary for keeping down the price of dairy products and bread.

8. The fire soon（consumed）the wooden buildings.

9. The firm went（bankrupt）before the building work was completed.

10. The manufacturers in some countries dumped their（surplus）commodities abroad.

Word List 4

音频

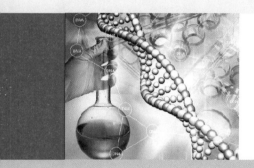

医 学(一)

医学（一）

acupuncture	[ˈækjupʌŋktʃər] n. 针刺（疗法）
adrenal	[əˈdriːnl] n. 肾上腺 adj. 肾上腺的
ambulance	[ˈæmbjələns] n. 救护车
amphetamine	[æmˈfetəmiːn] n. 苯丙胺，安非他明
analgesic	[ˌænəlˈdʒiːzɪk] n. 镇痛剂（pain-killer）
anesthetic	[ˌænəsˈθiːtɪk] adj. 麻醉的；麻木的 n. 麻醉剂

【派】anesthesia(n. 麻醉；麻木)

antipsychotic	[ˌæntisaɪˈkɑːtɪk] adj. 抑制精神的（preventing or treating psychosis）n. 安定药
astringent	[əˈstrɪndʒənt] n. 止血药；收敛剂 adj. 止血的；收敛的；严厉的（hard, severe）

【例】He had an *astringent* style of writing.

cancerous	[ˈkænsərəs] adj. 癌的，癌性的

【记】cancer(癌症) + ous → 癌的

clinical	[ˈklɪnɪkl] adj. 诊所的，医院的（relating to a clinic）
coronary angiography	冠状血管照相术
diagnose	[ˌdaɪəɡˈnoʊs] vt. 诊断；分析（analyze）

【例】A pathologist *diagnosed* the fatal virus.

【派】diagnosis(n. 诊断)

dope	[doʊp] n. 麻醉药 vt. 给…服麻醉药

【例】The girl had been *doped* and kidnapped.

dosage	[ˈdoʊsɪdʒ] n. (药的)剂量，服用量
dose	[doʊs] n. (药的)剂量；一服，一次投入量
disfunction	[dɪsˈfʌŋkʃn] n. 机能障碍，机能不良（abnormality in the function of an organ）
erythromycin	[ɪˌrɪθroʊˈmaɪsɪn] n. 红霉素
hypertherm	[ˈhaɪpəθɜːrm] n. 人工发热(治疗)器
immunology	[ˌɪmjuˈnɑːlədʒi] n. 免疫学
infectious	[ɪnˈfekʃəs] adj. 传染的（contagious）；感染性的，易传播的；有损害的

【记】infect(传染) + ious → 传染的

【例】Flu is highly *infectious*.

【派】infection(*n.* 传染)

infirmary [ɪnˈfɜːrməri] *n.* 医务室，医院(hospital)

influenza [ˌɪnfluˈenzə] *n.* 流行性感冒(flu)

inherited [ɪnˈherɪtɪd] *adj.* 遗传的(病等)

【例】How many of these traits are genetically *inherited*?

inhibitor [ɪnˈhɪbɪtər] *n.* 抑制剂，抑制者

inoculate [ɪˈnɑːkjuleɪt] *vt.* 预防注射

【例】All the children had been *inoculated* against hepatitis.

【派】inoculation(*n.* 预防接种)

inpatient [ˈɪnpeɪʃnt] *n.* 住院病人 *adj.* 夜间看病的

insomnia [ɪnˈsɑːmniə] *n.* 失眠，失眠症

【例】If you suffer from *insomnia*, you are not able to sleep.

insulin [ˈɪnsəlɪn] *n.* 胰岛素

【例】Diabetic patients require *insulin*.

intestine [ɪnˈtestɪn] *n.* 肠

【派】intestinal(*adj.* 肠的)

irritant [ˈɪrɪtənt] *n.* 刺激物 (something that keeps annoying you over a period of time) *adj.* 刺激的；引起发炎的

【例】Low flying aircraft are a constant *irritant* in this area.

kidney [ˈkɪdni] *n.* 肾，肾脏

【例】a *kidney* transplant

liver [ˈlɪvər] *n.* 肝，肝脏

malady [ˈmælədi] *n.* 疾病，弊病(a serious problem in society, an illness)

【记】mal(坏) + ady → 坏的东西 → 疾病

malaria [məˈleriə] *n.* 疟疾

manic [ˈmænɪk] *adj.* 狂躁的

【例】Mortimer continued to shoot, a *manic* grin on his face.

marijuana [ˌmærəˈwɑːnə] *n.* 大麻

marrow [ˈmæroʊ] *n.* 骨髓，脊髓 (the substance in the hollow center of bones)

measles [ˈmiːzlz] *n.* 麻疹

【派】measled(*adj.* 患麻疹的)

medication [ˌmedɪˈkeɪʃn] *n.* 敷药，施药；药物(medicine or drugs)

【例】He's on *medication* for high blood pressure.

migraine [ˈmaɪɡreɪn] *n.* 周期性偏头痛

morphine [ˈmɔːrfiːn] *n.* 吗啡

morphogenetic [ˌmɔːrfədʒəˈnetɪk] *adj.* 形态基因的

narcotic [nɑːrˈkɑːtɪk] *n.* 麻醉药，麻醉剂

nausea [ˈnɔːziə] *n.* 作呕，恶心(sick)

【例】A feeling of *nausea* suddenly came over me.

nicotine [ˈnɪkətiːn] *n.* 尼古丁

off-the-shelf (货品)现成常备的；非定制的

opiate [ˈoupiət] *n.* 鸦片制剂，麻醉剂(a drug that contains opium)

outpatient [ˈautpeɪʃnt] *n.* 门诊病人

【例】an *outpatient* department

panacea [ˌpænəˈsiːə] *n.* 万灵药(cure-all)

【例】There is no *panacea* for the country's economic problems.

paralysis [pəˈræləsɪs] *n.* 麻痹，瘫痪，中风(the loss of the ability to move all or part of your body)

【例】The snake's poison causes *paralysis*.

pediatric [ˌpiːdiˈætrɪk] *adj.* 儿科的 (the area of medicine that deals with children and their illnesses)

【例】a *pediatric* hospital

penicillin [ˌpenɪˈsɪlɪn] *n.* 青霉素，盘尼西林

pharmaceutical [ˌfɑːrməˈsuːtɪkl] *adj.* 制药的 (relating to the production of drugs and medicines)；卖药的

【例】the *pharmaceutical* industry

pharmacy [ˈfɑːrməsi] *n.* 药店 (a shop or a part of a shop where medicines are prepared and sold)

physician [fɪˈzɪʃn] *n.* 医师(doctor)

plague [pleɪɡ] *n.* 疫病(disease)，灾祸 *v.* 折磨，使苦恼

【例】The ceaseless war posed a big *plague* for those innocent. / Runaway inflation further *plagued* the salary' earner.

plaque [plæk] *n.* (用金属、象牙、陶瓷等制的)匾，饰；血小板

pneumonia [nuːˈmouniə] *n.* 肺炎

prescription [prɪˈskrɪpʃn] *n.* 处方，药方

【例】a *prescription* for sleeping pills

proprietary [prəˈpraɪəteri] *adj.* 业主的；专营的，专利的(under a trade name)

【例】a *proprietary* brand of insecticide

【派】proprietor (*n.* 所有人，业主)

psychiatric [ˌsaɪkiˈætrɪk] *adj.* 精神病的(relating to mental illness)

【例】Charles was suffering from a *psychiatric* disorder.

【派】psychiatrically(*adv.* 精神上) psychiatrist(*n.* 精神病专家)

psychoactive [ˌsaɪkoʊˈæktɪv] *adj.* (药剂)对神经起显著(或特殊)作用的

【例】*Psychoactive* drugs have an effect on your mind.

psychological [ˌsaɪkəˈlɑːdʒɪkl] *adj.* 心理的, 精神上的(relating to mind)

【例】Sleep disorders are a serious *psychological* problem.

【派】psychologically(*adv.* 心理上地) psychologist(*n.* 心理学家)

psychosis [saɪˈkoʊsɪs] *n.* 精神病(mental illness)

psychotherapy [ˌsaɪkoʊˈθerəpi] *n.* 心理疗法, 精神疗法

quarantine [ˈkwɔːrəntiːn] *n.* 隔离检疫期, 隔离

【例】The monkeys were kept in *quarantine* for 31 days.

remedy [ˈremədi] *n.* 治疗法, 药物 *vt.* 治疗(cure, rectify)

【例】The doctor tried all means to *remedy* the beloved man.

respiratory [ˈrespərətɔːri] *adj.* 呼吸的, 呼吸用的(relating to breathing)

【例】*respiratory* disease

respire [rɪˈspaɪər] *v.* 呼吸(breathe)

sanitary [ˈsænəteri] *adj.* 清洁的, 卫生的(clean); 保健的

【例】Diseases were spread through poor *sanitary* conditions.

sanitation [ˌsænɪˈteɪʃn] *n.* 卫生, 卫生设施(the protection of public health by removing and treating wast)

【例】Overcrowding and poor *sanitation* are common problems in prisons.

smallpox [ˈsmɔːlpɑːks] *n.* 天花, 痘(disease that causes spots)

spleen [spliːn] *n.* 脾; 脾气, 怒气(anger)

【例】Obviously you're annoyed, but that doesn't give you the right to vent your *spleen* on me.

surgeon [ˈsɜːrdʒən] *n.* 外科医生 (a doctor who does operations in a hospital)

surgical [ˈsɜːrdʒɪkl] *adj.* 外科的, 外科手术的 (relating to medical operations)

【例】*surgical* techniques

【派】surgically(*adv.* 外科手术上)

susceptible [səˈseptəbl] *adj.* 易受感染的(vulnerable, exposed)

【记】sus(下面) + cept(接受) + ible → 接受的 → 易受感染的

【例】Infants and the elderly are more *susceptible* to illness than other people.

【派】susceptibility(*n.* 敏感性)

sustenance [ˈsʌstənəns] *n.* 营养物

【例】For *sustenance*, the vegetarian ate fruits, nuts, and vegetables.

syndrome [ˈsɪndroʊm] *n.* 综合征；同时存在的事物

tablet [ˈtæblət] *n.* 药片；便笺簿；碑，匾

tardive [ˈtɑːrdɪv] *adj.* (疾病)延迟发作的

Every day I remind myself that my inner and outer life are based on the labors of other men, living and dead, and that I must exert myself in order to give in the same measure as I have received and am still receiving.

每天我都提醒着自己：我的精神生活和物质生活都是以别人的劳动为基础的，我必须尽力以同样的分量来报偿我所获得的和至今仍在接受着的东西。

——美国科学家 爱因斯坦(*Albert Einstein, American scientist*)

练 习 题

连线题

analgesic	机能障碍	intestine	门诊病人
infirmary	隔离检疫期	insomnia	住院病人
influenza	针刺（疗法）	smallpox	麻痹，瘫痪
pneumonia	疫病，灾祸	marrow	药片
ambulance	肺炎	liver	卫生的；保健的
acupuncture	流行性感冒	kidney	天花，痘
syndrome	外科医生	inpatient	肾，肾脏
quarantine	救护车	sanitary	麻疹
plague	疾病，弊病	tablet	药店
disfunction	止血药	outpatient	失眠症
malady	医务室	paralysis	骨髓，脊髓
astringent	镇痛剂	pharmacy	肠
surgeon	综合征	measles	肝，肝脏

选词填空

anesthetic	clinical	inherited	inoculate	nausea
pediatric	prescription	psychiatric	remedy	respiratory

1. The program gives the students experience in a _____ setting.

2. There is as yet no known _____ for cancer.

3. In order to improve children's health conditions, the government decides to establish more _____ hospitals.

4. The physician made a _____ against sea-sickness for him.

5. All pets should be _____against serious diseases before they are sold.

6. How many of these traits are genetically _____?

7. He was given a general _____ before the operation.

8. Early pregnancy is often accompanied by_____.

9. The old man suffers from _____ diseases and could not breathe smoothly.

10. Charles was suspected of mental illness and was sent to a _____ hospital.

练习题答案

连线题答案

analgesic	镇痛剂	intestine	肠
infirmary	医务室	insomnia	失眠症
influenza	流行性感冒	smallpox	天花，痘
pneumonia	肺炎	marrow	骨髓，脊髓
ambulance	救护车	liver	肝，肝脏
acupuncture	针刺（疗法）	kidney	肾，肾脏
syndrome	综合征	inpatient	住院病人
quarantine	隔离检疫期	sanitary	卫生的；保健的
plague	疫病，灾祸	tablet	药片
disfunction	机能障碍	outpatient	门诊病人
malady	疾病，弊病	paralysis	麻痹，瘫痪
astringent	止血药	pharmacy	药店
surgeon	外科医生	measles	麻疹

选词填空答案

anesthetic	clinical	inherited	inoculate	nausea
pediatric	prescription	psychiatric	remedy	respiratory

1. The program gives the students experience in a（clinical）setting.
2. There is as yet no known（remedy）for cancer.
3. In order to improve children's health conditions, the government decides to establish more（pediatric）hospitals.
4. The physician made a（prescription）against sea-sickness for him.
5. All pets should be（inoculated）against serious diseases before they are sold.
6. How many of these traits are genetically（inherited）?
7. He was given a general（anesthetic）before the operation.
8. Early pregnancy is often accompanied by（nausea）.
9. The old man suffers from（respiratory）diseases and could not breathe smoothly.
10.Charles was suspected of mental illness and was sent to a（psychiatric）hospital.

Word List 5

音频

医 学(二)
化 学

医学(二)&化学

thyroid	[ˈθaɪrɔɪd] *adj.* 甲状腺的 *n.* 甲状腺
tranquilizer	[ˈtræŋkwəlaɪzər] *n.* 镇静剂，止痛药
tuberculosis	[tuːˌbɜːrkjəˈloʊsɪs] *n.* 结核病，肺结核(略作TB)
typhoid	[ˈtaɪfɔɪd] *n.* 伤寒
ulcer	[ˈʌlsər] *n.* 溃疡；[喻]腐烂的事物，腐败的根源
vaccinate	[ˈvæksɪneɪt] *v.* 接种疫苗(immunize) 【例】All children should be *vaccinated* against measles. 【派】vaccination (*n.* 接种)
vaccine	[vækˈsiːn] *n.* 疫苗 【例】a polio *vaccine*
varicose	[ˈværɪkoʊs] *adj.* 静脉曲张的，治疗静脉曲张用的
vascular	[ˈvæskjələr] *adj.* 血管的 【例】*vascular* disease
venous	[ˈviːnəs] *adj.* 静脉的(relating to the veins)
vitamin	[ˈvaɪtəmɪn] *n.* 维生素 【例】*vitamin* A/B/C etc.
viral	[ˈvaɪrəl] *adj.* 病毒的，病毒引起的(relating to virus) 【例】a *viral* infection
virulent	[ˈvɪrələnt] *adj.* 剧毒的，致命的(poisonous, dangerous) 【例】a particularly *virulent* form of influenza 【派】virulently(*adv.* 恶毒地) virulence(*n.* 毒性，恶意)
virus	[ˈvaɪrəs] *n.* 病毒，病毒性感染；恶毒 【例】a *virus* infection
womb	[wuːm] *n.* 子宫；发源地 【例】from the *womb* to the tomb
yellow fever	黄热病
aluminium	[ˌæləˈmɪniəm] *n.* 铝
amalgam	[əˈmælgəm] *n.* 混合物；汞合金
arsenic	[ˈɑːrsnɪk] *n.* 砷，砒霜
brazen	[ˈbreɪzn] *adj.* 黄铜的 (made of brass)；无耻的，厚脸皮的

(shameless and bold)

bronze [brɑːnz] *n.* 青铜

buffer ['bʌfər] *n.* 缓冲器；起缓冲作用的人或物；缓冲剂 *v.* 缓冲，减轻

【例】Consumer spending is *buffering* the effects of the recession.

caffeine ['kæfiːn] *n.* 咖啡因

calcium ['kælsiəm] *n.* 钙

carbohydrate ['kɑːrbou'haɪdreɪt] *n.* 碳水化合物；糖类

carbon ['kɑːrbən] *n.* 碳

carotene ['kærətiːn] *n.* 胡萝卜素

catalyst ['kætəlɪst] *n.* 催化剂；促使事物发展的因素

【例】They hope his election will act as a *catalyst* for reform.

【派】catalytic(*adj.* 催化的) catalysis(*n.* 催化作用)

chemical ['kemɪkl] *n.* 化学药品 *adj.* 化学的

【派】chemistry(*n.* 化学) chemist(*n.* 化学家)

cholesterol [kə'lestərɔːl] *n.* 胆固醇

cocaine [kou'keɪn] *n.* 可卡因；古柯碱

cocoa ['koukou] *n.* 可可粉；可可茶；可可树；可可色

compound ['kɑːmpaund] *n.* 混合物，化合物 [kəm'paund] *v.* 使混合，使合成

【例】He *compounded* water, sand and soil and formed bricks.

dioxide [daɪ'ɑːksaɪd] *n.* 二氧化物

dispersant [dɪs'pɜːrsənt] *n.* 分散剂

ethylene ['eθɪliːn] *n.* 乙烯

formaldehyde [fɔːr'mældɪhaɪd] *n.* 甲醛

glycerol ['glɪsəroul] *n.* 甘油

graphite ['græfaɪt] *n.* 石墨

helium ['hiːliəm] *n.* 氦

hemoglobin [ˌhiːmə'gloubɪn] *n.* 血红蛋白

herpesvirus ['hɜːrpiːz'vaɪrəs] *n.* 疱疹病毒

hormone ['hɔːrmoun] *n.* (刺激生长的)荷尔蒙，激素

【派】hormonal(*adj.* 荷尔蒙的)

hydrocarbon [ˌhaɪdrə'kɑːrbən] *n.* 烃，碳氢化合物

hydrogen ['haɪdrədʒən] *n.* 氢

insecticide [ɪn'sektɪsaɪd] *n.* 杀虫剂 (a chemical substance used for killing insects)

metabolize [mə'tæbəlaɪz] *vt.* (使)产生代谢变化

【派】metabolite(*n.* 代谢物) metabolic(*adj.* 新陈代谢的) metabolism
(*n.* 新陈代谢)

methane ['miːθeɪn] *n.* 甲烷，沼气

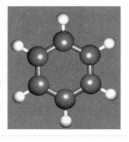

mineral ['mɪnərəl] *n.* 矿物，矿石

【派】mineralization(*n.* 矿化)

molecule ['mɑːlɪkjuːl] *n.* 分子

【记】mole("摩尔") + cule("小"的后缀)
→ 分子

【派】molecular(*adj.* 分子的)

nitrogen ['naɪtrədʒən] *n.* 氮

nucleotide ['nuːklɪətaɪd] *n.* 核苷酸

ocher ['oʊkər] *n.* 【矿】赭石；(黄)褐色

oligosaccharide ['ɔlɪɡoʊ 'sækəraɪd] *n.* 寡糖

ore [ɔːr] *n.* 矿，矿砂，矿石

【例】*ore* body

oxide ['ɑːksaɪd] *n.* 氧化物(substance combined with oxygen)

ozone ['oʊzoʊn] *n.* 臭氧；<口>新鲜空气；能使人兴奋的力量

particulates [pɑːr 'tɪkjələts] *n.* [*pl.*] 微粒 (harmful dust in the air, especially
produced by car engines)

pesticide ['pestɪsaɪd] *n.* 杀虫剂

petroleum [pə 'troʊlɪəm] *n.* 石油

【例】*petroleum* products

phosphate ['fɑːsfeɪt] *n.* 磷酸，磷酸盐

【例】*phosphate* fertilizer

pigment ['pɪɡmənt] *n.* 天然色素，干粉颜料

plutonium [pluː 'toʊnɪəm] *n.* 钚

pollutant [pə 'luːtənt] *n.* 污染物质

polymorph ['pɑːlimɔːrf] *n.* 多形体；多晶形物

potassium [pə 'tæsiəm] *n.* 钾

precipitation [prɪˌsɪpɪ 'teɪʃn] *n.* 沉淀作用；降雨量；仓促；猛然落下

preservative [prɪ 'zɜːrvətɪv] *n.* 防腐剂 (chemical substance to prevent from
decaying)

protein ['proʊtiːn] *n.* 蛋白质 *adj.* 蛋白质的

pseudomer ['suːdəmər] *n.* 假异构体

radon	[ˈreɪdɑːn] *n.* 氡	
ribosome	[ˈraɪbəsoʊm] *n.* 核糖体	
sodium	[ˈsoʊdiəm] *n.* 钠	
sulfur	[ˈsʌlfər] *n.* 硫黄	
uranium	[juˈreɪniəm] *n.* 铀	
cinder	[ˈsɪndər] *n.* 余烬，矿渣	

char [tʃɑːr] *n.* 炭，木炭 *v.* 把…烧成炭，烧焦，烧黑（scorch）

【例】The meat was slightly *charred*.

【派】charcoal(*n.* 炭，木炭)

crystallize [ˈkrɪstəlaɪz] *v.* 结晶 （to form or cause to form crystals）；计划成型；具体化

【例】The liquid will *crystallize* at 50 degrees centigrade.

A man is not old as long as he is seeking something. A man is not old until regrets take the place of dreams.

只要一个人还有所追求，他就没有老。直到后悔取代了梦想，一个人才算老。

——美国演员 巴里穆尔(*J. Barrymore, American actor*)

练 习 题

连线题

vascular	血管的	cinder	咖啡因
typhoid	黄热病	arsenic	硫黄
tuberculosis	碳	brazen	青铜
hydrogen	胆固醇	dispersant	砒霜
virus	二氧化物	venous	氧化物
particulates	结核病	hormone	甲烷, 沼气
yellow fever	铝	caffeine	静脉的
dioxide	伤寒	methane	矿物, 矿石
carbon	石油	bronze	胡萝卜素
cholesterol	钙	carotene	荷尔蒙
aluminum	氢	oxide	余烬, 矿渣
calcium	病毒	sulfur	黄铜的
petroleum	微粒	mineral	分散剂

选词填空

vaccinate	catalyst	chemical	compound	ozone
pesticide	protein	crystallize	preservative	molecule

1. _____ exists in food such as meat and rice. Your body needs it in order to grow and remain strong and healthy.

2. The _____ layer surrounding the earth protects our skin from being hurt by the ultraviolet rays.

3. Were you _____ against smallpox as a child?

4. The liquid will _____ at 50 degrees centigrade.

5. The workers' demand for better conditions was a _____ for social change.

6. The structure of _____ can be seen under an electron microscope.

7. The _____ was spread over the vegetable plot to prevent insect damage.

8. The food is treated with _____ to prevent decay.

9. Sulfur dioxide is a _____ of sulfur and oxygen.

10. Many cleaning products contain _____ that are harmful to human beings.

连线题答案

vascular	血管的	cinder	余烬, 矿渣
typhoid	伤寒	arsenic	砒霜
tuberculosis	结核病	brazen	黄铜的
hydrogen	氢	dispersant	分散剂
virus	病毒	venous	静脉的
particulates	微粒	hormone	荷尔蒙
yellow fever	黄热病	caffeine	咖啡因
dioxide	二氧化物	methane	甲烷, 沼气
carbon	碳	bronze	青铜
cholesterol	胆固醇	carotene	胡萝卜素
aluminum	铝	oxide	氧化物
calcium	钙	sulfur	硫黄
petroleum	石油	mineral	矿物, 矿石

选词填空答案

vaccinate	catalyst	chemical	compound	ozone
pesticide	protein	crystallize	preservative	molecule

1. （Protein）exists in food such as meat and rice. Your body needs it in order to grow and remain strong and healthy.
2. The （ozone）layer surrounding the earth protects our skin from being hurt by the ultraviolet rays.
3. Were you （vaccinated）against smallpox as a child?
4. The liquid will （crystallize）at 50 degrees centigrade.
5. The workers' demand for better conditions was a （catalyst）for social change.
6. The structure of （molecules）can be seen under an electron microscope.
7. The （pesticide）was spread over the vegetable plot to prevent insect damage.
8. The food is treated with （preservative）to prevent decay.
9. Sulfur dioxide is a （compound）of sulfur and oxygen.
10. Many cleaning products contain （chemicals）that are harmful to human beings.

Word List 6

音频

动物学
人类学

动物学 & 人类学

anole [ə'nouli] *n.* 变色龙，变色蜥蜴

anopheles [ə'nɑ:fəli:z] *n.* 疟蚊；按蚊属

antenna [æn'tenə] *n.* 触角，触须；天线

ape [eɪp] *n.* 无尾猿；类人猿；模仿者；粗野的大汉

avian ['eɪviən] *adj.* 鸟的，鸟类的

bipedalism [ˌbaɪ'pedəlɪzəm] *n.* 二足类

【记】bi(二，双) + pedal(足) + ism → 二足类

carnivore ['kɑ:rnɪvɔ:r] *n.* 食肉动物，食虫植物

caterpillar ['kætərpɪlər] *n.* 毛毛虫

chameleon [kə'mi:liən] *n.* 变色龙，蜥蜴

condor ['kɑ:ndɔ:r] *n.* (南美产)神鹰，秃鹰

dinosaur ['daɪnəsɔ:r] *n.* 恐龙

fauna ['fɔ:nə] *n.* 动物区系

fledgling ['fledʒlɪŋ] *n.* (刚学会飞的)幼鸟；无经验的人 *adj.* 无经验的

gorilla [gə'rɪlə] *n.* 大猩猩；[俚]打手；暴徒

hamster ['hæmstər] *n.* 仓鼠

herbivore ['hɜ:rbɪvɔ:r] *n.* 食草动物

herring ['herɪŋ] *n.* 鲱鱼

hippo ['hɪpoʊ] *n.* 河马

invertebrate [ɪn'vɜ:rtɪbrət] *n.* 无脊椎动物(a living creature that does not have a backbone)

lactation [læk'teɪʃn] *n.* 哺乳期 (the production of milk by a woman or female animal)

larva ['lɑ:rvə] *n.* (昆虫的)幼虫，幼体

【派】larvae(*n.* larva的复数形式)

leaven ['levn] *v.* 使(面团)发酵 *n.* 酵母

【派】leavened(*adj.* 加酵母的)

lepidopter [ˌlepɪ'dɑ:ptər] *n.* (尾虫)鳞翅目

livestock ['laɪvstɑ:k] *n.* (总称)家畜，牲畜

lobster ['lɑ:bstər] *n.* 龙虾

mammal	[ˈmæml] *n.* 哺乳动物
	【记】mamma(乳) + 1 → 哺乳动物
	【派】mammalian(*adj.* 哺乳动物的)
microbe	[ˈmaɪkroʊb] *n.* 微生物, 细菌(bacteria)
mosquito	[məˈskiːtoʊ] *n.* 蚊子
moth	[mɔːθ] *n.* 蛾
neuron	[ˈnʊrɑːn] *n.* 神经元, 神经细胞
	【派】neuroscientist(*n.* 神经系统科学家) neurotransmitter(*n.* 神经传递素)
parasite	[ˈpærəsaɪt] *n.* 寄生虫; 寄生植物
	【记】para(旁边) + site(坐) → 坐在旁边的 → 寄生虫
	【派】parasitic(*adj.* 寄生的)
pelvis	[ˈpelvɪs] *n.* 骨盆
	【派】pelvic(*adj.* 骨盆的)
plankton	[ˈplæŋktən] *n.* 浮游生物（the very small forms of plant and animal life that live in water)
plasma	[ˈplæzmə] *n.* 血浆, 淋巴液; 原生质; 等离子区
poultry	[ˈpoʊltri] *n.* 家禽(birds such as chickens and ducks that are kept on farms)
predator	[ˈpredətər] *n.* 食肉动物（an animal that kills and eats other animals)
prey	[preɪ] *n.* 被捕食的动物; 牺牲品, 战利品
primate	[ˈpraɪmeɪt] *n.* 灵长类(动物)
pupation	[pjuːˈpeɪʃn] *n.* 化蛹
quadrupedal	[kwɑːˈdruːpɪdəl] *adj.* 四足动物的
raccoon	[ræˈkuːn] *n.* 浣熊; 浣熊毛皮
reptile	[ˈreptaɪl] *n.* 爬行动物
	【派】reptilian(*adj.* 爬虫类的)
rhinoceros	[raɪˈnɑːsərəs] *n.* 犀牛, 犀属
rodent	[ˈroʊdnt] *n.* 啮齿类动物
saliva	[səˈlaɪvə] *n.* 唾液, 口水
	【派】salivary(*adj.* 分泌唾液的)
scavenger	[ˈskævɪndʒər] *n.* 清洁工
silkworm	[ˈsɪlkwɜːrm] *n.* 蚕(worm producing silk thread)
skull	[skʌl] *n.* 头脑, 头骨(bones of head)

specimen	['spesɪmən] *n.* 标本，样品（sample, instance）
spine	[spaɪn] *n.* 脊骨；脊柱（backbone）；书脊；[喻]中心；支持因素
squirrel	['skwɜːrəl] *n.* 松鼠 *vt.* 储藏，贮存（put away）
	【例】By December I had $300 *squirreled* away.
strain	[streɪn] *n.* 血统；（动物、昆虫等的）种（a type of animal etc.）
	【例】different *strains* of wheat
swarm	[swɔːrm] *n.* （蜜蜂、蚂蚁等）群（throng, crowd, horde）
tadpole	['tædpoʊl] *n.* 蝌蚪
vegetarian	[ˌvedʒə'teriən] *n.* 素食者，食草动物 *adj.* 素食者的
	【例】a *vegetarian* restaurant
	【派】vegetarianism（*n.* 素食主义）
vertebrate	['vɜːrtɪbrət] *n.* 脊椎动物（creature with backbone）*adj.* 有脊椎的
vessel	['vesl] *n.* 血管；船只（vein; boat）
wasp	[wɑːsp] *n.* 黄蜂；刻毒的人
weevil	['wiːvl] *n.* 象鼻虫
woodpecker	['wʊdpekər] *n.* 啄木鸟
yeast	[jiːst] *n.* 酵母，酵母菌，发面粉
anthropology	[ˌænθrə'pɑːlədʒi] *n.* 人类学
	【派】anthropologist（*n.* 人类学家）anthropological（*adj.* 人类学的）
orthogenetic	[ˌɔːrθədʒə'netɪk] *adj.* 直向演化的；直生现象的
overlord	['oʊvərlɔːrd] *n.* 封建领主（someone with great power over a large number of people, especially in the past）
paleolithic	[ˌpeɪliou'lɪθɪk] *adj.* 旧石器时代的
posterity	[pɑː'sterəti] *n.* 后代（offspring, descendant）
	【记】post(后) + erity → 后代
prehistoric	[ˌpriːhɪ'stɔːrɪk] *adj.* 史前的
	【例】*prehistoric* animals
sacralization	[ˌseɪkrəlaɪ'zeɪʃn] *n.* 神化
sexist	['seksɪst] *n.* 性别歧视（someone who believes that one sex is weaker）
	【例】My father was a complete *sexist*. He thought a woman's place was in the kitchen.
throne	[θroʊn] *n.* 王座，王权（the position and power as king）

【例】He is next in line to the *throne*.

sovereign [ˈsɑːvrən] *n.* 君主，元首 *adj.* 有至高无上的权力的（having the highest power）；完全独立的（independent）

【例】The Queen has *sovereign* power.

【派】sovereignty（*n.* 主权）

hominid [ˈhɑːmɪnɪd] *n.* 原始人类

You have to believe in yourself. That's the secret of success.

人必须相信自己，这是成功的秘诀。

——美国演员 卓别林（*Charles Chaplin, American actor*）

练 习 题

连线题

antenna	食肉动物	caterpillar	动物区系
hominid	大猩猩	lobster	啄木鸟
spine	食草动物	microbe	神经元, 神经细胞
sovereign	变色龙	lactation	头脑, 头骨
herbivore	家禽	raccoon	爬行动物
tadpole	河马	parasite	哺乳期
leaven	脊骨, 脊柱	throne	龙虾
gorilla	史前的	reptile	蚕
poultry	触角	neuron	毛毛虫
anole	原始人类	skull	寄生虫
carnivore	酵母	silkworm	王座, 王权
hippo	君主, 元首	fauna	微生物
prehistoric	蝌蚪	woodpecker	浣熊

选词填空

avian	dinosaur	mammal	mosquito	predator
vegetarian	specimen	anthropology	posterity	sexist

1. No one has come up with a convincing explanation of why _____ die out.
2. This is a priceless work of art that must be kept for _____.
3. _____ flu is an infectious disease that spreads very quickly among birds.
4. Whales are _____ that live in the sea.
5. The birds cannot afford to relax their vigilance against _____.
6. It is _____ to say that women are less intelligent than men.
7. Diseases could spread when _____ sucks the blood of people and animal.
8. The _____ of the future will not be concerned above all else with primitives.
9. The traveler brought back some _____ of the rocks from the mountains.
10. The old man takes only _____ food, since meat is hard to digest for him.

练习题答案

连线题答案

antenna	触角	caterpillar	毛毛虫
hominid	原始人类	lobster	龙虾
spine	脊骨，脊柱	microbe	微生物
sovereign	君主，元首	lactation	哺乳期
herbivore	食草动物	raccoon	浣熊
tadpole	蝌蚪	parasite	寄生虫
leaven	酵母	throne	王座，王权
gorilla	大猩猩	reptile	爬行动物
poultry	家禽	neuron	神经元，神经细胞
anole	变色龙	skull	头脑，头骨
carnivore	食肉动物	silkworm	蚕
hippo	河马	fauna	动物区系
prehistoric	史前的	woodpecker	啄木鸟

选词填空答案

avian	dinosaur	mammal	mosquito	predator
vegetarian	specimen	anthropology	posterity	sexist

1. No one has come up with a convincing explanation of why（dinosaur）die out.

2. This is a priceless work of art that must be kept for（posterity）.

3. （Avian）flu is an infectious disease that spreads very quickly among birds.

4. Whales are（mammals）that live in the sea.

5. The birds cannot afford to relax their vigilance against（predators）.

6. It is（sexist）to say that women are less intelligent than men.

7. Diseases could spread when（mosquito）sucks the blood of people and animal.

8. The（anthropology）of the future will not be concerned above all else with primitives.

9. The traveler brought back some（specimens）of the rocks from the mountains.

10. The old man takes only（vegetarian）food, since meat is hard to digest for him.

Word List 7

音频

物 理
农 业

物理 & 农业

adhesive [əd'hi:sɪv] n. 黏合剂 adj. 可黏着的, 黏性的(sticky, adherent)
【例】Would you give me an *adhesive* stamp?
【派】adhesion(n. 黏合)

alloy [ə'lɔɪ] v. 将…铸成合金 ['ælɔɪ] n. 合金

amplitude ['æmplɪtu:d] n. 广阔, 广大(greatness of extent; magnitude); 振幅

ballistic [bə'lɪstɪk] adj. 弹道(学)的, 发射的; 衡量冲击强度的

blind spot 盲点; 静区

conductive [kən'dʌktɪv] adj. 传导性的(able to conduct electricity, heat, etc.)
【例】Copper is a very *conductive* metal.
【派】conductor(n. 导体) conduction(n. 传导, 导热, 导电)

deform [dɪ'fɔ:rm] vt. 使变形(disfigure, distort)
【记】de(坏) + form(形状) → 使变形
【例】A constant wind *deformed* the tree.
【派】deformation(n. 变形, 畸形; 残疾)

density ['densəti] n. 密度; 稠密, 密集

dynamics [daɪ'næmɪks] n. 动力学, 力学

elastic [ɪ'læstɪk] adj. 有弹性的 n. 松紧带, 橡皮圈
【例】Children's bones are far more *elastic* than adults'.
【派】elasticity(n. 弹力, 弹性)

electrical [ɪ'lektrɪkl] adj. 与电有关的, 电学的(relating to electricity)
【例】an *electrical* engineer

electric [ɪ'lektrɪk] adj. 用电的
【例】*electric* light / kettle / cooker

electricity [ɪˌlek'trɪsəti] n. 电流

electromagnet [ɪ'lektroʊmægnət] n. 电磁体
【派】electromagnetic(adj. 电磁的)

electron [ɪ'lektrɑːn] n. 电子

electronic [ɪˌlek'trɑːnɪk] adj. 电子的
【例】*electronic* component

elliptical [ɪ'lɪptɪkl] adj. 椭圆的
【例】The Earth's path round the Sun is *elliptical*.

【派】ellipse(n. 椭圆)

flexible ['fleksəbl] adj. 有弹性的;灵活的(agile);变通的

【记】flex(弯曲)+ ible → 灵活的

【例】Jane easily bent the *flexible* wire into a loop.

【派】flexibility(n. 弹性;适应性)

gel [dʒel] n. 凝胶(体),冻胶

globular ['glɑːbjələr] adj. 球状的(shaped like a globe)

gradient ['greɪdiənt] n. 道路的斜面、斜坡;坡度,梯度;斜率

【例】The car slid down the steep *gradient* into the river.

gravitation [ˌgrævɪ'teɪʃn] n. 地心引力,引力作用

gravitational [ˌgrævɪ'teɪʃənl] adj. 万有引力的,重力的

gravity ['grævəti] n. 引力;严重性;严肃(graveness, sobriety, solemnity)

【例】An apple falls down because of *gravity*.

inelasticity [ˌɪnɪlæ'stɪsəti] n. 无伸缩性,无弹力

inertia [ɪ'nɜːrʃə] n. 惯性;不活动,惰性

infrared [ˌɪnfrə'red] n. 红外线

【例】*Infrared* is widely used in industry and medical science.

ion ['aɪɑːn] n. 离子

isotope ['aɪsətoʊp] n.【核】同位素

laser ['leɪzər] n. 激光;激光器

leverage ['levərɪdʒ] n. 杠杆作用;影响 vt. 促使改变

【例】the use of public funds to *leverage* private investment

magnetic [mæg'netɪk] adj. 有磁性的;有吸引力的 (having the power of a magnet or behaving like a magnet)

【例】The iron has lost its *magnetic* force.

【派】magnetically(adv. 有磁力地)

mass [mæs] n. 质量

mechanics [mə'kænɪks] n. 力学,机械学

【派】mechanism(n. 机械装置)

molten ['moʊltən] adj. 熔化的;熔融的

【例】*molten* iron

nucleus ['nuːkliəs] n. 原子核;中心;细胞核

opaque [oʊ'peɪk] n. 不透明物 adj. 不透明的(difficult to see through and often thick);不传热的

【例】a shower with an *opaque* glass door

【派】opaqueness(*n.* 不透明度)

parallax ['pærəlæks] *n.* 视差

particle ['pɑːrtɪkl] *n.* 颗粒，微粒
【记】比较article(*n.* 文章)

photon ['foʊtɑːn] *n.* 光子；【医】见光度

prism ['prɪzəm] *n.* 三棱镜；三棱柱

proton ['proʊtɑːn] *n.* 质子

pulsation [pʌl'seɪʃn] *n.* 跳动；有节奏的鼓动；脉动

quanta ['kwɑːntə] *n.* 量子；量，份额

radioactive ['reɪdioʊ'æktɪv] *adj.* 放射性的
【例】the problem of how to dispose of *radioactive* waste

reactor [rɪ'æktər] *n.* 核反应堆
【例】a nuclear *reactor*

reflex ['riːfleks] *n.* 反射作用；反应能力 (the natural ability to react)
【例】*reflex* action
【派】reflexed(*adj.* 反折的)

refraction [rɪ'frækʃn] *n.* 折射(程度)，折射角

semiconductor [ˌsemɪkən'dʌktər] *n.* 半导体

speed velocity 临界速度

sphere [sfɪr] *n.* 球；天体；领域(ball shape; field)
【例】The Earth is usually represented by a *sphere*.

transistor [træn'zɪstər] *n.* 晶体管，晶体管收音机

vacuum ['vækjuəm] *n.* 真空(gap, void)

velocity [və'lɑːsəti] *n.* 速度，迅速(speed)
【例】a high *velocity* bullet

rubbery ['rʌbəri] *adj.* 橡胶似的(looking or feeling like rubber)；有弹性的
【例】*rubbery* lips

agrarian [ə'grerɪən] *adj.* 耕地的；土地的，土地所有的；农民的 *n.* 主张平均地权的人
【例】People are leaving an *agrarian* way of life to go to the city.

arable ['ærəbl] *adj.* 适于耕种的(farmable)
【记】ara(耕种) + ble → 适于耕种的
【例】*arable* land

cereal ['sɪriəl] *n.* 谷物，谷类食物

cultivate	[ˈkʌltɪveɪt] *vt.* 耕种；培养（till; foster, train）	

【例】The botanist *cultivated* tropical flowers.

【派】cultivation（*n.* 耕种；培养）cultivated（*adj.* 耕种的，栽植的；有教养的）

fertilizer	[ˈfɜːrtəlaɪzər] *n.* 肥料
graft	[ɡræft] *n.* 接穗，嫁接；移植
graze	[ɡreɪz] *vt.* 喂草，放牧

【例】This field will *graze* 30 head of cattle.

niche	[nɪtʃ] *n.* 小生态环境
nomad	[ˈnoʊmæd] *n.* 流浪者，游牧部落的人

【派】nomadic（*adj.* 部落的）

plantation	[plænˈteɪʃn] *n.* 耕地；种植园，大农场（a large area of land, a large group of trees grown to produce wood）
specialty	[ˈspeʃəlti] *n.* 专业；特产

【例】Johnson's *specialty* is medieval European history.

pasture	[ˈpæstʃər] *n.* 牧场，牧草 *v.* 放牧

【例】large areas of rough upland *pasture*

Trouble is only opportunity in work clothes.
困难只是穿上工作服的机遇。

——美国实业家 凯泽（*H.J. Kaiser, American businessman*）

练 习 题

连线题

dynamics	电磁体	elastic	力学，机械学
proton	导电的	cereal	电子
infrared	原子核	plantation	椭圆的
velocity	密度	leverage	地心吸力
reflex	振幅	laser	流浪者
density	惯性	nomad	谷类食物
nucleus	合金	elliptical	有弹性的
alloy	反射作用	pasture	耕地，种植园
electromagnet	质子	gravitation	特产
prism	速度	electron	接穗，嫁接
amplitude	动力学，力学	mechanics	激光
conductive	红外线	specialty	杠杆作用
inertia	三棱镜	graft	牧场，牧草

选词填空

radioactive	deform	electrical	electronic	flexible
vacuum	arable	fertilizer	cultivate	gravity

1. We have a large population but not enough _____ land.

2. The government needs a more _____ approach to education.

3. The disappearance of religious beliefs has left a _____ in many people's lives.

4. The _____ material is stored in a special radiation-proof container.

5. Wearing badly-fitting shoes can _____ your feet.

6. An apple falls down because of _____.

7. The trees would grow better if you get some more _____ for them.

8. One should _____ good manners from childhood.

9. Most kids love _____ games.

10. There is something wrong with the electric instrument, so he sends it to an _____ engineer for repair.

练习题答案

连线题答案

dynamics	动力学，力学	elastic	有弹性的
proton	质子	cereal	谷类食物
infrared	红外线	plantation	耕地，种植园
velocity	速度	leverage	杠杆作用
reflex	反射作用	laser	激光
density	密度	nomad	流浪者
nucleus	原子核	elliptical	椭圆的
alloy	合金	pasture	牧场，牧草
electromagnet	电磁体	gravitation	地心吸力
prism	三棱镜	electron	电子
amplitude	振幅	mechanics	力学，机械学
conductive	导电的	specialty	特产
inertia	惯性	graft	接穗，嫁接

选词填空答案

radioactive	deform	electrical	electronic	flexible
vacuum	arable	fertilizer	cultivate	gravity

1. We have a large population but not enough (arable) land.
2. The government needs a more (flexible) approach to education.
3. The disappearance of religious beliefs has left a (vacuum) in many people's lives.
4. The (radioactive) material is stored in a special radiation-proof container.
5. Wearing badly-fitting shoes can (deform) your feet.
6. An apple falls down because of (gravity).
7. The trees would grow better if you get some more (fertilizer) for them.
8. One should (cultivate) good manners from childhood.
9. Most kids love (electronic) games.
10. There is something wrong with the electric instrument, so he sends it to an (electrical) engineer for repair.

Word List 8

音频

地　理
植物学

地理 & 植物学

algae	[ˈældʒiː]	n. [alga的复数]水藻, 海藻
cashew	[ˈkæʃuː]	n. 腰果树, 腰果
coriander	[ˌkɔːriˈændər]	n. 芫荽, 香菜
escarole	[ˈeskəroʊl]	n. 苣荬
flora	[ˈflɔːrə]	n. (某地区或某时期的)植物群
foliage	[ˈfoʊliɪdʒ]	n. [集合词]叶子
forage	[ˈfɑːrɪdʒ]	n. 草料; 饲料
hemp	[hemp]	n. 大麻
husk	[hʌsk]	n. (果类或谷物的)外壳
intracellular	[ˌɪntrəˈseljələr]	adj. 细胞内部的
laurel	[ˈlɑːrəl]	n. 月桂树, 桂冠
maize	[meɪz]	n. 玉米
membrane	[ˈmembreɪn]	n. 薄膜, 细胞膜
mitochondria	[ˌmaɪtoʊˈkɑːndriə]	n. [mitochondrion的复数]线粒体
organelle	[ˌɔːrgəˈnel]	n. 细胞器

organic [ɔːrˈgænɪk] *adj.* 有机的; 器官性的 (relating to the organs of the body, produced by or from living things)
【例】Adding *organic* matter such as manure can improve the soil.
【派】organically(*adv.* 有机地) organism(*n.* 有机物)

palm [pɑːm] *n.* 手掌; 棕榈(树); 胜利 *vt.* (戏法)把…藏在手心(to hide something in the palm of your hand)

Basic Photosynthesis

photosynthesis [ˌfoʊtoʊˈsɪnθəsɪs] *n.* 光合作用
【派】photosynthesize(*v.* 光合作用)

pollen [ˈpɑːlən] *n.* 花粉(a fine powder produced by flowers)

pollinate [ˈpɑːləneɪt] *vt.* 对…授粉
【例】Many crops require bees to *pollinate* them.
【派】pollination(*n.* 授粉)

protoplasm	[ˈproʊtəplæzəm]	n. 原生质, 原浆; 细胞质
rib	[rɪb]	n.【解】肋骨; (叶)脉, 主脉;【动】翅脉
runner	[ˈrʌnər]	n. 蔓藤植物, 长葡茎

species	['spi:ʃi:z] *n.* 物种
spinach	['spɪnɪtʃ] *n.* 菠菜
squash	[skwɑːʃ] *n.* 南瓜；西葫芦
stem	[stem] *n.* 茎，干(stalk)；词干
sugarcane	['ʃʊgərˌkeɪn] *n.* 甘蔗
tissue	['tɪsjuː] *n.* 组织

【例】The *tissues* of the body constitute the organ.

unicellular	[ˌjuːnɪ'seljələr] *adj.* 单细胞的
vegetation	[ˌvedʒə'teɪʃn] *n.* 植物(总称)；(尤指某地的)植被，草木(plants)

【例】Lefkas has an abundance of lush green *vegetation*.

alluvial	[ə'luːviəl] *adj.* (河流、洪水)冲积的；淤积的 *n.* 冲积层
arctic	['ɑːrktɪk] *adj.* 北极的(north polar)；极冷的 *n.* 北极

【派】antarctic(*adj.* 南极的 *n.* 南极)

aseismic	[eɪ'saɪzmɪk] *adj.* 无地震的(free of earthquakes)；耐震的

【例】*aseismic* design

clay	[kleɪ] *n.* 黏土，泥土
delta	['deltə] *n.* (河流的)三角洲
desert	['dezərt] *n.* 沙漠 [dɪ'zɜːrt] *v.* 舍弃，遗弃(to forsake, abandon)

【例】Never *desert* a friend in need.

【派】deserted(*adj.* 荒芜的；为人所弃的)

domain	[doʊ'meɪn] *n.* 领土，领域(field, region)
epicenter	['epɪsentər] *n.* 震中；中心，集中点
equator	[ɪ'kweɪtər] *n.* 赤道
Eurasian	[ju'reɪʃn] *adj.* 欧亚的
geography	[dʒi'ɑːgrəfi] *n.* 地理(学)；地形，地势

【派】geographic(*adj.* 地理学的)

geology	[dʒi'ɑːlədʒi] *n.* 地质学

【派】geological(*adj.* 地质学的) geologist(*n.* 地质学者)

hemisphere	['hemɪsfɪr] *n.* 半球；地球的半球

【例】the Northern *hemisphere*

latitude	['lætɪtuːd] *n.* 纬度

【例】The birds breed in Northern *latitudes*.

leeway	['liːweɪ] *n.* 风压差；余地
limestone	['laɪmstoʊn] *n.* 石灰岩
longitudinal	[ˌlɑːndʒə'tuːdnl] *adj.* 经度的；纵向的；纵观的

【例】*longitudinal* stripes

【派】longitudinally（*adv.* 纵向地）

lunar ['lu:nər] *adj.* 月球的，有关月球的

【例】a *lunar* eclipse

magma ['mægmə] *n.* (有机物或矿物的)稀糊；岩浆

magnitude ['mægnɪtu:d] *n.* 震级；巨大；重要性(the great size or importance of something)

【例】They didn't seem to appreciate the *magnitude* of the problem.

marine [mə'ri:n] *adj.* 海的；海上的；海军的；海运的

【记】mari(海) + ne → 海的

【例】Human beings are natural enemies of *marine* mammals.

meteorite ['mi:tiəraɪt] *n.* 陨石(a piece of rock or metal from space that has landed on Earth)

peninsula [pə'nɪnsələ] *n.* 半岛

【派】peninsular(*adj.* 半岛的)

prairie ['preri] *n.* 大草原

ranch [rænʃ] *n.* 大农场(large farm)

【派】rancher(*n.* 大农场主)

rapid ['ræpɪd] *n.* [常*pl.*]急流，湍流

salinity [sə'lɪnəti] *n.* 盐分；盐度

seismic ['saɪzmɪk] *adj.* 地震的

【例】*seismic* wave

seismology [saɪz'mɑ:lədʒi] *n.* 地震学

【派】seismologist(*n.* 地震学家)

semi-arid [ˌsemi'ærɪd] *adj.* 半干旱的

slant [slænt] *n.* 斜面 *vt.* 使倾斜(tilt, slope)

【例】The roof was built at a *slant* so rain would run off it.

solar ['soulər] *adj.* 太阳的

【例】*solar* system / *solar* corona / *solar* eclipse / *solar* radiation

stratigraphy [strə'tɪgrəfi] *n.* 地层学

【派】stratigraphical(*adj.* 地层学的) stratigraphically(*adv.* 地层学地)

theodolite [θi'ɑ:dəlaɪt] *n.* 经纬仪

topographical [ˌtɑ:pə'græfɪkl] *adj.* 地形的；地形学的；地形测量的

topsoil ['tɑ:psɔɪl] *n.* 表层土；耕作层

transatlantic [ˌtrænzət'læntɪk] *adj.* 横跨大西洋的(crossing the Atlantic Ocean)

【例】*transatlantic* flights

	tributary	['trɪbjəteri] *n.* 支流 (river that flows into larger river)
	tropical	['trɑːpɪkl] *adj.* 热带的
		【例】the *tropical* rain forests
	Yare	[jɑːr] *n.* 耶尔河
	terrain	[təˈreɪn] *n.* 地形 (type of land)
		【例】rocky *terrain*
	zoning	[ˈzoʊnɪŋ] *n.* 分区制
		【例】*zoning* in urban area

If you would go up high, then use your own legs! Do not let yourselves carried aloft; do not seat yourselves on other people's backs and heads.

如果你想要走到高处，就要使用自己的两条腿！不要让别人把你抬到高处；不要坐在别人的背上和头上。

——德国哲学家 尼采 (*F. W. Nietzsche, German philosopher*)

练 习 题

连线题

alluvial	岩浆	latitude	月桂树, 桂冠
forage	植物群	membrane	赤道
peninsula	甘蔗	photosynthesis	陨石
cashew	花粉	equator	南瓜; 西葫芦
maize	(河流)淤积的	ranch	地形
clay	叶子	squash	纬度
pollen	草料; 饲料	laurel	经度的
flora	黏土, 泥土	geology	大农场
magma	腰果树, 腰果	terrain	光合作用
foliage	半岛	meteorite	地震的
delta	菠菜	longitudinal	地质学
sugarcane	(河流的)三角洲	seismic	经纬仪
spinach	玉米	theodolite	薄膜, 细胞膜

选词填空

arctic	domain	epicenter	magnitude	solar
tropical	organic	species	stem	tributary

1. I hadn't realized the _____ of the problem.

2. This question comes into the _____ of philosophy.

3. A _____ of the Columbia River runs through this city.

4. Many people think that _____ food is better for health.

5. He brought some _____ fruits when he came back from Africa.

6. Paris has become the _____ of the world fashion industry.

7. The _____ of the plant is broken and it falls on the ground.

8. Laws have been passed to protect panda and other endangered _____.

9. Will _____ energy replace coal as a power source in electricity production in the future?

10. Polar bear lives in the _____ Circle.

连线题答案

alluvial	（河流)淤积的	latitude	纬度
forage	草料；饲料	membrane	薄膜，细胞膜
peninsula	半岛	photosynthesis	光合作用
cashew	腰果树，腰果	equator	赤道
maize	玉米	ranch	大农场
clay	黏土，泥土	squash	南瓜；西葫芦
pollen	花粉	laurel	月桂树，桂冠
flora	植物群	geology	地质学
magma	岩浆	terrain	地形
foliage	叶子	meteorite	陨石
delta	（河流的)三角洲	longitudinal	经度的
sugarcane	甘蔗	seismic	地震的
spinach	菠菜	theodolite	经纬仪

选词填空答案

arctic	domain	epicenter	magnitude	solar
tropical	organic	species	stem	tributary

1. I hadn't realized the （magnitude）of the problem.
2. This question comes into the （domain）of philosophy.
3. A （tributary）of the Columbia River runs through this city.
4. Many people think that （organic）food is better for health.
5. He brought some （tropical）fruits when he came back from Africa.
6. Paris has become the （epicenter）of the world fashion industry.
7. The （stem）of the plant is broken and it falls on the ground.
8. Laws have been passed to protect panda and other endangered （species）.
9. Will（solar）energy replace coal as a power source in electricity production in the future?
10. Polar bear lives in the （Arctic）Circle.

Word List 9

音频

法　律
语言学
文　学

法律 & 语言学 & 文学

enact [ɪˈnækt] *vt.* 制定(法律),通过(法案)

【例】They're trying to *enact* a "nationality" bill.

enforce [ɪnˈfɔːrs] *vt.* 实施,执行(法律或规定);迫使(to force)

【例】The police *enforce* the law.

investigate [ɪnˈvestɪɡeɪt] *vt.* 调查,研究(research, survey)

【例】The police would *investigate* this accident.

【派】investigation(*n.* 调查,侦查)

judgment [ˈdʒʌdʒmənt] *n.* 判决(verdict, decision)

【记】judg(判断)+ ment → 判决

jurisdiction [ˌdʒʊrɪsˈdɪkʃn] *n.* 司法权

【记】juris(法律)+ dict(说,命令)+ ion → 法律的命令 → 司法权

【例】The committee has *jurisdiction* over all tax measures.

justify [ˈdʒʌstɪfaɪ] *vt.* 证明…是正当的(defend, vindicate)

【记】just(公正的)+ ify → 证明…是正当的

【例】How can you *justify* what you did yesterday?

lawsuit [ˈlɔːsuːt] *n.* 诉讼

【记】law(法律)+ suit(诉讼)→ 诉讼

legacy [ˈleɡəsi] *n.* 遗产(bequest, heritage),遗物

【例】My farm is a *legacy* from my grandfather.

legislature [ˈledʒɪsleɪtʃər] *n.* 立法机关(an institution that has the power to make or change laws)

【例】the state *legislature* of Virginia

legitimate [lɪˈdʒɪtɪmət] *adj.* 合情合理的;合法的(fair, reasonable, acceptable or allowed by law)

【例】That's a perfectly *legitimate* question. / Most scientists believe it is *legitimate* to use animals in medical research.

【派】legitimately(*adv.* 合理地)legitimacy(*n.* 合理,合法)

liability [ˌlaɪəˈbɪləti] *n.* 责任,义务(legal responsibility);倾向

【例】Tenants have legal *liability* for any damage they cause.

lien [ˈliːən] *n.* 留置权,扣押权(the legal right to keep something that belongs to someone who owes you money, until the debt has been paid)

| litigant | [ˈlɪtɪgənt] *adj.* (人)在诉讼中的 *n.* 诉讼当事人 |
| malpractice | [ˌmælˈpræktɪs] *n.* 不法行为，利用职权营私舞弊；玩忽职守；治疗失当 |

【例】Her doctor was found guilty of *malpractice*.

| motion | [ˈmoʊʃn] *n.* 动议(a proposal that is made formally at a meeting, and then is usually decided on by voting) |
| obligation | [ˌɑːblɪˈgeɪʃn] *n.* 义务，责任(a moral or legal duty to do something) |

【例】Employers have an *obligation* to treat all employees equally.

| ordinance | [ˈɔːrdɪnəns] *n.* 条例，法令，指示(law, order) |

【例】city *ordinance* that says parks must be closed at 11 p.m.

| parole | [pəˈroʊl] *n.* 假释 *vt.* 假释，使获假释 (allow someone to leave prison on the condition that they promise to behave well) |

【例】He was *paroled* last week.

| penalize | [ˈpiːnəlaɪz] *vt.* 对…予以惩罚(punish) |

【例】Two students were *penalized* very differently for the same offence.

【派】penalty(*n.* 处罚，罚款)

| perpetrate | [ˈpɜːrpətreɪt] *vt.* 犯罪 (to do something that is morally wrong or illegal)；施行(欺骗、谋杀等) |

【例】Who could have *perpetrated* such a dreadful crime?

【派】perpetrator(*n.* 作恶者, 犯罪者) perpetration(*n.* 犯罪)

| plaintiff | [ˈpleɪntɪf] *n.* 原告(complainant) |

【记】plain(哀诉) + tiff → 原告

| probate | [ˈproʊbeɪt] *n./v.* 遗嘱检验(to prove that a will is legal) |
| prosecute | [ˈprɑːsɪkjuːt] *v.* 起诉；检举(accuse, charge) |

【例】Trespassers will be *prosecuted*.

【派】prosecution(*n.* 起诉)

| purge | [pɜːrdʒ] *v.* 洗清(罪等) |

【记】比较pure(*adj.* 纯的)

【例】The old tycoon did a lot of good deeds to *purge* away his sins.

| recess | [rɪˈses] *vi.* 休息；休会，休庭 (officially stop work for a period of time) |

【派】recessed(*adj.* 凹的)

| recoup | [rɪˈkuːp] *vt.* 扣除；赔偿，偿还(get back money) |

【例】The movie will have to be a huge hit to *recoup* its cost.

| respondent | [rɪˈspɑːndənt] *n.* (尤指离婚案的)被告；调查对象(someone who defends their case in a law court) |

sentinel	['sentɪnl] *n.* 岗哨，哨兵(sentry)
session	['seʃn] *n.* 会议，会期；开庭；[*pl.*] 法庭；一段时间 (a period of time)
statute	['stætjuːt] *n.* 法令，章程，条例(law, rules)
sue	[suː] *v.* 控告，控诉(make claims against)

【例】If the builders don't fulfil their side of the contract, we'll *sue*.

superintendent	[ˌsuːpərɪn'tendənt] *n.* 主管，负责人，指挥者(supervisor, manager)

【记】super(上面) + intendent(监督) → 主管

tribunal	[traɪ'bjuːnl] *n.* 特别法庭(a type of court)；裁决，公断
vendor	['vendər] *n.* 小贩；卖主(seller)

【例】the shouts of street *vendors*

subterfuge	['sʌbtərfjuːdʒ] *n.* 诡计；托词(trick)

【例】Sereni was lured to Moscow by *subterfuge*.

tactic	['tæktɪk] *n.* (达到目的的)手段，战术(method, strategy)

【派】tactical(*adj.* 手段的，战术的)

practitioner	[præk'tɪʃənər] *n.* 开业者(医生、律师等)(someone who works as a doctor or a lawyer)；实践者
defendant	[dɪ'fendənt] *n.* 被告

【记】defend(辩护) + ant → 被告

bilingual	[ˌbaɪ'lɪŋgwəl] *adj.* 双语的；能说两种语言的 *n.* 能说两种语言的人

【记】bi(二，双) + lingua(语言) + l → 双语的

【例】She works as a *bilingual* secretary for an insurance company.

clause	[klɔːz] *n.* 【语法】从句；(法律文件等的)条款

【例】A confidentiality *clause* was added to the contract.

conjunction	[kən'dʒʌŋkʃn] *n.* 连词；结合，联合
countable	['kaʊntəbl] *adj.* 可计算的 (capable of being counted) *n.* 可数名词
dialect	['daɪəlekt] *n.* 方言
etymology	[ˌetɪ'mɑːlədʒi] *n.* 语源学
figurative	['fɪgjərətɪv] *adj.* 【修辞手法】比喻的

【例】He imprisoned her, in a *figurative* sense.

idiomatic [ˌɪdiə'mætɪk] *adj.* 含有习语的；符合语言习惯的，地道的

【记】idiom(习语，成语) + atic → 含有习语的

【例】Their books are translated into *idiomatic* English.

【派】idiomatically(*adv.* 惯用地)

infinitive [ɪn'fɪnətɪv] *n.* 【动词】不定式；不定词 *adj.* 不定式的

【例】Modal verbs generally take the bare *infinitive*.

lingo ['lɪŋgoʊ] *n.* 外国话(贬义)；行话；方言；隐语

【例】academic *lingo*

linguistics [lɪŋ'gwɪstɪks] *n.* 语言学

【记】lingu(语言) + istics(学科后缀) → 语言学

【派】linguist(*n.* 语言学家) linguistic(*adj.* 语言学的)

lyrical ['lɪrɪkl] *adj.* 抒情的，抒情诗的(beautifully expressed in words, poetry, or music)

【例】*lyrical* love poetry

【派】lyrically(*adv.* 抒情地)

methodology [ˌmeθə'dɑ:lədʒi] *n.* 方法学，方法论

【例】There are some differences in *methodology* between the two studies.

【派】methodological(*adj.* 方法论的) methodologically(*adv.* 方法论地)

non-verbal [nɑ:n'vɜ:rbl] *adj.* 不用言辞表达的(not using words)

【例】*non-verbal* forms of communication

【派】non-verbally(*adv.* 非语言地)

paradox ['pærədɑ:ks] *n.* 似非而是的论点；有矛盾特点的人(事物、情况)(a situation or statement that seems strange because it involves two different ideas or qualities)

【例】It's a *paradox* that in such a rich country there can be so much poverty.

【派】paradoxical(*adj.* 自相矛盾的)

parenthetical [ˌpærən'θetɪkl] *adj.* 作为插入语的，放在括号里的；[喻]插曲的

passive ['pæsɪv] *adj.* 被动的，消极的；漠然的；被动语态的

【例】Kathy seems to take a very *passive* role in the relationship.

【派】passively(*adv.* 被动地) passivity(*n.* 被动)

polygraph ['pɑ:ligræf] *n.* 多产作家；测谎器(lie detector)

【例】The suspect was given a *polygraph* test.

poststructuralism [ˌpoʊst'strʌktʃərəlɪzəm] *n.* 后结构主义

punctuation [ˌpʌŋktʃu'eɪʃn] *n.* 标点；全部标点符号

rhetoric	[ˈretərɪk] *n.* 花言巧语（art or language used to influence people）；修辞学
	【例】The speech was dismissed by some people as merely political *rhetoric*.
skim	[skɪm] *vt.* 略读(scan)
	【例】He *skims* the book and says it has no use.
	【派】skimming(*n.* 略读)
syllable	[ˈsɪləbl] *n.* 音节
synonymous	[sɪˈnɑːnɪməs] *adj.* 同义的(with same meanings)
	【例】Nixon's name has become *synonymous* with political scandal.
	【派】synonymously(*adv.* 同义地)
tag	[tæg] *n.* 附加语；标签(label, tab)
transitive	[ˈtrænsətɪv] *n.* 及物动词 *adj.* 及物的；过渡的；转变的
	【派】transitively(*adv.* 及物地) transitivity(*n.* 及物性)
typology	[taɪˈpɑːlədʒi] *n.* 类型学；象征论
vocal	[ˈvoʊkl] *adj.* 有声的；口述的；畅言无忌的(outspoken)
	【例】Foley has been particularly *vocal* in his criticism of the government.
	【派】vocally(*adv.* 口头地) vocality(*n.* 声音，声乐)
morphology	[mɔːrˈfɑːlədʒi] *n.* 形态学
	【派】morphological(*adj.* 形态学的；词法的) morphologically(*adv.* 形态上地)

terminology	[ˌtɜːrməˈnɑːlədʒi] *n.* 术语，术语学
	【派】terminological(*adj.* 术语学的)
anthology	[ænˈθɑːlədʒi] *n.* 诗集，文选
autobiography	[ˌɔːtəbaɪˈɑːgrəfi] *n.* 自传
composition	[ˌkɑːmpəˈzɪʃn] *n.* 构成；混合物；写作，作曲，作文
epic	[ˈepɪk] *n.* 史诗，叙事诗 *adj.* 史诗(般)的，宏大的
	【例】I read the *epic* work *War and Peace*.
fiction	[ˈfɪkʃn] *n.* 小说
pornography	[pɔːrˈnɑːgrəfi] *n.* 色情文学，色情画
mythology	[mɪˈθɑːlədʒi] *n.* 神话（set of ancient myths）；虚构的事实
	【例】characters from classical *mythology*
	【派】mythological(*adj.* 虚构的)

70

练 习 题

连线题

defendant	休息；休会，休庭	terminology	条例，法令
liability	作曲；作文	tribunal	音节
rhetoric	司法权	parenthetical	术语
dialect	诉讼	ordinance	语言学
recess	修辞学	epic	标点符号
plaintiff	立法	methodology	神话
jurisdiction	责任，义务	punctuation	特别法庭
passive	自传	legitimate	史诗
lawsuit	抒情的	linguistics	作为插入语的
composition	被动语态的	synonymous	合法的
legislature	方言	syllable	方法学
lyrical	原告	parole	同义的
autobiography	被告	mythology	假释

选词填空

enforce	legacy	sue	penalize	malpractice
bilingual	figurative	paradox	anthology	idiomatic

1. We should always critically inherit _____ of history.

2. The _____ is that fisherman would catch more fish if they fished less.

3. Governments make laws and the police _____ them.

4. He is virtually _____ in Spanish and Portuguese.

5. The composition of the _____ of American literature took a long time and great efforts.

6. People who drive when they are drunk should be heavily _____.

7. In our reading we should always be alert for_____ expressions.

8. If the builders don't fulfill their side of the contract, we will _____ .

9. He imprisoned her, in a _____ sense.

10. The patient died due to _____ of the doctor.

练习题答案

连线题答案

defendant	被告	terminology	术语
liability	责任，义务	tribunal	特别法庭
rhetoric	修辞学	parenthetical	作为插入语的
dialect	方言	ordinance	条例，法令
recess	休息；休会，休庭	epic	史诗
plaintiff	原告	methodology	方法学
jurisdiction	司法权	punctuation	标点符号
passive	被动语态的	legitimate	合法的
lawsuit	诉讼	linguistics	语言学
composition	作曲；作文	synonymous	同义的
legislature	立法	syllable	音节
lyrical	抒情的	parole	假释
autobiography	自传	mythology	神话

选词填空答案

enforce	legacy	sue	penalize	malpractice
bilingual	figurative	paradox	anthology	idiomatic

1. We should always critically inherit (legacy) of history.
2. The (paradox) is that fisherman would catch more fish if they fished less.
3. Governments make laws and the police (enforce) them.
4. He is virtually (bilingual) in Spanish and Portuguese.
5. The composition of the (anthology) of American literature took a long time and great efforts.
6. People who drive when they are drunk should be heavily (penalized).
7. In our reading we should always be alert for (idiomatic) expressions.
8. If the builders don't fulfill their side of the contract, we will (sue).
9. He imprisoned her, in a (figurative) sense.
10. The patient died due to (malpractice) of the doctor.

Word List 10

音频

生物学
军事
宗教

生物学 & 军事 & 宗教

amino acid	氨基酸
anatomy	[əˈnætəmi] *n.* 解剖；分析；解剖学
	【派】anatomical(*adj.* 结构上的；解剖的)
ankle	[ˈæŋkl] *n.* 踝，踝关节
	【例】He sprained his *ankle* when playing football.
antibiotic	[ˌæntibaɪˈɑːtɪk] *n.* 抗生素 *adj.* 抗菌的
	【派】antibiotics(*n.* 抗生学) antibody(*n.* 抗体)
antidote	[ˈæntidoʊt] *n.* 解毒药
appendix	[əˈpendɪks] *n.* 附录；阑尾
bacteria	[bækˈtɪəriə] *n.* [bacterium的复数]细菌
biofeedback	[ˌbaɪoʊˈfiːdbæk] *n.* 生物反馈
biological	[ˌbaɪəˈlɑːdʒɪkl] *adj.* 生物学的，生物的
	【派】biology(*n.* 生物学) biologist(*n.* 生物学家)
biota	[baɪˈoʊtə] *n.* 生物区系
bloodstream	[ˈblʌdstriːm] *n.* 血流，体内循环的血液
bronchial	[ˈbrɑːŋkiəl] *adj.* 支气管的
	【派】bronchitis(*n.* 支气管炎)
carcass	[ˈkɑːrkəs] *n.* (尤指动物的)尸体，骨架
chordate	[ˈkɔːrdeɪt] *n.* 脊索动物 *adj.* 有脊索的
chromosome	[ˈkroʊməsoʊm] *n.* 染色体
clavicle	[ˈklævɪkl] *n.* 锁骨
crest	[krest] *n.* 鸟冠，羽冠；(波浪等的)顶，峰
cytology	[saɪˈtɑːlədʒi] *n.* 细胞学
cytoplasm	[ˈsaɪtoʊplæzəm] *n.* 细胞质
embryo	[ˈembrioʊ] *n.* 胚，胚胎(fetus)
enzyme	[ˈenzaɪm] *n.* 酶
fetal	[ˈfiːtl] *adj.* 胎儿的
	【派】fetus(*n.* 胎儿)
fossil	[ˈfɑːsl] *n.* 化石；顽固不化的人
fungi	[ˈfʌŋgaɪ] *n.* [fungus的复数]真菌
gene	[dʒiːn] *n.* 基因

genetic [dʒə'netɪk] *adj.* 遗传(学)的(genetical)

【例】It's very difficult to treat *genetic* diseases.

gland [glænd] *n.* 腺

hereditary [hə'redɪteri] *adj.* (生物学中)遗传的；世袭的，承袭的 (inherited)

【例】She believes that *hereditary* peerages should be abolished.

histidine ['hɪstɪdiːn] *n.* 组氨酸

admiral ['ædmərəl] *n.* 海军将领，舰队司令

【派】admiralty(*n.* 海军部)

ammunition [ˌæmju'nɪʃn] *n.* 弹药，军火

array [ə'reɪ] *n.* 队列，排列(order, display) *v.* 排列(to arrange in order)

【例】The soldiers *arrayed* themselves before the general.

battalion [bə'tæliən] *n.* (陆军之)一营(大约有一千兵士)

demobilization [dɪˌmoʊbələ'zeɪʃn] *n.* 遣散(军人)，复员

enlist [ɪn'lɪst] *v.* 使入伍；从军；征募(enroll)

【记】en + list(列入名单) → 征募

【例】I *enlisted* Mary and Bill to help decorate the party room.

fortress ['fɔːrtrəs] *n.* 堡垒，要塞

levy ['levi] *n.* 课税 *v.* 征收(collect, charge)；征兵

【例】The Empire *levied* heavy taxes upon its colonies.

maneuver [mə'nuːvər] *vt.* 调遣(move) *n.* 策略(tactic)

【记】man(手) + euver(劳动) → 用手劳动 → 调遣

【例】At the last moment, the basketball player made a clever *maneuver* that allowed a goal to be made.

martial ['mɑːrʃl] *adj.* 军事的，战争的(connected with war and fighting)

【例】*martial* music

militancy ['mɪlɪtənsi] *n.* 战斗性，交战状态

【例】an increase in trade union *militancy*

missile ['mɪsl] *n.* 投射出的物体或武器；导弹

nuclear ['nuːkliər] *adj.* 原子的，核武器的

【例】concern about the country's *nuclear* weapons program

rear-echelon ['rɪr'eʃəlɑːn] *n.* 后方指挥所

recruit [rɪ'kruːt] *vt.* 征兵，征募(enlist, enroll)

【例】He was *recruited* into the army.

【派】recruiter(*n.* 征兵人员)

regiment ['redʒɪmənt] *n.* (军)团(a large group of soldiers)
【例】a *regiment* of ants
【派】regimental(*adj.* 团的)

samurai ['sæmuraɪ] *n.* (日本)武士阶层；陆军军官(powerful military class)

sheathe [ʃiːð] *vt.* (将刀剑)入鞘(cover, encase)
【例】He *sheathes* his sword.
【派】sheath(*n.* 鞘, 套)

sniper ['snaɪpər] *n.* 狙击手
【例】*sniper* scope

strategic [strə'tiːdʒɪk] *adj.* 战略的, 对全局有重要意义的(tactical)
【例】Marseilles was of great *strategic* importance.
【派】strategically(*adv.* 战略上)

strategy ['strætədʒi] *n.* 战略, 策略(a planned series of actions)

wage [weɪdʒ] *vt.* 开展运动, 作战(launch, fight against)
【例】The police are *waging* war on drug pushers in the city.

warrior ['wɔːriər] *n.* 战士, 斗士(soldier)

defensive [dɪ'fensɪv] *adj.* 防御用的, 防守的 (protecting sb./sth. against attack) *n.* 防守, 守势
【例】The prince drew up his forces in a strong *defensive* position.

baptism ['bæptɪzəm] *n.* (基督教的)洗礼, 浸礼；(轮船等)命名礼
【派】baptize(*v.* 给…施洗礼) baptist(*n.* 施洗者)

Buddha ['budə] *n.* 佛
【派】Buddhist (*adj.* 佛教的 *n.* 佛教徒) Buddhism(*n.* 佛教)

cult [kʌlt] *n.* 宗派；崇拜

divine [dɪ'vaɪn] *adj.* 神的；神性的；天赐的；非凡的
【例】Jesus is believed by Christians to have been *divine*.
【派】divinity(*n.* 神, 上帝)

doctrine ['dɑːktrɪn] *n.* 教义(dogma)；学说(theory)
【例】How are the *doctrines* of the two churches different?

dogma ['dɔːgmə] *n.* 教义, 教条(belief, view)
【例】Tom rejected the *dogma* of his church and joined another.
【派】dogmatic(*adj.* 教条的；武断的；固执己见的)

Islam [ɪz'lɑːm] *n.* 伊斯兰教, 穆斯林(the Muslim religion)

【派】Islamic(*adj.* 伊斯兰教的) Islamist(*n.* 伊斯兰教主义者)

mosque [mɑːsk] *n.* 伊斯兰教寺院, 清真寺（a building in which Muslims worship）

mundane [mʌnˈdeɪn] *adj.* 现世的, 世俗的(worldly)

【例】He seemed very calm and far removed from *mundane* concerns.

parable [ˈpærəbl] *n.* （圣经中的）寓言故事(short simple story that teaches a moral lesson in *the Bible*)

parish [ˈpærɪʃ] *n.* 教区, 教区全体居民(the area that a priest in some Christian churches is responsible for)

Puritan [ˈpjʊrɪtən] *n.* 清教徒；[p-]极端拘谨的人 *adj.* 清教徒的

【例】the *Puritan* work ethic

religious [rɪˈlɪdʒəs] *adj.* 宗教的, 虔诚的(relating to religion)

【例】I don't share her *religious* beliefs.

【派】religiously(*adv.* 虔诚地)

secular [ˈsekjələr] *adj.* 世俗的, 非宗教的(not connected with churches)

【例】*secular* education

When an end is lawful and obligatory, the indispensable means to it are also lawful and obligatory.

如果一个目的是正当而必须做的, 则达到这个目的的必要手段也是正当而必须采取的。

——美国政治家 林肯(*Abraham Lincoln, American statesman*)

练 习 题

连线题

missile	锁骨	bloodstream	（圣经中的）寓言故事
baptism	支气管的	antidote	附录；阑尾
ankle	导弹	admiral	（军队的）营
dogma	鸟冠，羽冠	martial	胚，胚胎
fossil	弹药，军火	chromosome	狙击手
fungi	踝关节	sniper	解毒药
ammunition	堡垒，要塞	bacteria	佛
antibiotic	真菌	battalion	军事的，战争的
clavicle	（基督教的）洗礼	appendix	细菌
crest	教义，教条	Buddha	战士，斗士
bronchial	抗菌的	embryo	血流
fortress	清教徒	parable	海军将领，舰队司令
Puritan	化石	warrior	染色体

选词填空

anatomy	enzyme	genetic	enlist	array
maneuver	nuclear	doctrine	secular	divine

1. It was said that washing powders containing _____ remove stains more efficiently.

2. At the outbreak of war, he was _____ in the army.

3. They tried by diplomatic _____ to obtain an agreement.

4. Knowledge of human _____ is essential to figure drawing.

5. The United Nations has expressed concern about the country's _____ weapons program.

6. Christians are supposed to follow the _____ of Christianity.

7. The _____ structure of the plants has been changed so that they would not be affected by particular diseases or harmful insects.

8. The soldiers _____ themselves before the general.

9. Jesus is believed by Christians to have been _____.

10. Renaissance undermined the importance of religion in people's lives and put more emphasis on _____ matters.

练习题答案

连线题答案

missile	导弹	bloodstream	血流
baptism	(基督教的)洗礼	antidote	解毒药
ankle	踝关节	admiral	海军将领，舰队司令
dogma	教义，教条	martial	军事的，战争的
fossil	化石	chromosome	染色体
fungi	真菌	sniper	狙击手
ammunition	弹药，军火	bacteria	细菌
antibiotic	抗菌的	battalion	(军队的)营
clavicle	锁骨	appendix	附录；阑尾
crest	鸟冠，羽冠	Buddha	佛
bronchial	支气管的	embryo	胚，胚胎
fortress	堡垒，要塞	parable	(圣经中的)寓言故事
Puritan	清教徒	warrior	战士，斗士

选词填空答案

anatomy	enzyme	genetic	enlist	array
maneuver	nuclear	doctrine	secular	divine

1. It was said that washing powders containing (enzymes) remove stains more efficiently.
2. At the outbreak of war, he was (enlisted) in the army.
3. They tried by diplomatic (maneuvers) to obtain an agreement.
4. Knowledge of human (anatomy) is essential to figure drawing.
5. The United Nations has expressed concern about the country's (nuclear) weapons program.
6. Christians are supposed to follow the (doctrines) of Christianity.
7. The (genetic) structure of the plants has been changed so that they would not be affected by particular diseases or harmful insects.
8. The soldiers (arrayed) themselves before the general.
9. Jesus is believed by Christians to have been (divine).
10. Renaissance undermined the importance of religion in people's lives and put more emphasis on (secular) matters.

Word List 11

音频

航天/天体
术治他
艺政其

航天/天体 & 艺术 & 政治 & 其他

aeronautics	[ˌerə'nɔːtɪks] *n.* 航空学，航空术
	【派】aeronautic(*adj.* 航空的)
airborne	['erbɔːrn] *adj.* 空降的，空运的，空中飞行的；通过电视传送的
asteroid	['æstərɔɪd] *n.* （尤指火星和木星轨道间运行的)小行星
astronaut	['æstrənɔːt] *n.* 太空人，宇航员
astronomer	[ə'strɑːnəmər] *n.* 天文学家
	【派】astronomy（*n.* 天文学）astronomical（*adj.* 天文学的；极大的）
aviation	[ˌeɪvi'eɪʃn] *n.* 航空，航空学
black hole	黑洞
celestial	[sə'lestiəl] *adj.* 天上的，天空的（relating to sky）；天国的，神圣的(heavenly, divine, spiritual)
	【例】Angels are *celestial* beings.
comet	['kɑːmət] *n.* 彗星
	【派】cometary/cometic(*adj.* 彗星的，彗星似的)
cosmic	['kɑːzmɪk] *adj.* 宇宙的
	【例】*cosmic* radiation / *cosmic* rays
eclipse	[ɪ'klɪps] *n./v.* 日食，月食
envelope	['envəloup] *n.* 包层
	【例】air *envelope*
galaxy	['gæləksi] *n.* 银河系
	【派】galactic(*adj.* 银河的)
neutron star	中子星
planetary	['plænəteri] *adj.* （似)行星的
	【例】*planetary* probe
spherical	['sferɪkl] *adj.* 球形的，天体的(round)
	【例】a *spherical* object
supernova	[ˌsuːpər'noʊvə] *n.* 超新星
carol	['kærəl] *n.* 赞美诗，颂歌(尤指基督教的)
chant	[tʃænt] *n.* 歌，单调的歌；赞美诗 *v.* 咏唱，吟诵
choreography	[ˌkɔːri'ɑːgrəfi] *n.* 舞蹈，舞蹈编排(the composition of dance steps

and sequences)

concert [ˈkɑːnsərt] *n.* 一致；协作；音乐会

concerto [kənˈtʃɜːrtoʊ] *n.* 协奏曲

debut [deɪˈbjuː] *n.* (演员的)首次演出；初进社交界

ethnomusicology [ˈeθnoʊˌmjuːzɪˈkɑːlədʒi] *n.* 民族音乐(学)

finale [fɪˈnɑːli] *n.* 终曲，乐曲的最后部分

foreshorten [fɔːrˈʃɔːrtn] *vt.* (绘画中)按照透视法缩短

instrument [ˈɪnstrəmənt] *n.* 乐器
【例】Flute, piano and violin are all musical *instruments*.

orchestra [ˈɔːrkɪstrə] *n.* 管弦乐队

renaissance [ˈrenəsɑːns] *n.* [R-]文艺复兴(时期)；复兴(a new interest in something)
【例】a *renaissance* in wood carving over the last few years

rendition [renˈdɪʃn] *n.* 演唱，表演(performance)
【例】He gave a moving *rendition* of Lennon's *Imagine*.

repertory [ˈrepərtɔːri] *n.* 全部剧目，轮演剧目
【例】a *repertory* company

rhythmic [ˈrɪðmɪk] *adj.* 有韵律的，有节奏的
【例】the *rhythmic* thud of the bass drum

rhythmical [ˈrɪðmɪkl] *adj.* 有节奏的，有节拍的
【派】rhythmically(*adv.* 有节奏地)

statue [ˈstætʃuː] *n.* 雕像(sculpture)

calligraphy [kəˈlɪɡrəfi] *n.* 书法
【派】calligraphic(*adj.* 书法的)

apolitical [ˌeɪpəˈlɪtɪkl] *adj.* 不关心政治的，与政治无关的(without political attitudes, content, or bias, unpolitical)

autonomy [ɔːˈtɑːnəmi] *n.* 自治权(independence)
【记】auto(自己) + nomy(统治) → 自己统治 → 自治权
【例】The nation's *autonomy* was compromised by the treaty.
【派】autonomous(*adj.* 自治的，自主的)

bipartisan [ˌbaɪˈpɑːrtɪzn] *adj.* 由两党成员组成的；被两党支持的
【记】bi(二，双) + partisan(党派) → 由两党成员组成的

bureaucrat [ˈbjʊrəkræt] *n.* 官僚，官僚主义者，官僚作风的人
【派】bureau(*n.* 局，办事处) bureaucracy(*n.* 政府机构；官僚作风) bureaucratic(*adj.* 官僚主义的)

| franchise | [ˈfræntʃaɪz] n. 选举权；参政权 |
| municipal | [mjuːˈnɪsɪpl] adj. 市政的，市立的；地方性的，地方自治的(relating to or belonging to the government of a town or city) |

【例】the *municipal* waste dump

【派】municipally(*adv.* 市政上地)

NATO (North Atlantic Treaty Organization) 北大西洋公约组织

| non-partisan | [nɑːnˈpɑːrtəzn] adj. 无党无派的，超乎党派的(not supporting the ideas of any political party or group) |

【例】a *non-partisan* research group

| partisan | [ˈpɑːrtəzn] n. 党派支持者 adj. 党派的，派系感强的(strongly supporting a particular political party) |

【例】Her *partisan* speech angered the opposing party.

| polyarchy | [ˈpɑːliˌɑːrki] n. 多头政治 |
| regime | [reɪˈʒiːm] n. 政权 |

【记】regi(统治) + me → 政权

| suffrage | [ˈsʌfrɪdʒ] n. 选举权，投票权(the right to vote) |
| terrestrial | [təˈrestriəl] adj. 领土的 |

【例】*terrestrial* heat / *terrestrial* magnetism

| territory | [ˈterətɔːri] n. 领土，版图，地域 |

【派】territorial(*adj.* 领地的)

| totalitarian | [touˌtæləˈteriən] n. 极权主义者 adj. 极权主义的 |

【例】a *totalitarian* state / regime

【派】totalitarianism(*n.* 极权主义)

| archaeology | [ˌɑːrkiˈɑːlədʒi] n. 考古学 |

【派】archaeologist(*n.* 考古学家) archaeological(*adj.* 考古学的)

| climatology | [ˌklaɪməˈtɑːlədʒi] n. 气候学(the study of climate) |

【派】climatologist(*n.* 气候学家)

| demography | [dɪˈmɑːgrəfi] n. 人口统计学 |

【派】demographic(*adj.* 人口统计学的)

| empirical | [ɪmˈpɪrɪkl] adj. 以观察或实验为依据的 |

【例】We now have *empirical* evidence that the Moon is covered with dust.

| ethics | [ˈeθɪks] n. 伦理学；道德规范 |

【例】professional *ethics*

graphics	['græfɪks] *n.* 制图法，制图学
iconography	[ˌaɪkə'nɑːgrəfi] *n.* 肖像画法；肖像学；插画，图解
qualitative	['kwɑːləteɪtɪv] *adj.* 性质上的，定性的(relating to quality)

【例】a *qualitative* study of educational services

【派】qualitatively(*adv.* 质量上地)

tentative	['tentətɪv] *adj.* 试验性的(trial)

【记】tent=test(测试) + ative → 试验性的

【例】*Tentative* measures have been taken to settle these refugees.

【派】tentatively(*adv.* 试验性地) tentativeness(*n.* 固定)

theoretical	[ˌθiːə'retɪkl] *adj.* 理论的(academic)

【例】She has *theoretical* knowledge of teaching, but no practical experience.

【派】theoretically(*adv.* 在理论上)

analytical	[ˌænə'lɪtɪkl] *adj.* 分析的，分析法的(analytic, using analysis)

【例】During the course, students will develop their *analytical* skills.

【派】analyst(*n.* 分析家，化验员) analytics(*n.* 分析论，解析学)

conceptual	[kən'septʃuəl] *adj.* 观念的(relating to concepts)；抽象的(abstract)

【例】The mall's plans are still in the *conceptual* stage.

concrete	['kɑːŋkriːt] *adj.* 具体的，有形的(substantial, tangible) *n.* 混凝土

【例】Bill prefers *concrete* facts to abstract ideas.

applied	[ə'plaɪd] *adj.* (尤指某种科学)应用的

【例】*applied* mathematics / *applied* art

hygiene	['haɪdʒiːn] *n.* 卫生(sanitation)

【例】The dentist instructed his patients on dental *hygiene*.

【派】hygienic(*adj.* 卫生的；清洁的)

连线题

asteroid	黑洞	theoretical	乐器
archaeology	与政治无关的	comet	宇宙的
astronomer	航空学	statue	音乐会
conceptual	政权	non-partisan	人口统计学
ethics	管弦乐队	bureaucrat	彗星
calligraphy	选举权；参政权	galaxy	多头政治
aeronautics	书法	totalitarian	理论的
graphics	道德规范	analytical	官僚
apolitical	小行星	cosmic	雕像
regime	观念的	concert	银河系
black hole	天文学家	polyarchy	分析的
orchestra	考古学	demography	无党无派的
franchise	制图法	instrument	极权主义者

选词填空

astronaut	eclipse	celestial	autonomy	suffrage
municipal	territory	debut	rhythmic	tentative

1. You need to wear protective glasses to view a solar _____.
2. She made her _____ album in 1973 which was an instant success.
3. We've made a _____ plan for the vacation but haven't really decided yet.
4. He works in the _____ government.
5. The _____ was welcomed with joyous, resounding acclaim when he went out of the spacecraft.
6. Angels are _____ beings.
7. The _____ stamping of the heels is characteristic of Spanish flamenco dance.
8. Taiwan is the inseparable _____ of China.
9. Branch managers have full _____ in their own areas.
10. The _____ movement campaigned for votes for women in Britain and the U.S.

练习题答案

连线题答案

asteroid	小行星	theoretical	理论的
archaeology	考古学	comet	彗星
astronomer	天文学家	statue	雕像
conceptual	观念的	non-partisan	无党无派的
ethics	道德规范	bureaucrat	官僚
calligraphy	书法	galaxy	银河系
aeronautics	航空学	totalitarian	极权主义者
graphics	制图法	analytical	分析的
apolitical	与政治无关的	cosmic	宇宙的
regime	政权	concert	音乐会
black hole	黑洞	polyarchy	多头政治
orchestra	管弦乐队	demography	人口统计学
franchise	选举权；参政权	instrument	乐器

选词填空答案

astronaut	eclipse	celestial	autonomy	suffrage
municipal	territory	debut	rhythmic	tentative

1. You need to wear protective glasses to view a solar（eclipse）.
2. She made her（debut）album in 1973 which was an instant success.
3. We've made a（tentative）plan for the vacation but haven't really decided yet.
4. He works in the（municipal）government.
5. The（astronaut）was welcomed with joyous, resounding acclaim when he went out of the spacecraft.
6. Angels are（celestial）beings.
7. The（rhythmic）stamping of the heels is characteristic of Spanish flamenco dance.
8. Taiwan is the inseparable（territory）of China.
9. Branch managers have full（autonomy）in their own areas.
10. The（suffrage）movement campaigned for votes for women in Britain and the U.S.

GMAT
按意群分类
Subjects

Word List 12

音频

社会事物（一）

社会事物(一)

器　具

antifreeze [ˈæntifriːz] *n.* 抗冻剂

ceramic [səˈræmɪk] *adj.* 陶器的，与陶器有关的

【例】Some *ceramic* works of art are shown in this exhibition.

【派】ceramics(*n.* 陶器；制陶工艺)

apparatus [ˌæpəˈrætəs] *n.* 运动器械，仪器；器官(organ)

【例】The breathing *apparatus* includes the nose, throat and lungs.

apparel [əˈpærəl] *n.* 衣服，服饰；外观，外表；船上的用具

appliance [əˈplaɪəns] *n.* 器具，器械(device, instrument, utensil)

chisel [ˈtʃɪzl] *n./v.* 凿

【例】He *chiseled* a hole in the door to fit a new lock.

component [kəmˈpoʊnənt] *n.* 组成部分；零件

constituent [kənˈstitjuənt] *n.* 成分(component)；选民

device [dɪˈvaɪs] *n.* 器械，装置（machine, equipment）；设计(scheme, ploy)

【例】Dave bought a special *device* to peel potatoes.

equipment [ɪˈkwɪpmənt] *n.* 设备(facility, fixture)

hinge [hɪndʒ] *n.* 铰链(joint, pivot) *vi.* 依…而定(depend, rely)

【例】This plan *hinges* on her approval.

implement [ˈɪmplɪment] *vt.* 实现，执行（carry out, fulfil, execute）

[ˈɪmplɪmənt] *n.* 工具(device, instrument, facility)

【记】im(进入) + ple(满) + ment → 使圆满 → 实现

【例】Once we made a plan, the remaining task would be to *implement* it.

【派】implementation(*n.* 执行)

latch [lætʃ] *n.* 闩；弹簧锁 *vt.* 用闩把…闩上（to fasten a door, gate etc.）

【例】Remember to *latch* the gate behind you.

microwave [ˈmaɪkrəweɪv] *n.* 微波，微波炉

mute [mjuːt] *adj.* 沉默的(silent) *n.* 弱音器

【例】Billy continued to stand there, *mute* and defiant.

panel	['pænl] *n.* 讨论小组（group of people）；仪表板
	【例】A *panel* of experts has looked at the proposal.
phonograph	['foʊnəgræf] *n.* 留声机，唱机（record player）
pliers	['plaɪərz] *n.* 钳子，老虎钳
plug	[plʌg] *n.* 塞子；插头
plywood	['plaɪwʊd] *n.* 胶合板，夹板
porcelain	['pɔːrsəlɪn] *n.* 瓷，瓷器（china）
pottery	['pɑːtəri] *n.* 陶器，陶器制品（objects made out of baked clay）
receptor	[rɪ'septər] *n.* 受体；接收器
shuttle	['ʃʌtl] *n.* （织机的）梭；穿梭运输工具（a plane, bus, or train, etc.）
	【例】He took the Washington–New York *shuttle*.
sickle	['sɪkl] *n.* 镰刀
staple	['steɪpl] *n.* 订书钉
throttle	['θrɑːtl] *n.* 节流阀 *vt.* 掐脖子，扼杀（strangle）
	【例】He grabbed her by the throat and began *throttling* her.
trench	[trentʃ] *n.* 沟，壕沟（a long narrow hole）
scale	[skeɪl] *n.* 规模；尺度；天平
	【例】I'll be glad when I tip the *scales* at a few pounds less.
telescope	['telɪskoʊp] *n.* 望远镜 *v.* 变短（shorten）
	【例】The whole legal process was *telescoped* into a few weeks.
wrapper	['ræpər] *n.* 包装纸，封套
	【例】old sweet *wrappers*

称　呼

recipient	[rɪ'sɪpiənt] *n.* 接受者（receiver, payee）
anonymous	[ə'nɑːnɪməs] *adj.* 匿名的（unknown by name）
	【例】$50,000 has been given to the charity by an *anonymous* donor.
	【派】anonymity（*n.* 匿名）
apologist	[ə'pɑːlədʒɪst] *n.* 辩护士（尤指卫护基督教教义的辩护者）
arbitrator	['ɑːrbɪtreɪtər] *n.* 公断人，仲裁人
	【派】arbitration（*n.* 仲裁）
artisan	['ɑːrtəzn] *n.* 技工，工匠

attorney [əˈtɜːrni] *n.* 代理人，辩护律师（lawyer）

【例】Bob hired an *attorney* to get a patent for his invention.

authorship [ˈɔːθərʃɪp] *n.* 作者身份（职业）；原作者；来源

【例】What is the *authorship* of that novel?

bandit [ˈbændɪt] *n.* 土匪，强盗

benefactor [ˈbenɪfæktər] *n.* 行善者，捐助者

【派】beneficiary（*n.* 受益者，受惠者）

burglar [ˈbɜːrglər] *n.* 窃贼，破门盗窃者

cartographer [kɑːrˈtɑːgrəfər] *n.* 制图员，地图制作者

【派】cartography（*n.* 制图学，制图法）

celebrity [səˈlebrəti] *n.* 名人，知名人士

chef [ʃef] *n.* 厨师

clerical [ˈklerɪkl] *adj.* 文书的，办事员的（relating to office work）；牧师的（relating to clergy）

【例】She had a *clerical* assistant to do her paperwork.

comedian [kəˈmiːdiən] *n.* 喜剧演员，丑角

【派】comedy（*n.* 喜剧）

consultant [kənˈsʌltənt] *n.* 顾问（advisor）

contractor [kənˈtræktər] *n.* 承包人

courier [ˈkʊriər] *n.* 送急件的人，信使

distributor [dɪˈstrɪbjətər] *n.* 发行人

donor [ˈdoʊnər] *n.* 捐献者

dropout [ˈdrɑːpaʊt] *n.* 辍学者；中途退出的人；拒绝传统社会的人

emperor [ˈempərər] *n.* 皇帝，君主

【派】empress（*n.* 女王，皇后）

entrepreneur [ˌɑːntrəprəˈnɜːr] *n.* 企业家

entrepreneurship [ˌɑːntrəprəˈnɜːrʃɪp] *n.* 企业家的身份、地位、职权、能力、精神等

executioner [ˌeksɪˈkjuːʃənər] *n.* 刽子手

gourmet [ˈɡʊrmeɪ] *n.* 讲究吃喝的人，美食家

gymnast [ˈdʒɪmnæst] *n.* 体操家，体育家

gynecologist [ˌɡaɪnəˈkɑːlədʒɪst] *n.* 妇科医生

historian [hɪˈstɔːriən] *n.* 历史学家，史学工作者

hypnotist [ˈhɪpnətɪst] *n.* 催眠师

signature [ˈsɪɡnətʃər] *n.* 签名，鲜明特征（name written, character）

tenant [ˈtenənt] *n.* 租户，房客（occupant, inhabitant）

victor ['vɪktər] *n. /adj.* 胜利者(的), 获胜者(的)(winner)

建 筑

architect ['ɑːrkɪtekt] *n.* 建筑师, 设计师
【派】architecture(*n.* 建筑, 建筑学)

archive ['ɑːrkaɪv] *n.* 档案文件 *v.* 存档
【派】archives(*n.* 档案, 档案馆)

auditorium [ˌɔːdɪ'tɔːriəm] *n.* 大礼堂
【记】audi(听) + t + orium(名词词尾, 表示场所、地点)→ 大礼堂
【例】The new *auditorium* had velvet seats.

baroque [bə'rouk] *adj.* (艺术、建筑等)巴洛克风格的; 高度装饰的, 过分
雕琢的

basement ['beɪsmənt] *n.* 地下室

buttress ['bʌtrəs] *n.* 撑墙, 扶壁 *v.* 支撑, 加固(to sustain)

cathedral [kə'θiːdrəl] *n.* 总教堂, 大教堂

chamber ['tʃeɪmbər] *n.* 卧室; 议院 *adj.* 室内的; 小规模的
【例】*chamber* music

cornerstone ['kɔːrnərstoun] *n.* 墙角石, 奠基石;[喻]柱石, 基础

pantheon ['pænθiɑːn] *n.* 万神殿, 先贤祠(a religious building that is built in
honor of all gods)

tectonic [tek'tɑːnɪk] *adj.* 构造的, 建筑的

tubular ['tuːbjələr] *adj.* 管的, 由管构成的(made of tubes)
【例】*tubular* metal furniture

threshold ['θreʃhould] *n.* 门槛(doorsill, entrance); 开端
【例】Eighty percent of the vote was the *threshold* for approval of the
plan.

练 习 题

连线题

telescope	铰链	tenant	大礼堂
ceramic	建筑师	bandit	留声机
distributor	代理人,辩护律师	microwave	档案文件
apparatus	地下室	hypnotist	技工,工匠
comedian	陶器的	staple	辍学者
constituent	刽子手	donor	微波炉
basement	企业家	phonograph	妇科医生
celebrity	知名人士	dropout	瓷器
attorney	喜剧演员	auditorium	租户,房客
architect	运动器械,仪器	porcelain	土匪,强盗
entrepreneur	发行人	artisan	催眠师
hinge	成分	gynecologist	订书钉
executioner	望远镜	archive	捐献者

选词填空

appliance	implement	scale	anonymous	authorship
consultant	signature	cathedral	cornerstone	historian

1. We have decided to _____ the committee's recommendations in full.
2. These two _____ are very similar. Can you tell them apart?
3. There is no evidence to dispute his claim to the _____ of these books.
4. Photography is strictly forbidden in the _____, the holy place for worship.
5. Wage control is the _____ of the government's economic policy.
6. Jack is a famous American _____ who published numerous works on the colonial period.
7. He is a _____ on law affairs to the mayor.
8. There has been housing development on a mass _____ since 1980.
9. Washing machine is one of the must-have household _____ today.
10. According to one employee, who wishes to remain _____, the company engaged in illegal activities.

连线题答案

telescope	望远镜	tenant	租户，房客
ceramic	陶器的	bandit	土匪，强盗
distributor	发行人	microwave	微波炉
apparatus	运动器械，仪器	hypnotist	催眠师
comedian	喜剧演员	staple	订书钉
constituent	成分	donor	捐献者
basement	地下室	phonograph	留声机
celebrity	知名人士	dropout	辍学者
attorney	代理人，辩护律师	auditorium	大礼堂
architect	建筑师	porcelain	瓷器
entrepreneur	企业家	artisan	技工，工匠
hinge	铰链	gynecologist	妇科医生
executioner	刽子手	archive	档案文件

选词填空答案

appliance	implement	scale	anonymous	authorship
consultant	signature	cathedral	cornerstone	historian

1. We have decided to（implement）the committee's recommendations in full.

2. These two（signatures）are very similar. Can you tell them apart?

3. There is no evidence to dispute his claim to the（authorship）of these books.

4. Photography is strictly forbidden in the（cathedral）, the holy place for worship.

5. Wage control is the（cornerstone）of the government's economic policy.

6. Jack is a famous American（historian）who published numerous works on the colonial period.

7. He is a（consultant）on law affairs to the mayor.

8. There has been housing development on a mass（scale）since 1980.

9. Washing machine is one of the must-have household（appliances）today.

10. According to one employee, who wishes to remain（anonymous）, the company engaged in illegal activities.

Word List 13

音频

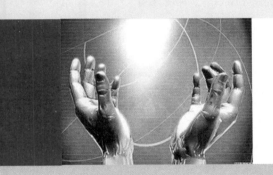

社会事物(二)

社会事物(二)

交　通

congested [kən'dʒestɪd] *adj.* 拥挤的，堵车的（over-crowded）
【例】The roads out of Cornwall were heavily *congested*.
【派】congestion（*n.* 拥挤，堵车）

embark [ɪm'bɑːrk] *vi.* 乘船 *vt.* 装载
【例】Passengers with cargo must *embark* first. / This ship *embarked* cargoes.

automatic [ˌɔːtə'mætɪk] *adj.* （机器或行为）自动的（activating, moving or regulating by itself）
【例】The movements of machines are completely *automatic*, you only need to start and stop the machines.
【派】automation（*n.* 自动操作，自动化）

automobile ['ɔːtəməbiːl] *n.* 机动车，车辆
【记】auto（自己）+ mobile（动）→ 机动车

braking ['breɪkɪŋ] *n.* 刹车，制动

chaise [ʃeɪz] *n.* 两轮（或四轮）轻便马车

cylinder ['sɪlɪndər] *n.* 圆筒，圆柱体；汽缸

diesel ['diːzl] *n.* 柴油，柴油机机车（或船等）

freeway ['friːweɪ] *n.* 高速公路，快车道

gasoline ['gæsəliːn] *n.* 汽油（petroleum）

headlight ['hedlaɪt] *n.* （汽车等的）前灯

navigation [ˌnævɪ'geɪʃn] *n.* 航海
【派】navigational（*adj.* 航海的）navigator（*n.* 领航员）

pedal ['pedl] *n.* 脚踏板

pedestrian [pə'destriən] *n.* 步行者，行人（someone who is walking, especially along a street）

reef [riːf] *n.* 暗礁 *vt.* 收帆（to tie up part of a sail）

relay ['riːleɪ] *n.* 驿马；补充物资；接替人员
【例】work in *relays*

sedan [sɪ'dæn] *n.* 轿子；轿车（car）；单舱汽艇（boat）

steerage	[ˈstɪrɪdʒ] n. 驾驶；操纵；下等客舱
supersonic	[ˌsuːpərˈsɑːnɪk] adj. 超声的，超音速的（faster than the speed of sound）
	【例】*supersonic* aircraft
windshield	[ˈwɪndʃiːld] n. 挡风玻璃(windscreen)

其他事物

bakery	[ˈbeɪkəri] n. 面包房
barrel	[ˈbærəl] n. 桶；照相机的镜头 vt. 把…装桶
	【例】The cement is *barreled*.
basketry	[ˈbæskɪtrɪ] n. (篮、篓、筐等的)编织术；[总称](篮子等)编织物
beverage	[ˈbevərɪdʒ] n. 饮料
bookkeeping	[ˈbʊkkiːpɪŋ] n. 簿记
boomerang	[ˈbuːməræŋ] n. 回飞棒，飞去来器
booth	[buːθ] n. 售货亭，摊位
bottleneck	[ˈbɑːtlnek] n. 瓶颈口；[喻]交通易阻塞的狭口；妨碍生产流程的一环
bouquet	[buˈkeɪ] n. 花束
brewery	[ˈbruːəri] n. 啤酒厂，酿酒厂
brine	[braɪn] n. 海水；浓盐水，卤水
	【派】briny(*adj.* 盐水的，很咸的；海水的)
buoy	[ˈbɔɪ] n. 浮标，航标 v. 使浮起；使振奋，使有信心
	【例】They were *buoyed* up by hopes of success.
	【派】buoyant(*adj.* 有浮力的；轻快的，活泼的) buoyancy(*n.* 浮力)
bust	[bʌst] n. 半身塑像
cabin	[ˈkæbɪn] n. (简陋的)小屋；船舱，机舱
cache	[kæʃ] n. 土窖，藏物处；贮藏物
camcorder	[ˈkæmkɔːrdər] n. (VCR)摄像机
candidate	[ˈkændɪdət] n. 候选人，报考者，求职者
canopy	[ˈkænəpi] n. 悬于上空的覆盖物，华盖，罩棚
canvas	[ˈkænvəs] n. 粗帆布；帐篷；一幅油画
censorship	[ˈsensərʃɪp] n. 审查员的职权；审查(制度)
	【记】censor(审查员) + ship → 审查员的职权
census	[ˈsensəs] n. 人口普查

commuter	[kəˈmjuːtər] n. (远距离)上下班往返的人

【例】The congested highway made many *commuters* late for work.

【派】commute(v. 通勤)

container	[kənˈteɪnər] n. 容器；集装箱
cork	[kɔːrk] n. 软木塞
detergent	[dɪˈtɜːrdʒənt] n. 洗涤剂
domesticity	[ˌdoʊmeˈstɪsəti] n. 家庭生活(family life)
fiberglass	[ˈfaɪbərglæs] n. 玻璃纤维，玻璃丝
funnel	[ˈfʌnl] n. 漏斗；(轮船、火车等的)烟囱
fuse	[fjuːz] n. 保险丝；导火线 v. 合并(to blend, combine)；熔化

【例】The wax from the two candles *fused* as they burned.

【派】fusion(n. 熔合；合并)

helicopter	[ˈhelɪkɑːptər] n. 直升机
ideology	[ˌaɪdiˈɑːlədʒi] n. 意识形态，思想体系

【例】The *ideology* has great influence in the world.

recreation	[ˌrekriˈeɪʃn] n. 消遣(pastime, amusement)

【例】For *recreation*, I like to go hiking and camping.

【派】recreational(adj. 娱乐的)

insurance	[ɪnˈʃʊrəns] n. 保险，保险费，保险业，保险措施

【例】Do you have *insurance* on your house and its contents?

ceremonious	[ˌserəˈmoʊniəs] adj. 隆重的；正式的，恭敬的(formal, solemn)

【例】The symphony conductor took a *ceremonious* bow.

饮　食

braise	[breɪz] vt. 炖，焖
palatable	[ˈpælətəbl] adj. 味美的(savory, flavorous)

【记】palat(e)(上颚)+ able → 与上颚有关 → 味美的

【例】very *palatable* wine

【派】palatability(n. 美味，风味)

cater	[ˈkeɪtər] v. 供应饮食及服务(to provide what is required or desired)；迎合，投合

【例】We *catered* for forty guests but only twenty came.

caviar	['kæviɑːr] *n.* 鱼子酱；不为一般人所欣赏的雅品	

caviar ['kæviɑːr] *n.* 鱼子酱；不为一般人所欣赏的雅品

【例】*caviar* to the general

chocolate ['tʃɑːklət] *n.* 巧克力

clam [klæm] *n.* 蛤；蛤肉；寡言的人

culinary ['kʌlɪneri] *adj.* 厨房的，烹饪的（relating to kitchen or cookery）

dietary ['daɪəteri] *adj.* 与饮食有关的，饮食的（relating to a diet）

【例】Will there be any special *dietary* requirements?

digest [daɪ'dʒest] *v.* 消化 ['daɪdʒest] *n.* 文摘，汇编

【例】Cheese doesn't *digest* easily.

【派】digestion(*n.* 消化) digestive(*adj.* 消化的)

dine [daɪn] *v.* 吃饭；招待…吃饭；(房子、桌子)可容…吃饭

dough [doʊ] *n.* 生面团

edible ['edəbl] *adj.* 可食的(eatable, comestible)

【记】ed(吃) + ible → 可食的

【例】The cake was garnished with *edible* decorations.

【派】edibility(*n.* 可食性)

ingest [ɪn'dʒest] *vt.* 摄取，咽下(to take food or other substances into your body)

【派】ingestion(*n.* 摄取)

oatmeal ['oʊtmiːl] *n.* 燕麦片

processed food 腌制食品

recipe ['resəpi] *n.* 食谱(a set of instructions for cooking)；处方，秘诀

sandwich ['sænwɪtʃ] *vt.* 把…做成三明治；夹入，挤进(squeeze)

【例】A layer of transparent material is *sandwiched* between the pieces of glass.

sweetener ['swiːtnər] *n.* 食糖，果糖，糖浆，甜味剂

练 习 题

连线题

gasoline	洗涤剂	windshield	燕麦片
processed food	柴油	supersonic	人口普查
cylinder	保险丝	pedestrian	食谱
automobile	刹车，制动	booth	食糖，甜味剂
culinary	汽油	ceremonious	暗礁
freeway	腌制食品	reef	可食的
insurance	机动车	census	步行者，行人
diesel	面包房	sweetener	隆重的
fuse	鱼子酱	recreation	售货亭
braking	厨房的，烹饪的	bouquet	超音速的
caviar	汽缸	oatmeal	花束
detergent	保险	edible	消遣，娱乐
bakery	高速公路	recipe	挡风玻璃

选词填空

congested	automatic	navigation	beverage	candidate
censorship	commute	ideology	dietary	digest

1. _____ is difficult on this river because of hidden rocks.

2. We do not sell alcoholic _____ to teenagers.

3. The city streets were _____ with vehicles.

4. He interviewed many _____ for the job but found none qualified.

5. It often takes a long time to _____ new ideas.

6. The government has imposed strict _____ on the press.

7. Patients with special _____ requirements should be given special attention.

8. Barbara lives in the suburb and works in the downtown, so she _____ between the two places every day.

9. A boy who has good manners stands up in an _____ movement when a lady enters the room.

10. The _____ based on individualism has great influence in the world.

练习题答案

连线题答案

gasoline	汽油	windshield	挡风玻璃
processed food	腌制食品	supersonic	超音速的
cylinder	汽缸	pedestrian	步行者，行人
automobile	机动车	booth	售货亭
culinary	厨房的，烹饪的	ceremonious	隆重的
freeway	高速公路	reef	暗礁
insurance	保险	census	人口普查
diesel	柴油	sweetener	食糖，甜味剂
fuse	保险丝	recreation	消遣，娱乐
braking	刹车，制动	bouquet	花束
caviar	鱼子酱	oatmeal	燕麦片
detergent	洗涤剂	edible	可食的
bakery	面包房	recipe	食谱

选词填空答案

congested	automatic	navigation	beverage	candidate
censorship	commute	ideology	dietary	digest

1. （Navigation）is difficult on this river because of hidden rocks.
2. We do not sell alcoholic（beverages）to teenagers.
3. The city streets were（congested）with vehicles.
4. He interviewed many（candidates）for the job but found none qualified.
5. It often takes a long time to（digest）new ideas.
6. The government has imposed strict（censorship）on the press.
7. Patients with special（dietary）requirements should be given special attention.
8. Barbara lives in the suburb and works in the downtown, so she（commutes）between the two places every day.
9. A boy who has good manners stands up in an（automatic）movement when a lady enters the room.
10. The（ideology）based on individualism has great influence in the world.

Word List 14

音频

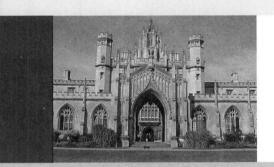

社会事物(三)

社会事物(三)

文　书

boldface ['bouldfeis] *n.* 黑体字,粗体字

【派】boldfaced(*adj.* 粗体字的;厚颜的,冒失的)

portfolio [pɔːrt'fouliou] *n.* 文件夹;系列产品;(求职时用以证明资历的)作品(flat case, pieces of work)

brochure [brou'ʃur] *n.* 小册子

catalogue ['kætəlɔːg] *n.* (图书或商品)目录 *vt.* 为…编目录;按目录分类(同 catalog)

【例】The librarians *catalogued* the new books.

charter ['tʃɑːrtər] *n.* 宪章,纲领,许可证;租赁

chronicle ['krɑːnɪkl] *n.* 年代记,编年史;历史,记事 *vt.* 把…载入编年史

【例】History *chronicles* important events of the past.

chronology [krə'nɑːlədʒi] *n.* 年代学;年表(an account of past events in the order in which they happened)

【例】The book includes a *chronology* of his life and works.

【派】chronological(*adj.* 按时间前后顺序排列的)

compendium [kəm'pendiəm] *n.* 纲要,摘要(a concise summary of a larger work)

context ['kɑːntekst] *n.* (文章的)上下文;背景(background)

【例】You can always tell the meaning of a word from its *context*.

contraction [kən'trækʃn] *n.* 订约(making a contract);收缩(compression, condensation)

【例】*Contraction* of the timbers left gaps in the fence.

contractual [kən'træktʃuəl] *adj.* 契约的(relating to contracts)

【例】They have a *contractual* obligation to research and publish.

convention [kən'venʃn] *n.* 协定;会议(conference);习俗,惯例(custom, tradition)

diploma [dɪ'ploumə] *n.* 毕业文凭,学位证书;执照

editorial [ˌedɪ'tɔːriəl] *adj.* 编辑的(relating to editing or editors) *n.* 社论,时评

【例】Sharon is an *editorial* assistant in the

sports department.

episode ['epɪsoʊd] *n.* 插曲，片断；(电视)一集

guideline ['gaɪdlaɪn] *n.* 指导方针，准则(rules or instructions)

manuscript ['mænjuskrɪpt] *n.* 手稿，原稿，底稿 (a book or piece of writing before it is printed)

【例】I read his novel in *manuscript*.

memoir ['memwɑːr] *n.* [*pl.*]回忆录，自传；传略

【例】Lady Thatcher had just published her *memoirs*.

memorandum [ˌmeməˈrændəm] *n.* (备忘的)记录，便函(memo, a short legal document that contains the important details of an agreement)

notification [ˌnoʊtɪfɪˈkeɪʃn] *n.* 通 知 ，通 知 单 (official information about something)

【例】I was given no prior *notification*.

pamphlet ['pæmflət] *n.* 小册子(leaflet)

【例】a political *pamphlet*

paperwork ['peɪpərwɜːrk] *n.* 日常文书工作 (work such as writing letters or reports)

petition [pəˈtɪʃn] *n.* 请愿 *vt.* 向…请愿 (to ask the government or an organization to do something)

【记】pet(寻求) + ition → 向…请愿

【例】Villagers *petitioned* the local authority to provide better bus services.

protocol ['proʊtəkɔːl] *n.* 协议，协定，草案(a system of rules)

【例】a breach of diplomatic *protocol*

referendum [ˌrefəˈrendəm] *n.* 公民投票；请示书

【派】referenda(*n.* referendum的复数)

version ['vɜːrʒn] *n.* 译本，改写本，版本

民　众

civic ['sɪvɪk] *adj.* 城市的；市民的，公民的 (of or relating to a city, citizens, or citizenship)

【例】It is your *civic* duty to vote in the local elections.

civil ['sɪvl] *adj.* 公民的，民用的 (of the ordinary life of citizens as distinguished from military or legal affairs)；文明的，有教养的

【例】Voting is the exercise of a *civil* right.

【派】civilian(*n.* 平民，百姓)

civilization [ˌsɪvələ'zeɪʃn] *n.* 文明，文化

【派】civilized(*adj.* 文明的，有教养的)

compatriot [kəm'peɪtriət] *n.* 同胞，同国人

congregation [ˌkɑːŋgrɪ'geɪʃn] *n.* 集合在一起的群众

congress ['kɑːŋgrəs] *n.* (代表)大会；国会，议会

denationalization [diːˌnæʃnələ'zeɪʃn] *n.* 剥夺国籍，剥夺公民权利

electorate [ɪ'lektərət] *n.* 全体选民；选民区，选举区

inhabitant [ɪn'hæbɪtənt] *n.* 居民，住户(resident, occupant)

【记】inhabit (居住)+ ant(表人) → 居民

lot [lɑːt] *n.* 一批，某一类的人

【例】The last *lot* of people offered £70,000.

mainstream ['meɪnstriːm] *n.* (思想或行为的)主流(the most usual ideas or methods，or the people who have these ideas or methods)

【例】Environmental ideas have been absorbed into the *mainstream* of European politics.

monarch ['mɑːnərk] *n.* 君主，最高统治者

【记】mon(单个) + arch(统治者) → 君主

phenomenon [fə'nɑːmɪnən] *n.* 现象(something that happens or exists in society)；非凡的人

【例】Homelessness is not a new *phenomenon*.

mason ['meɪsn] *n.* 石匠

组　织

gregarious [grɪ'geriəs] *adj.* 群居的，喜社交的 (enjoying the company of others)

【例】These animals are highly *gregarious*.

commission [kə'mɪʃn] *vt.* 委任，委托制作(画像等) *n.* 委员会；佣金

【例】Macmillan *commissioned* her to illustrate a book by Spike Milligan.

committee [kə'mɪti] *n.* 委员会，全体委员

【例】The *committee* planned the club's budget for next year.

corporation [ˌkɔːrpə'reɪʃn] *n.* 公司(enterprise, company)

division [dɪ'vɪʒn] *n.* 部门，科；区域；【军】师

faction	[ˈfækʃn] *n.* 派系，组织中的小派别	
federal	[ˈfedərəl] *adj.* 联邦(制)的；联邦政府的	
guild	[gɪld] *n.* 同业公会（an organization, club, or fellowship）	

资 格

eligible [ˈelɪdʒəbl] *adj.* 有资格的(qualified)；合适的(fit, suitable)
【例】Over 500,000 18-year-olds will become *eligible* to vote this year.
【派】eligibility(*n.* 合格，适任)

entitled [ɪnˈtaɪtld] *adj.* 有资格的(eligible, qualified)；名字为…的
【例】Are you *entitled* to unemployment benefit? / a book *entitled Jane Eyre*

时 代

contemporary [kənˈtempəreri] *adj.* 当代的，同时代的（belonging to the same period of time）*n.* 同代人
【例】I'm not very impressed by the works of many *contemporary* artists.

epochal [ˈepəkl] *adj.* (新)时代的，划时代的
【例】an *epochal* shift
【派】epoch(*n.* 时代；纪元)

era [ˈerə] *n.* 时代，年代；纪元

juvenile [ˈdʒuːvənl] *adj.* 青少年的(adolescent, young)
【记】juven(年青) + ile → 青少年的
【例】The clerk directed Jane and her mother to the *juvenile* clothing section of the store.

medieval [ˌmiːdˈiːvl] *adj.* 中世纪的
【例】These spices were first brought to Italy from the East in *medieval* times.

millennium [mɪˈleniəm] *n.* 一千年，千禧年
【派】millennia(*n.* millenium的复数)

outdated [ˌaʊtˈdeɪtɪd] *adj.* 过时的(old-fashioned)
【例】His writing style is now boring and *outdated*.

outmoded [ˌaʊtˈmoʊdɪd] *adj.* (式样等)过时了的，废弃了的(no longer

fashionable or useful）

【例】*outmoded* ideas

overdue [ˌoʊvərˈduː] *adj.* 迟到的，延误的；过期的（not done, paid, returned, etc. by the time expected）

【例】The library books are *overdue*.

种　族

desegregation [diːˌsegrɪˈɡeɪʃn] *n.* 取消种族隔离

gypsy [ˈdʒɪpsi] *n.* 吉卜赛人，吉卜赛语 *adj.* 吉卜赛的

enslave [ɪnˈsleɪv] *vt.* 使…成为奴隶，奴役

【记】en + slave(奴隶) → 奴役

【例】The addict was *enslaved* by drugs.

ethnic [ˈeθnɪk] *adj.* 种族的(racial, national)；具有民族特色的

【记】ethn(种族) + ic → 种族的

【例】The chef prepared many *ethnic* dishes.

ethnicity [eθˈnɪsəti] *n.* 种族划分，种族关系

ethnocentric [ˌeθnoʊˈsentrɪk] *adj.* 种族(或民族)中心主义的；种族(或民族)优越感的

【记】ethno(种族) + centric(中心的) → 种族中心主义的

ethnographic [ˌeθnəˈɡræfɪk] *adj.* 人种史的，人种论的

ethnology [eθˈnɑːlədʒi] *n.* 人种学，民族学

【派】ethnologist(*n.* 人种学者)

interracial [ˌɪntəˈreɪʃl] *adj.* 人种间的（between different races of people）

【例】*interracial* marriage

minority [maɪˈnɔːrəti] *n.* 少数；少数民族

【记】minor（小，少） + ity → 少的状态 → 少数

racist [ˈreɪsɪst] *n.* 种族主义者（someone discriminating other races）

tribal [ˈtraɪbl] *adj.* 部落的，宗族的（relating to a tribe）

【例】*tribal* dance

Spaniard [ˈspænjərd] *n.* 西班牙人(Spanish)

练习题

连线题

civilization	中世纪的	version	居民，住户
memoir	千禧年	guideline	君主，最高统治者
boldface	手稿，原稿	commission	编年史
ethnology	同业公会	chronicle	奴役
paperwork	黑体字，粗体字	monarch	指导方针，准则
guild	人种学	juvenile	联邦政府的
brochure	少数民族	compendium	同胞，同国人
medieval	回忆录	charter	版本
millennium	取消种族隔离	tribal	纲要，摘要
manuscript	订约	inhabitant	部落的
minority	小册子	compatriot	青少年的
desegregation	文明，文化	enslave	宪章，纲领
contraction	日常文书工作	federal	委员会

选词填空

convention	diploma	editorial	petition	congress
mainstream	entitled	outdated	ethnic	racist

1. Many of us conform to the _____ customs laid down by our forebears.
2. Their views lie outside the _____ of current medical opinion.
3. Full-time employees are _____ to receive health insurance.
4. She worked hard to earn a _____ in her double major.
5. Alexander is a _____ who refuses to employ blacks.
6. Japan has signed a _____ of peace with a neighboring country.
7. Mary holds a /an _____ position with a publishing company.
8. There were some days to wait before the National People's _____.
9. Everyone signed the _____ to the County Council for a new school in our village.
10. The students are from a variety of _____ backgrounds.

练 习 题 答 案

连线题答案

civilization	文明，文化	version	版本
memoir	回忆录	guideline	指导方针，准则
boldface	黑体字，粗体字	commission	委员会
ethnology	人种学	chronicle	编年史
paperwork	日常文书工作	monarch	君主，最高统治者
guild	同业公会	juvenile	青少年的
brochure	小册子	compendium	纲要，摘要
medieval	中世纪的	charter	宪章，纲领
millennium	千禧年	tribal	部落的
manuscript	手稿，原稿	inhabitant	居民，住户
minority	少数民族	compatriot	同胞，同国人
desegregation	取消种族隔离	enslave	奴役
contraction	订约	federal	联邦政府的

选词填空答案

convention	diploma	editorial	petition	congress
mainstream	entitled	outdated	ethnic	racist

1. Many of us conform to the（outdated）customs laid down by our forebears.

2. Their views lie outside the（mainstream）of current medical opinion.

3. Full-time employees are（entitled）to receive health insurance.

4. She worked hard to earn a（diploma）in her double major.

5. Alexander is a（racist）who refuses to employ blacks.

6. Japan has signed a（convention）of peace with a neighboring country.

7. Mary holds a /an（editorial）position with a publishing company.

8. There were some days to wait before the National People's（Congress）.

9. Everyone signed the（petition）to the County Council for a new school in our village.

10. The students are from a variety of（ethnic）backgrounds.

Word List 15

音频

社会事物（四）

社会事物(四)

亲　属

clan [klæn] *n.* 家族；宗派

ancestor [ˈænsestər] *n.* 祖先(forefather, progenitor)；起源(origin)
【例】This machine is the *ancestor* of the modern computer.
【派】ancestral(*adj.* 祖先的；祖传的，遗传的)

forebear [ˈfɔːrber] *n.* 祖先，祖宗

fraternal [frəˈtɜːrnl] *adj.* 兄弟的，兄弟般的；友爱的(brotherly; cordial)
【记】fratern(兄弟) + al → 兄弟的
【例】They fought side by side, and developed *fraternal* love to each other.

kinship [ˈkɪnʃɪp] *n.* (家属或亲属)关系，类似家属的密切关系

lineage [ˈlɪniɪdʒ] *n.* 血统，世系
【例】a family of ancient *lineage*

marital [ˈmærɪtl] *adj.* 婚姻的(wedded, conjugal)
【例】*marital* problems

maternal [məˈtɜːrnl] *adj.* 母亲(般)的(typical of the way a good mother behaves or feels)；母系的
【例】Annie was wonderfully warm and *maternal*.
【派】maternally(*adv.* 母亲般地)

matrilineal [ˌmætrɪˈlɪniəl] *adj.* 母系的
【例】*matrilineal* society

paternal [pəˈtɜːrnl] *adj.* 父亲(般)的(like a father)；父系的
【例】Dan took a *paternal* interest in my work.
【派】paternalism(*n.* 家长式统治，家长作风) paternally(*adv.* 父亲般地)

paternity [pəˈtɜːrnəti] *n.* 父亲的身份/地位
【例】The *paternity* of the child is in dispute.

patriarchal [ˌpeɪtriˈɑːrkl] *adj.* 家长(式)的，族长(式)的；由男人统治或控制

的（ruled or controlled only by men）；威严的

【例】a *patriarchal* society

patrilineal ［ˌpætrɪˈlɪniəl］ *adj.* 父系的

【例】*patrilineal* society

spouse ［spaʊs］ *n.* 配偶（partner, mate）

货　物

cargo ［ˈkɑːrgoʊ］ *n.* 货物（goods carried by a ship, aircraft, or other vehicle; freight）

freight ［freɪt］ *n.* 货运，货物

importation ［ˌɪmpɔːrˈteɪʃn］ *n.* 进口；输入品

处　所

dwelling ［ˈdwelɪŋ］ *n.* 住所（a place of residence）

habitat ［ˈhæbɪtæt］ *n.* （动物的）栖息地，住处

【例】This creature's natural *habitat* is the jungle.

habitation ［ˌhæbɪˈteɪʃn］ *n.* 居住；住所，家（a dwelling place）

【例】These houses are not fit for human *habitation*.

haven ［ˈheɪvn］ *n.* 安息所，避难所

locale ［loʊˈkæl］ *n.* 场所，现场（setting）

【例】people who see the countryside as a *locale* for recreation

refinery ［rɪˈfaɪnəri］ *n.* 精炼厂（a factory where oil or sugar is made purer）

reservoir ［ˈrezərvwɑːr］ *n.* 水库，蓄水池（artificial lake）

roller coaster 娱乐场中的环滑车道，过山车

sanctuary ［ˈsæŋktʃueri］ *n.* 圣堂；避难所（refuge）

sewage ［ˈsuːɪdʒ］ *n.* 下水道；污水

sewer ［ˈsuːər］ *n.* 阴沟；污水管

运　动

hockey	[ˈhɑːki] *n.* 曲棍球
jog	[dʒɑːg] *v.* 慢跑；轻敲，轻碰(bump)
	【例】You *jogged* my elbow.
jolt	[dʒəʊlt] *vt.* 摇动(shake, jar)
	【例】The coach stops and starts *jolting* the passengers.
outdistance	[ˌaʊtˈdɪstəns] *vt.* (指赛跑或竞争中)把…远远抛在后面(to run, ride, etc. faster than other people)
	【例】Lewis quickly *outdistanced* the other runners.
outfield	[ˈaʊtfiːld] *n.* (棒球或垒球等)外场
	【派】outfielder(*n.* 外场手)
plummet	[ˈplʌmɪt] *vt.* 骤然跌落，直线下降 (suddenly and quickly decrease in value or amount)
	【例】Profits *plummeted* from £49 million to £11 million.
slowdown	[ˈsloʊdaʊn] *n.* 减速，减缓(reduction in speed)
	【例】a *slowdown* in the U.S. economy
soar	[sɔːr] *vi.* 高飞(fly high up)，向上；高耸(look tall)；猛增(increase quickly)
	【例】The price of petrol has *soared* in recent weeks.
spiral	[ˈspaɪrəl] *vi.* 盘旋上升(或下降)(move in a continuous curve)；(物价等)不断急剧地上升(或下降)
	【例】The damaged plane *spiralled* to the ground.
	【派】spiralling(*n.* 螺旋运动)
stride	[straɪd] *v.* 跨越(step, pace)
	【例】He *strode* angrily into the classroom.
traverse	[trəˈvɜːrs] *vt.* 横过，扫过(move across)
	【记】tra(横) + verse(转) → 横过
	【例】two minutes to *traverse* the park

思　想

insight	[ˈɪnsaɪt] *n.* 洞察力，洞悉，见识(understanding)；【心】顿悟
	【例】The article gives us a real *insight* into the causes of the present economic crisis.

intention [ɪn'tenʃn] n. 意图，意旨（a plan or desire to do something）

【例】They went into town with the *intention* of visiting the library.

【派】intentional（adj. 有意的，故意的）

orientation [ˌɔːriən'teɪʃn] n. 定向，目标；态度；倾向（attitude; direction, inclination）

【例】The company needs to develop a stronger *orientation* towards marketing its products.

parental leave 父母亲的同意；父母假

receptive [rɪ'septɪv] adj. （对新的思想等）善于接受的（willing to consider new ideas, etc.）

【例】You might find them in a more *receptive* mood tomorrow.

【派】receptivity（n. 接受能力）receptiveness（n. 感受性）

retentive [rɪ'tentɪv] adj. 有记忆力的，记忆性强的

【例】a *retentive* memory

【派】retentiveness（n. 好记性）

sentiment ['sentɪmənt] n. 思想感情，情绪；观点（opinion; feelings）

【派】sentimental（adj. 多愁善感的）

standpoint ['stændpɔint] n. 立场，观点（point of view）

【例】Let's look at the questions from an economic *standpoint*.

prestige [pre'stiːʒ] n. 威望，声望（fame, reputation）

【例】Our mayor's *prestige* is known throughout the state.

残留物

residue ['rezɪduː] n. 残余（remains, leftover, remnant）

sediment ['sedɪmənt] n. 沉淀物，沉积

【例】a thick layer of *sediment*

vestige ['vestɪdʒ] n. 痕迹，残余（trace）；【生】退化器官

【例】The new law removed the last *vestiges* of royal power.

wreckage ['rekɪdʒ] n. （坠毁物）残片，残骸（pieces of destroyed planes, etc.）

【例】Firemen managed to pull some survivors from the *wreckage*.

科学（家）

logistics [lə'dʒɪstɪks] n. 后勤学，后勤，物流

【例】the *logistics* of travelling with small children

nutrition [nuˈtrɪʃn] n. 营养；营养学（the process of giving or getting the right type of food for good health and growth）

【派】nutritious(adj. 有营养的) nutrient(n.营养物)

paleontologist [ˌpeɪliɑːnˈtɑːlədʒɪst] n. 古生物学家

parapsychology [ˌpærəsaɪˈkɑːlədʒi] n.【心】通灵学

pathology [pəˈθɑːlədʒi] n. 病理学

pharmacology [ˌfɑːrməˈkɑːlədʒi] n. 药理学，药物学（the scientific study of drugs and medicines）

【派】pharmacologist（n. 药理学家，药物学家）pharmacological（adj. 药理学的）

physiology [ˌfɪziˈɑːlədʒi] n. 生理，生理学

【派】physiological(adj. 生理的) physiologically(adv. 生理上地)

pseudoscience [ˈsuːdoʊˈsaɪəns] n. 伪科学

socio-economic [ˌsoʊsioʊˌekəˈnɑːmɪk] adj. 社会经济学的（based on a combination of social and economic conditions）

【派】socio-economically(adv. 社会经济上地)

sociology [ˌsoʊsiˈɑːlədʒi] n. 社会学（the scientific study of societies and people）

【派】sociologist（n. 社会学家）sociological（adj. 社会学的）sociologically(adv. 社会学地)

wholesale [ˈhoʊlseɪl] n./vt. 批发 adj. 批发的

【例】*wholesale* prices

顶　点

culminate [ˈkʌlmɪneɪt] v. 达到极点（to reach a final or climactic stage）

【例】All his efforts *culminate* in failure.

peak [piːk] n. 高峰；尖端（mountain top; summit, top）

【例】At the *peak* of their labor, they could lay five miles of rails a day.

pinnacle [ˈpɪnəkl] n. 顶峰，顶点，极点（the most successful, powerful, exciting etc. part of something, mountain top）

【例】the *pinnacle* of academic achievement

vertices [ˈvɜːrtɪsiːz] n. [vertex 的复数]顶点，头顶

出 售

auction [ˈɔːkʃn] *n.* 拍卖
【例】His paintings were put up for *auction*.

bargain [ˈbɑːrgən] *v.* 讲条件，谈判 *n.* 廉价货；好交易
【例】*bargain* on doing sth.

bid [bɪd] *n./v.* 出价，喊价(尤指拍卖中)；投标
【例】She *bid* £100 for a Victorian chair.
【派】bidding(*n.* 喊价；投标；吩咐，命令)

If you put out your hands, you are a laborer; if you put out your hands and mind, you are a craftsperson; if you put out your hands, mind, heart and soul, you are an artist.

如果你用双手工作，你是一个劳力；如果你用双手和头脑工作，你是一个工匠；如果你用双手和头脑工作，并且全身心投入，你就是一个艺术家。

——美国电影 *American Heart and Soul*

练 习 题

连线题

refinery	批发	auction	沉淀物
forebear	父系的	nutrition	住所
standpoint	生理, 生理学	habitat	后勤, 物流
sociology	立场, 观点	wreckage	病理学
hockey	祖先, 祖宗	peak	场所, 现场
lineage	精炼厂	locale	货物
wholesale	下水道; 污水	pathology	盘旋上升(或下降)
spouse	配偶	cargo	进口
sentiment	血统, 世系	spiral	高峰, 尖端
marital	思想感情, 情绪	dwelling	营养; 营养学
physiology	社会学	sediment	拍卖
sewage	婚姻的	importation	栖息地
paternal	曲棍球	logistics	残片, 残骸

选词填空

kinship	maternal	patriarchal	reservoir	jog
slowdown	soar	insight	orientation	prestige

1. Every woman has _____ instinct.

2. This article gives us a real _____ into the causes of the present economic crisis.

3. The _____ in domestic demand was offset by an increase in exports.

4. The contract will affect the _____of our university in the country.

5. She watched the dove _____ above the chestnut trees.

6. Women have no say in a _____ society in which men have all the power.

7. Keep _____ for half an hour every morning is good to your health.

8. The winding trail caused the hikers to lose their _____.

9. Enterprise must have a _____ of cheap labor.

10.He felt a sense of _____with the only other Chinese in the company.

连线题答案

refinery	精炼厂	auction	拍卖
forebear	祖先，祖宗	nutrition	营养；营养学
standpoint	立场，观点	habitat	栖息地
sociology	社会学	wreckage	残片，残骸
hockey	曲棍球	peak	高峰，尖端
lineage	血统，世系	locale	场所，现场
wholesale	批发	pathology	病理学
spouse	配偶	cargo	货物
sentiment	思想感情，情绪	spiral	盘旋上升（或下降）
marital	婚姻的	dwelling	住所
physiology	生理，生理学	sediment	沉淀物
sewage	下水道；污水	importation	进口
paternal	父系的	logistics	后勤，物流

选词填空答案

kinship	maternal	patriarchal	reservoir	jog
slowdown	soar	insight	orientation	prestige

1. Every woman has （maternal）instinct.

2. This article gives us a real （insight）into the causes of the present economic crisis.

3. The （slowdown）in domestic demand was offset by an increase in exports.

4. The contract will affect the （prestige）of our university in the country.

5. She watched the dove （soar）above the chestnut trees.

6. Women have no say in a （patriarchal）society in which men have all the power.

7. Keep （jogging）for half an hour every morning is good to your health.

8. The winding trail caused the hikers to lose their （orientation）.

9. Enterprise must have a （reservoir）of cheap labor.

10. He felt a sense of （kinship）with the only other Chinese in the company.

Word List 16

音频

自然事物
普通状态（一）

自然事物

气 象

humid ['hju:mɪd] *adj.* 潮湿的(damp, moist)
【例】The *humid* weather made everyone sticky and uncomfortable.
【派】humidity(*n.* 潮湿，湿气)

inclement [ɪn'klemənt] *adj.* (天气)恶劣的(指寒冷的、潮湿的等)
【记】in(非) + clement(温暖的，温和的) → (天气)恶劣的
【例】Predictions of *inclement* weather proved to be wrong.

meteorologist [ˌmi:tiəˈrɑ:lədʒɪst] *n.* 气象学家

paleoclimatologist ['peɪliouˌklaɪməˈtɑ:lədʒɪst] *n.* 古生物气象学家

precipitate [prɪ'sɪpɪteɪt] *v.* 凝结(形成雨、雪)
【记】pre(提前) + cipit(落下) + ate → 凝结
【例】It's supposed to *precipitate* today, so bring an umbrella.
【派】precipitation(*n.* 降水)

smog [smɑ:g] *n.* 烟雾

stratosphere ['strætəsfɪr] *n.*【天】平流层

其 他

amber ['æmbər] *n.* 琥珀，琥珀色

hail [heɪl] *v.* 向…欢呼，欢迎(acclaim, applaud) *n.* 冰雹
【例】Birds are singing, *hailing* the coming of the spring.

atmosphere ['ætməsfɪr] *n.* 气氛；大气层
【例】Smith's favorite restaurant has a friendly, relaxed *atmosphere*.

aurora [ɔ:'rɔ:rə] *n.* 极光(南北极夜晚所放彩光)

avalanche ['ævəlæntʃ] *n.* 雪崩

blast [blæst] *n.* 一阵(疾风)；爆炸

crater ['kreɪtər] *n.* 火山口；弹坑

deluge ['delju:dʒ] *n.* 大洪水，暴雨

ecological systems 生态系统(ecosystem)

ecology [i'kɑ:lədʒi] *n.* 生态学

【派】ecological(*adj.* 生态学的)

glacier ['gleɪsɪə(r)] *n.* 冰河，冰川

granite ['grænɪt] *n.* 花岗岩，花岗石

hurricane ['hɜːrəkən] *n.* 飓风

【派】twister(*n.* 龙卷风) tornado(*n.* 龙卷风)

普通状态(一)

正　机

commonplace ['kɑːmənpleɪs] *adj.* 平凡的，陈腐的 *n.* 平常话，平常的事物

orthodox ['ɔːrθədɑːks] *adj.* 规范的；公认的(generally accepted)；正统的

【例】He challenged the *orthodox* views on education.

routine [ruːˈtiːn] *adj.* 常规的(regular, conventional, usual)

【例】Anne took a *routine* coffee break at 2:30 p.m.

【派】routinely(*adv.* 惯常地)

异　常

abnormal [æbˈnɔːrml] *adj.* 异常的(not normal, exceptional)

【记】ab(离开) + normal(正常的) → 异常的

【例】My parents thought it was *abnormal* for a boy to be interested in ballet.

anomalous [əˈnɑːmələs] *adj.* 不规则的，反常的(irregular, abnormal, unusual)

【例】This phenomenon may explain the *anomalous* results of our research.

【派】anomaly(*n.* 反常，不规则；畸形)

exotic [ɪgˈzɑːtɪk] *adj.* 外来的；有异国风味的(unusual, foreign)

【记】exo(外面) + tic → 外来的

【例】Susan and Bill love to eat spicy and *exotic* food.

extraterrestrial [ˌekstrətəˈrestriəl] *adj.* 地球外的 *n.* 外星人

【记】extra(外部) + terrestrial(地球的) → 地球外的

heretical [həˈretɪkl] *adj.* 异教的，异端的(pagan, unorthodox)

【派】heretic(*n.* 异教徒，持异端者)

infrequent [ɪnˈfriːkwənt] *adj.* 很少的，不常的(not happen often, rare)

【例】They would make *infrequent* visits to the house.

【派】infrequency(*n.* 很少发生，罕见)

inverse [ˌɪn'vɜːrs] *adj.* 反的(contrary, opposite)

【记】in(反) + verse(转) → 反的

【例】Clearly, the amount of money people save increases in *inverse* proportion to the amount they spend.

【派】inversely(*adv.* 相反地)

lopsided [ˌlɑːp'saɪdɪd] *adj.* 不平等的，两侧不匀称的(unequal, uneven)

【例】a *lopsided* grin

miracle ['mɪrəkl] *n.* 奇迹

【例】It's a *miracle* you weren't killed!

nontarget [nɑːn'tɑːrgɪt] *n.* 不属预定目标

novelty ['nɑːvlti] *n.* 新颖；新奇的事物(newness, unusualness)

【记】novel(新) + ty → 新颖

paranormal [ˌpærə'nɔːrml] *adj.* 超自然的，异常的(supernatural)

【例】ghosts and other *paranormal* phenomena

unconventional [ˌʌnkən'venʃənl] *adj.* 自由的(free)

【例】*unconventional* political views

unpredictable [ˌʌnprɪ'dɪktbl] *adj.* 不可预测的，捉摸不透的

【例】*unpredictable* weather

【派】unpredictably(*adv.* 捉摸不透地) unpredictability(*n.* 不可预测性)

unrealistic [ˌʌnriːə'lɪstɪk] *adj.* 不切实际的(unreasonable)

【例】It is *unrealistic* to expect these changes to happen overnight.

untenable [ʌn'tenəbl] *adj.* 难以防守的，站不住脚的(unable to be defended)

【例】The scandal put the President in an *untenable* position.

【派】untenably(*adv.* 难以承受地)

slip [slɪp] *n.* 疏忽，错误(a small mistake)；溜走(escape)

【例】a *slip* of the pen/tongue

随　机

accidental [ˌæksɪ'dentl] *adj.* 偶然的(occasional)

【例】Our meeting in New York was quite *accidental*.

arbitrary ['ɑːrbətreri] *adj.* 随意的(random)；主观的(subjective)；专横的，独断的(despotic or dictatorial)

【例】A good judge does not make *arbitrary* decisions.

【派】arbitrariness(*n.* 任意；专横，武断)

contingent [kən'tɪndʒənt] *adj.* 可能发生的(depending on something that may happen in the future)

【例】Further investment is *contingent* upon the company's profit performance.

haphazard [hæp'hæzərd] *adj.* 偶然的；随便的(casual, random, indiscriminate)

【记】hap + hazard(偶然，运气)→ 偶然的

【例】I didn't mean to meet my old friend at the airport—it is just a *haphazard* meeting.

unbridled [ʌn'braɪdld] *adj.* (马等)脱缰的；放纵的，无约束的(uncontrolled)

【例】*unbridled* greed

精　确

accurate ['ækjərət] *adj.* 准确的，正确的(exact, correct)

【例】Your statements about the cost of the house were not *accurate*.

【派】accuracy(*n.* 准确性)

literal ['lɪtərəl] *adj.* 照字面的，原义的(basic, original meanings)

【例】A trade war is not a war in the *literal* sense.

【派】literally(*adv.* 逐字地；确实地)

sophisticated [sə'fɪstɪkeɪtɪd] *adj.* 老于世故的；见多识广的；先进的；高雅的(experienced; advanced; complicated)

【例】a *sophisticated*, witty American

【派】sophistication(*n.* 强词夺理)

对　立

adversary ['ædvərseri] *n.* 敌人，对手(enemy, foe)

【派】adversarial(*adj.* 敌对的，对抗性的)

adverse [əd'vɜːs] *adj.* 敌对的；不利的(hostile; unfavorable, negative)

【例】The *adverse* weather conditions made travel difficult.

antagonism [æn'tægənɪzəm] *n.* 对抗，敌对(mutual opposition, enmity, hostility)

【例】 There is *antagonism* between the army and other military groups.

【派】 antagonise(*v.* 引起敌对，使成为敌人) antagonist(*n.* 对立者，对手) antagonistic(*adj.* 敌对的，对抗性的)

antithesis [ænˈtɪθɪsɪs] *n.* 对立面，相对(the exact opposite)

archenemy [ˈɑːrtʃˈenəmi] *n.* 主要敌人(a chief enemy)；[A-]撒旦(Satan)

foe [foʊ] *n.* 敌人，敌军；危害物

【例】 a *foe* to health

hostile [ˈhɑːstl] *adj.* 敌对的，不友好的(antagonistic, unfriendly)

【例】 The *hostile* cat hissed whenever I came near.

【派】 hostility(*n.* 敌意，敌对状态)

exclusionary [ɪkˈskluːʒənri] *adj.* 排斥的

【例】 *exclusionary* business practices

模　糊

ambiguous [æmˈbɪɡjuəs] *adj.* 含糊的，模棱两可的(vague, equivocal, obscure)

【例】 The language in the Minister's statement is highly *ambiguous*.

【派】 ambiguity(*n.* 歧义；模棱两可) unambiguous(*adj.* 不含糊的，清楚的)

blur [blɜːr] *vt.* 使模糊(become indistinct)

【例】 His eyes were *blurred* with tears.

【派】 blurry(*adj.* 模糊的)

equivocal [ɪˈkwɪvəkl] *adj.* 模棱两可的，意义不清的(ambiguous)

【记】 equi(平的) + voc(声音) + al → 用平平的声音 → 意义不清的

【例】 She was rather *equivocal* about her work.

loom [luːm] *vi.* 隐隐呈现；赫然耸现，逼近(to appear as a large unclear shape, especially in a threatening way)

【例】 Suddenly a mountain *loomed* up in front of them.

obscure [əbˈskjʊr] *adj.* 模糊的(unclear)

【记】 ob(离开) + scure(跑) → 东西跑开 → 模糊的

【例】 Alchemists made these symbols purposely *obscure*. They don't want people know all this.

【派】 obscurely(*adv.* 模糊地)

potential [pəˈtenʃl] *adj.* 可能的，潜在的(possible, conceivable)

【例】 The inventor determined *potential* markets for the new product.

【派】 potentially(*adv.* 潜在地)

vague [veɪg] *adj.* 模糊的, 含糊的(imprecise, obscure, ambiguous)
【例】Tom evaded Jane's question by giving her a *vague* answer.
【派】vagueness(*n.* 含糊)

清　晰

appreciable [əˈpriːʃəbl] *adj.* 看得出的, 可估计的(large enough to be noticed or considered important)
【例】There's no *appreciable* change in the patient's condition.
【派】appreciably(*adv.* 略微, 有一点儿)

clarify [ˈklærəfaɪ] *v.* 澄清(to make clear)
【例】The explanation *clarified* the details of the plan.
【派】clarification(*n.* 澄清) clarity(*n.* 清楚, 明晰)

explicit [ɪkˈsplɪsɪt] *adj.* 明确的; 清楚的(straightforward)
【例】The new tax law is *explicit*.
【派】explicitly(*adv.* 明确地)

expressly [ɪkˈspresli] *adv.* 清楚地(clearly); 特意地(deliberately)
【例】The building is *expressly* designed to conserve energy.

manifestation [ˌmænɪfeˈsteɪʃn] *n.* 显示; 表明; 表示 (a very clear sign that a particular situation or feeling exists)
【例】These latest riots are a clear *manifestation* of growing discontent.

patent [ˈpætnt] *n.* 专利, 专利权 *adj.* 专利的; 明显的(obvious)
【例】It is *patent* to all that this is a good chance.
【派】patently(*adv.* 公然地)

pronounced [prəˈnaʊnst] *adj.* 明显的(notable, prominent)
【记】pronounce(发音) + d →(人人都能) 发的音 → 明显的
【例】The result will become *pronounced* after two weeks' medication.

remarkable [rɪˈmɑːrkəbl] *adj.* 值得注意的(striking, considerable)
【例】It's a *remarkable* achievement for the company.
【派】remarkably(*adv.* 明显地)

specific [spəˈsɪfɪk] *adj.* 具体的, 明确的(detailed and exact); 特写的
【例】Could you be more *specific* about what you're looking for?
【派】specifically(*adv.* 明确地)

平　衡

balance [ˈbæləns] *n./v.* 平衡(equilibrium)
【例】I lost my *balance* and fell.

bias [ˈbaɪəs] *vt.* 使…偏离 *n.* 偏见(prejudice, partiality)
【例】The government used newspapers and the radio to *bias* the opinions of the people.
【派】biased(*adj.* 有偏见的) unbiased(*adj.* 没有偏见的)

equilibrium [ˌiːkwɪˈlɪbriəm] *n.* 平衡状态(balance);(心情、感情等)平静
【例】The gymnast has perfect *equilibrium*.

marginalize [ˈmɑːrdʒɪnəlaɪz] *vt.* 使边缘化(to make someone unimportant and powerless in an unfair way)
【例】Female employees complained of being *marginalized* by management.
【派】marginalized(*adj.* 边缘化的) marginalization(*n.* 边缘化)

stabilize [ˈsteɪbəlaɪz] *v.* (使)稳定,(使)稳固(become firm, steady)
【例】The patient's condition has now *stabilized*.
【派】stabilization(*n.* 稳定性)

tendency [ˈtendənsi] *n.* 趋势(inclination, trend)
【例】Some people may inherit a *tendency* to alcoholism.

tilt [tɪlt] *v.* (使)倾斜(slant, slope)
【例】My mother *tilted* her head and smiled.
【派】tilted(*adj.* 倾斜的)

Jovons saw the kettle boil and cried out with the delighted voice of a child; Marshal too had seen the kettle boil and sat down silently to build an engine.
杰文斯看见壶开了,高兴得像孩子似地叫了起来;马歇尔也看见壶开了,却悄悄地坐下来造了一部蒸气机。
——英国经济学家 凯恩斯(*John Maynard Keynes, British economist*)

练 习 题

连线题

tendency	偏见	adversary	平衡
unrealistic	反的	heretical	雪崩
unpredictable	气象学家	extraterrestrial	烟雾
amber	专利，专利权	deluge	具体的，明确的
obscure	潮湿的	avalanche	冰川
ecology	琥珀	specific	模棱两可的
patent	准确的	aurora	飓风
atmosphere	不可预测的	clarify	外星人
humid	不切实际的	smog	敌人，对手
inverse	趋势	balance	极光
bias	气氛；大气层	glacier	异教的
meteorologist	生态学	equivocal	澄清
accurate	模糊的	hurricane	大洪水

选词填空

stabilize	abnormal	novelty	accidental	arbitrary
literal	hostile	ambiguous	sophisticated	potential

1. It was quite a _____ to spend my holidays working on a boat.

2. His account was deliberately _____ .

3. Their _____ looks showed that he was unwelcome.

4. The patient's condition has now _____ under the doctor's help.

5. It's important to draw out a child's _____ capacities.

6. My parents thought it was _____ for a boy to be interested in ballet.

7. I want to buy insurance for my car that covers _____ damage.

8. She has become very _____ since she began to work in the government.

9. A trade war is not a war in the _____ sense.

10. It's difficult to predict his behavior, since he often makes _____ decisions.

练习题答案

连线题答案

tendency	趋势	adversary	敌人，对手
unrealistic	不切实际的	heretical	异教的
unpredictable	不可预测的	extraterrestrial	外星人
amber	琥珀	deluge	大洪水
obscure	模糊的	avalanche	雪崩
ecology	生态学	specific	具体的，明确的
patent	专利，专利权	aurora	极光
atmosphere	气氛；大气层	clarify	澄清
humid	潮湿的	smog	烟雾
inverse	反的	balance	平衡
bias	偏见	glacier	冰川
meteorologist	气象学家	equivocal	模棱两可的
accurate	准确的	hurricane	飓风

选词填空答案

stabilize	abnormal	novelty	accidental	arbitrary
literal	hostile	ambiguous	sophisticated	potential

1. It was quite a（novelty）to spend my holidays working on a boat.
2. His account was deliberately（ambiguous）.
3. Their（hostile）looks showed that he was unwelcome.
4. The patient's condition has now（stabilized）under the doctor's help.
5. It's important to draw out a child's（potential）capacities.
6. My parents thought it was（abnormal）for a boy to be interested in ballet.
7. I want to buy insurance for my car that covers（accidental）damage.
8. She has become very（sophisticated）since she began to work in the government.
9. A trade war is not a war in the（literal）sense.
10. It's difficult to predict his behavior, since he often makes（arbitrary）decisions.

Word List 17

音频

普通状态（二）

普通状态(二)

奇 怪

awkward [ˈɔːkwərd] *adj.* 笨拙的(clumsy); 尴尬的
【例】The growing teenager went through an *awkward* stage.
【派】awkwardness(*n.* 笨拙; 不雅)

bizarre [bɪˈzɑːr] *adj.* 古怪的(odd, eccentric)
【例】They saw a *bizarre* animal in the lake.

erratic [ɪˈrætɪk] *adj.* 古怪的(odd, eccentric); 飘忽不定的;(运动或行为)不规则的
【例】Bill's *erratic* moods upset everyone in our office.
【派】erratically(*adv.* 不规律地, 不定地)

一 致

coincide [ˌkoʊɪnˈsaɪd] *vi.* 同时发生(to occur or exist simultaneously); 相符, 一致(to be the same)
【例】Our opinion of the question *coincided*.
【派】coincidence(*n.* 巧合; 符合; 一致) coincidental(*adj.* 巧合的; 同时发生的)

consensus [kənˈsensəs] *n.* 一致(unanimity)
【例】The school board could not reach a *consensus* on the curriculum.

consistent [kənˈsɪstənt] *adj.* 始终如一的; 一致的, 符合的
【例】She is a *consistent* girl in her feeling. / The results are *consistent* with earlier research.
【派】consistency(*n.* 一致性; 连贯性)

intermingled [ˌɪntərˈmɪŋgld] *adj.* 互相交织的(to mix together or mix something with something else)
【例】The pain and the anger were *intermingled*.

nexus [ˈneksəs] *n.* (看法等)联系; 联结(connections)
【例】a *nexus* of social relationships

proportionate [prəˈpɔːrʃənət] *adj.* 成比例的; 均衡的(balanced)

【派】proportionally(*adv.* 适当地)

symmetry [ˈsɪmətri] *n.* 对称(性)，匀称(balance, harmony)

【记】sym(共同) + metry(测量) → 两边测量一样 → 对称

【派】symmetrical(*adj.* 对称的)

systematic [ˌsɪstəˈmætɪk] *adj.* 系统的，有条理的(methodical)

【例】a *systematic* approach to solving the problem

【派】systematically(*adv.* 有条不紊地)

tally [ˈtæli] *vi.* 符合(accord, agree)

【例】The report *tallies* with your description of the accident.

unification [ˌjuːnɪfɪˈkeɪʃn] *n.* 统一，联合，一致

【例】the *unification* of Germany

unison [ˈjuːnɪsn] *n.* 一致，调和(consensus)；【音】齐唱，齐奏

【例】"Good morning!" The kids replied in *unison*.

liken [ˈlaɪkən] *vt.* 把…比作；把…比拟成(compare)

【例】Critics have *likened* the new theater to a supermarket.

collide [kəˈlaɪd] *vi.* 碰撞，相撞(to crash)；抵触，不一致(to clash, disagree, have conflicts)

【例】The interests of the two countries *collide*.

【派】collision(*n.* 碰撞；冲突)

方　便

convenient [kənˈviːniənt] *adj.* 便利的，方便的

【例】Could we postpone the meeting until a more *convenient* time?

expedient [ɪkˈspiːdiənt] *adj.* 权宜的；方便的(suitable, convenient)

【例】*Expedient* solutions rarely solve long-term problems.

inconvenience [ˌɪnkənˈviːniəns] *n.* 不方便，麻烦

严厉、严肃

demure [dɪˈmjʊr] *adj.* 娴静的；羞涩的(quiet; bashful)

【例】Old photos of Maggie show her young and *demure*.

severe [sɪˈvɪr] *adj.* 严重的；严肃的(grave; grievous)

【例】She's suffering from *severe* depression.

【派】severity(*n.* 严重性)

stringent [ˈstrɪndʒənt] *adj.* 严格的(strict, rigid)；迫切的

【例】Our company has a *stringent* policy against smoking.

【派】stringently(*adv.* 严格地)

困 境

dilemma [dai'lemə] *n.* 左右为难，困境

【例】I have the *dilemma* of choosing a new car or a computer.

famine ['fæmɪn] *n.* 饥荒，饥饿；严重缺乏

impoverish [ɪm'pɑːvərɪʃ] *v.* 使贫穷(to make poor)

indigent ['ɪndɪdʒənt] *adj.* 贫穷的，贫困的(needy, poor)

【例】Even those almost totally *indigent* retained their pride.

irreconcilable [ɪˌrekən'saɪləbl] *adj.* 不能妥协的(unconformable, incompatible)

【记】ir(不) + reconcilable(可以和解的) → 不能妥协的

【例】The differences between the landowners and the conservationists were *irreconcilable* from the start.

quandary ['kwɑːndəri] *n.* 困惑，进退两难(a difficult situation or problem)

【例】Kate was in a *quandary* over whether to go or not.

混 乱

destabilize [ˌdiː'steɪbəlaɪz] *vt.* 使不稳定(to make unstable)

【例】The new policy threatens to *destabilize* the economy.

disorder [dɪs'ɔːrdər] *n.* 混乱；(身心)不适，异常

disrupt [dɪs'rʌpt] *vt.* 使混乱，扰乱(disturb, disorder)

【例】An emergency announcement *disrupted* the TV show.

disruptive [dɪs'rʌptɪv] *adj.* 使破裂的，分裂的(tumultuous, turbulent)

【例】Night work can be very *disruptive* to home life.

【派】disruption(*n.* 分裂，瓦解)

disturbance [dɪ'stɜːrbəns] *n.* 打扰，扰乱(the act of disturbing or the state of being disturbed)

havoc ['hævək] *n.* 大破坏，毁坏(destruction, devastation, ruin)

miscellaneous [ˌmɪsə'leɪniəs] *adj.* 多种多样的，混杂的

【例】They receive a grant of £1094 to cover the cost of *miscellaneous* expenses.

problematic [ˌprɑːblə'mætɪk] *adj.* 成问题的 (difficult to handle)；有疑问的；未定的

138

【例】The reforms could turn out to be highly *problematic*.

specious [ˈspiːʃəs] *adj.* 似是而非的(seeming to be true but actually false)

【例】a *specious* argument

turbulent [ˈtɜːrbjələnt] *adj.* 骚动的，骚乱的(violent)

【例】He has had a *turbulent* political career.

【派】turbulence(*n.* 动乱)

turmoil [ˈtɜːrmɔɪl] *n.* 骚动，混乱(disorder, chaos)

【记】tur + moil(喧闹) → 混乱

【例】The *turmoil* of exams made the students very irritable.

和　谐

dissonant [ˈdɪsənənt] *adj.* 不和谐的(inharmonious)

【例】He made *dissonant* and loud voices in the classroom.

【派】dissonance(*n.* 不一致，不调和)

harmonize [ˈhɑːrmənaɪz] *v.* 使和谐，使相称(to make or become harmonious)

We're all on this together.

【例】The colors do not seem to *harmonize* (with each other) at all.

incompatible [ˌɪnkəmˈpætəbl] *adj.* 不兼容的；不相配的(inconsistent, incongruous)

【记】in(不) + compatible(和谐的，融合的) → 不相配的

【例】His plan is *incompatible* with my intent.

reconcile [ˈrekənsaɪl] *vt.* 和解(conform, harmonize)

【例】Anne *reconciled* her disagreement with Mary.

【派】reconciliation(*n.* 和解)

solidarity [ˌsɑːlɪˈdærəti] *n.* 团结一致，休戚相关(loyalty, unity)

【例】an appeal for worker *solidarity*

sympathetic [ˌsɪmpəˈθetɪk] *adj.* 同情的(caring)，赞同的

【例】I'm *sympathetic* to parents who are worried about what their children see on television.

【派】sympathetically(*adv.* 悲悯地)

prospect [ˈprɑːspekt] *n.* 前景，期望(outlook, likelihood, possibility)

【记】pro(向前) + spect(看) → 向前看 → 前景

【例】Older people are always concerned by the *prospect* that an unprecedented depression would bring chaos again.

危　险

endanger [ɪnˈdeɪndʒər] *vt.* 危及（to put something or somebody in danger）
【记】en + danger（危险）→ 危及
【例】The animals that lived in the marsh were *endangered* by the drought.

hazardous [ˈhæzərdəs] *adj.* 危险的（dangerous, perilous）
【例】People hesitated whether to begin the *hazardous* journey to the unknown west or not.

imperil [ɪmˈperəl] *v.* 使陷于危险，危及（to endanger）
【例】The whole project is *imperiled* by lack of funds.

jeopardize [ˈdʒepərdaɪz] *vt.* 危及，危害（to risk losing or spoiling something important）
【例】large-scale military offensives which could *jeopardize* the UN peace process
【派】jeopardy（*n.* 危难）

menace [ˈmenəs] *vt.* 威吓，胁迫（threaten, intimidate）
【记】men（人）+ ace（王牌）→ 用手中的一张王牌 → 胁迫
【例】The people are being *menaced* by the threat of war.

precarious [prɪˈkeriəs] *adj.* 不确定的，不稳固的（unsteady）
【例】Her health remained *precarious*, despite the treatment.
【派】precariously（*adv.* 危险地）precariousness（*n.* 有危险）

venture [ˈventʃər] *n./vi.* 冒险（risk）；冒昧
【例】May I *venture* to ask you a question, sir?

灭　绝

exterminate [ɪkˈstɜːrmɪneɪt] *vt.* 消灭（eradicate, eliminate）
【记】ex + termin（范围）+ ate → 清除出范围 → 消灭
【例】The landlord *exterminated* the rats in the cellar.
【派】exterminator（*n.* 扑灭的人；害虫驱除剂）extermination（*n.* 消灭，根绝）

extinct [ɪkˈstɪŋkt] *adj.* 灭绝的；熄灭的
【例】Dinosaurs have been *extinct* for millions of years.

extinction [ɪkˈstɪŋkʃn] *n.* 灭绝

【例】What caused the *extinction* of dinosaurs?

extinguish [ɪk'stɪŋgwɪʃ] *vt.* 熄灭；消灭(exterminate)

【例】John *extinguished* the campfire with water.

mortality [mɔːr'tæləti] *n.* 必死性，死亡人数

【例】*Mortality* from heart disease varies widely across the world.

obituary [oʊ'bɪtʃʊeri] *n.* (常附死者传略的)讣告，讣闻

【例】I read Sewell's *obituary* in the *Daily News*.

perish ['perɪʃ] *vi.* 丧生，消亡，死亡(to die, especially in a terrible or sudden way)

【例】Hundreds *perished* when the ship went down.

【派】perishable(*adj.* 易变质的)

适　合

inappropriate [ˌɪnə'proʊpriət] *adj.* 不恰当的，不适宜的(not appropriate)

【例】A party dress is *inappropriate* for a hike.

inept [ɪ'nept] *adj.* 不适当的，不合场面的(inappropriate)；无能的(incompetent, inefficient)

【记】in(不) + ept(熟练的) → 无能的

【例】What an *inept* remark to make on such a formal occasion!

maladaptive [ˌmælə'dæptɪv] *adj.* 不适应的

强　烈

acute [ə'kjuːt] *adj.* 严重的(of extreme importance; serious)；敏锐的(sensitive, keen)；(病)急性的

【例】They think his mother's illness is *acute* rather than chronic.

cogent ['koʊdʒənt] *adj.* 强有力的；有说服力的(compelling; convincing)

【例】The defense attorney's *cogent* argument was persuasive.

【派】cogency(*n.* 说服力)

intense [ɪn'tens] *adj.* 强烈的；紧张的；热切的；认真的

【例】Under years of *intense* pressure, he finally gave up hope and committed suicide.

vehement ['viːəmənt] *adj.* 猛烈的，激烈的(passionate, ardent)

【例】Despite her *vehement* protests, he pulled her inside.

【派】vehemence(*n.* 热切，激烈)

空　白

untainted	[ʌnˈteɪntɪd] *adj.* 无污点的（unaffected by bad effects） 【例】a politician *untainted* by corruption
vacancy	[ˈveɪkənsi] *n.* 空白, 空缺, 空职 【例】There are still two *vacancies* on the school board.
vanish	[ˈvænɪʃ] *vi.* 消失（disappear, fade） 【记】van(空) + ish → 变空 → 消失 【例】The magician made the flowers *vanish* with a wave of his hand.

The supreme happiness of life is the conviction that we are loved.
生活中最大的幸福是坚信有人爱我们。

——法国小说家 雨果（*Victor Hugo, French novelist*）

连线题

disorder	联合	prospect	不和谐的
symmetry	不确定的	solidarity	空白
unison	古怪的	unification	两难困境
systematic	消灭	menace	统一，联合
obituary	饥荒	convenient	消失
consensus	古怪的	collide	猛烈的
exterminate	混乱	dilemma	团结一致
intermingled	对称	vehement	碰撞
erratic	不恰当的	demure	便利的
famine	一致	inept	前景，期望
bizarre	互相交织的	vanish	威吓，胁迫
precarious	讣告，讣闻	dissonant	不适当的
inappropriate	系统的，有条理的	vacancy	娴静的，羞涩的

选词填空

coincide	consistent	proportionate	extinct	impoverish
disruptive	turbulent	incompatible	sympathetic	endanger

1. His account of what happened was _____with what the witness had said.
2. The laser printer is _____with the new computer.
3. He was expelled from school for _____ behavior.
4. When our vacation _____ , we often go on holiday together.
5. People suffered a lot during the _____ times of the French Revolution.
6. The cost of the ticket is _____ to the distance you travel.
7. They were _____ by a prolonged spell of unemployment.
8. We are _____ to the flood sufferers.
9. Poison gas blew off and _____ the lives of hundreds of persons.
10.Dinosaurs have been _____ for millions of years.

练习题答案

连线题答案

disorder	混乱	prospect	前景，期望
symmetry	对称	solidarity	团结一致
unison	联合	unification	统一，联合
systematic	系统的，有条理的	menace	威吓，胁迫
obituary	讣告，讣闻	convenient	便利的
consensus	一致	collide	碰撞
exterminate	消灭	dilemma	两难困境
intermingled	互相交织的	vehement	猛烈的
erratic	古怪的	demure	娴静的，羞涩的
famine	饥荒	inept	不适当的
bizarre	古怪的	vanish	消失
precarious	不确定的	dissonant	不和谐的
inappropriate	不恰当的	vacancy	空白

选词填空答案

coincide	consistent	proportionate	extinct	impoverish
disruptive	turbulent	incompatible	sympathetic	endanger

1. His account of what happened was（consistent）with what the witness had said.
2. The laser printer is（incompatible）with the new computer.
3. He was expelled from school for（disruptive）behavior.
4. When our vacation（coincided）, we often go on holiday together.
5. People suffered a lot during the（turbulent）times of the French Revolution.
6. The cost of the ticket is（proportionate）to the distance you travel.
7. They were（impoverished）by a prolonged spell of unemployment.
8. We are（sympathetic）to the flood sufferers.
9. Poison gas blew off and（endangered）the lives of hundreds of persons.
10. Dinosaurs have been（extinct）for millions of years.

Word List 18

正向状态
负向状态

正向状态

快　乐

beatific	[ˌbiːəˈtɪfɪk] *adj.* 祝福的，有福的；快乐的
euphoria	[juːˈfɔːriə] *n.* 极度愉快的心情；过度兴奋的情绪
well-being	[ˈwelˈbiːɪŋ] *n.* 健康；幸福；福利（happiness, wealth）

【例】We are responsible for the care and *well-being* of all our patients.

负向状态

不　幸

aftermath	[ˈæftərmæθ] *n.* 后果（outcome, result）
calamity	[kəˈlæməti] *n.* 灾难，祸患（disaster）

【例】It would be a *calamity* for the farmers if the crops failed again.

【派】calamitous（*adj.* 多灾难的，不幸的）

casualty	[ˈkæʒuəlti] *n.* 意外伤亡，事故；伤亡者

【例】Jane saw a *casualty* on the highway and phoned the police.

catastrophe	[kəˈtæstrəfi] *n.* 灾难，灾祸

【派】catastrophic（*adj.* 悲惨的，灾难的）

doomed	[duːmd] *adj.* 命定的，注定失败的

【例】The marriage was *doomed* from the beginning.

【派】doom（*n.* 厄运，劫数）

烦　躁

agitate	[ˈædʒɪteɪt] *v.* 鼓动，煽动（to stir up, instigate）；使焦虑（to disturb, or worry）

【例】His fiery speech *agitated* the crowd.

【派】agitator（*n.* 煽动者）agitation（*n.* 煽动；焦虑）

infest [ɪnˈfest] v. 骚扰，扰乱

【例】The kitchen was *infested* with cockroaches.

【派】infestation[n. (害虫、盗贼等)群袭，出没，横行]

obsess [əbˈses] vt. 迷住(fascinate)；使困窘，使烦扰

【例】A lot of young girls are *obsessed* by their weight.

【派】obsession(n. 痴迷) obsessive(adj. 有执着想法的)

病　症

ailment [ˈeɪlmənt] n. 不适，小病(slight illness)

allergic [əˈlɜːrdʒɪk] adj. 过敏的；对…反感

【例】Alice is *allergic* to the fur of cats.

【派】allergy(n. 过敏症)

amnesia [æmˈniːziə] n. 健忘症

arthritis [ɑːrˈθraɪtɪs] n. 关节炎

asthma [ˈæzmə] n. 哮喘，气喘

convulsion [kənˈvʌlʃn] n. 痉挛

cramp [kræmp] n. 痉挛，抽筋

diabetes [ˌdaɪəˈbiːtiːz] n. 糖尿病

encephalitis [enˌsefəˈlaɪtəs] n. 脑炎

epidemic [ˌepɪˈdemɪk] n. 流行病

hypertension [ˌhaɪpərˈtenʃn] n. 高血压(high blood pressure)

obesity [oʊˈbiːsəti] n. 肥胖，过胖(very fat in a way that is unhealthy)

sunburn [ˈsʌnbɜːrn] n. 晒伤(red and painful skin)

trauma [ˈtraʊmə] n. 心灵创伤，挫折，损伤(mental state caused by unpleasant experience)

【例】the *trauma* of being a young refugee

厌　恶

aversion [əˈvɜːrʒn] n. 厌恶(dislike, distaste)

【例】Her *aversion* to buses makes it necessary for her to own a car.

nuisance [ˈnjuːsns] n. 讨厌的东西，麻烦事 (a person, thing, or situation that annoys you or causes problems)

【例】The dogs next door are a real *nuisance*.

repellent [rɪ'pelənt] *adj.* 令人反感的(very unpleasant)
【例】She found him physically *repellent*.

肮　脏

blemish ['blemɪʃ] *v.* 损害，玷污(defect, flaw) *n.* 瑕疵，缺点
【记】blem(弄伤)+ ish → 玷污
【例】One illness will *blemish* your perfect attendance record.

contaminate [kən'tæmɪneɪt] *vt.* 污染(defile, pollute)
【例】The Department of Resources notified the town council that the water supply was *contaminated*.
【派】contamination(*n.* 玷污，污染) contaminant(*n.* 污染物 *adj.* 污染的)

effluent ['efluənt] *n.* (注入河中的)污水，工业废水(wastewater, sewage)

landfill ['lændfɪl] *n.* 垃圾堆

notorious [noʊ'tɔːriəs] *adj.* 臭名昭著的(infamous)
【记】not(知道)+ orious(多) → 臭名昭著的
【例】Bill is a *notorious* loudmouth.
【派】notoriously(*adv.* 声名狼藉地)

odor ['oʊdər] *n.* 气味(a smell, especially an unpleasant one)

smear [smɪr] *vt.* 涂；弄脏
【例】The politician was *smeared* by his opponent's accusations.

stench [stentʃ] *n.* 臭气，恶臭(bad smell, stink)

沮　丧

melancholy ['melənkɑːli] *adj.* 忧郁的，令人悲伤的(very sad)
【例】The music suited her *melancholy* mood.

depress [dɪ'pres] *vt.* 使沮丧(deject, dispirit)
【记】de(加强)+ press(压) → 使沮丧
【例】He was *depressed* because he had not passed his examinations.
【派】depression(*n.* 沮丧；经济大萧条) depressive(*adj.* 郁闷的)

dismal ['dɪzməl] *adj.* 阴暗的；沮丧的（dark, gloomy, somber）

【例】Mary cried during the *dismal* movie.

frustrate [frʌ'streit] *vt.* 破坏；挫败（baffle, thwart）

【例】The failure in the first battle *frustrated* the soldiers.

【派】frustration（*n.* 挫败，受挫）frustrated（*adj.* 失败的，落空的）

可　怕

formidable ['fɔːrmɪdəbl] *adj.* 可畏惧的，可怕的（dreadful, frightening）

【例】He is kind, but unfortunately with a *formidable* face.

grim [grɪm] *adj.* 冷酷的；可怕的（cruel, merciless）

【例】His expression was *grim* when he told them they had lost their jobs.

horrendous [hɔː'rendəs] *adj.* 可怕的，恐怖的（horrific, direful, dreadful, fearful）；极讨厌的

【例】What *horrendous* weather!

nightmare ['naɪtmer] *n.* 噩梦，梦魇（a very frightening dream）；可怕的经历（a very difficult experience）

【例】Years after the accident I still have *nightmares* about it.

stun [stʌn] *vt.* 使昏倒，使目瞪口呆（astonish, daze, amaze）

【例】He was *stunned* when he knew he failed the exam, which he had been preparing for months.

【派】stunning（*adj.* 令人惊奇的）

superstition [ˌsuːpər'stɪʃn] *n.* 迷信

【例】Fear of the number 13 is an old *superstition*.

vindictive [vɪn'dɪktɪv] *adj.* 报复性的

【例】a bitter and *vindictive* old man

【派】vindictively（*adv.* 报复性地）vindictiveness（*n.* 报复）

stinging ['stɪŋɪŋ] *adj.* 刺人的；激烈的（fierce, sharp）

【例】Dr. Forwell made a *stinging* attack on government policy.

terrify ['terɪfaɪ] *vt.* 使恐怖，使惊吓

【例】The animals were *terrified* by the storm.

【派】terrified（*adj.* 吓坏了的）terrorism（*n.* 恐怖主义）

愤 怒

indignation [ˌɪndɪɡˈneɪʃn] *n.* 愤慨，愤怒(anger)
【例】The news aroused great *indignation*.

inflammatory [ɪnˈflæmətɔːri] *adj.* 使激怒的，煽动性的;【医】发炎的
【例】*inflammatory* remarks
【派】inflammation(*n.*【医】发炎，炎症)

infuriate [ɪnˈfjʊrieɪt] *vt.* 使大怒;激怒(to make someone extremely angry)
【例】Her actions *infuriated* her mother.
【派】infuriating(*adj.* 愤怒的)

irate [aɪˈreɪt] *adj.* 发怒的，愤怒的，激怒的(extremely angry)
【例】an *irate* customer

provocative [prəˈvɑːkətɪv] *adj.* 激怒人的，挑战的(intended to make people upset)
【例】She was accused of being deliberately *provocative*.
【派】provocatively(*adv.* 挑衅地) provocation(*n.* 挑衅)

rage [reɪdʒ] *vi.* 大怒(feel very angry) *n.* 激怒，愤怒(fury, anger)
【例】He was sorry he had *raged* at her earlier.

resent [rɪˈzent] *vt.* 憎恨(loathe, hate, detest)
【记】re(反) + sent(感情) → 相反的感情 → 憎恨
【例】I bitterly *resent* your criticism.
【派】resentment(*n.* 愤恨)

其 他

exhaust [ɪɡˈzɔːst] *vt.* 使疲倦;用尽，耗尽(use up, drain)
【例】The children thoroughly *exhausted* their mother's patience.

fatigue [fəˈtiːɡ] *n.* 劳累，疲劳(physical or mental exhaustion)
【例】The old lady can't bear the *fatigue* of a long journey.

deplore [dɪˈplɔːr] *vt.* 悲叹，痛惜(to grieve, lament, regret)
【例】They *deplore* the use of force as a solution to this problem.
【派】deplorable(*adj.* 可悲的，可叹的)

embarrass [ɪmˈbærəs] *vt.* 使困窘

【例】Anne's older brother tried to *embarrass* her in front of her friends.

【派】embarrassing(*adj.* 令人难堪的) embarrassment(*n.* 尴尬,难堪;令人难堪的事)

thwart [θwɔːrt] *vt.* 阻挠(prevent),使…受挫

【例】Fierce opposition *thwarted* the government's plans.

torture [ˈtɔːrtʃər] *n.* 酷刑,折磨 *vt.* 对…施以酷刑(deliberately hurt)

【例】Political opponents of the regime may be *tortured*.

【派】torturer(*n.* 虐待者)

tyrannical [tɪˈrænɪkl] *adj.* 专制的,专横的(bossy, dominating);暴君的

【例】a *tyrannical* parent

【派】tyrannically(*adv.* 专横地)

wasteful [ˈweɪstfl] *adj.* 浪费的,挥霍的,耗费的(using too much)

【例】The software is very *wasteful* of memory.

【派】wastefully(*adv.* 浪费地) wastefulness(*n.* 浪费)

And gladly would learn, and gladly teach.
勤于学习的人才能乐于施教。

——英国诗人 乔叟(*Chaucer, British poet*)

151

练 习 题

连线题

doomed	臭气，恶臭	effluent	臭名昭著的
repellent	噩梦	diabetes	肥胖，过胖
euphoria	不适，小病	amnesia	高血压
formidable	阴暗的；沮丧的	notorious	晒伤
aftermath	可怕的	arthritis	哮喘
odor	极度愉快的心情	frustrate	鼓动，煽动
landfill	令人反感的	convulsion	关节炎
catastrophe	心灵创伤	vindictive	工业废水
dismal	注定失败的	obesity	健忘症
stench	后果	hypertension	痉挛
ailment	气味	sunburn	报复性的
nightmare	灾难，灾祸	asthma	糖尿病
trauma	垃圾堆	agitate	挫败

选词填空

well-being	casualty	obsess	allergic	epidemic
aversion	contaminate	melancholy	superstition	blemish

1. They are _____ the minds of our young people with these subversive ideas.

2. Miranda has been _____ with some handsome lifeguard for months.

3. In spite of his _____ to publicity, he still accepts the interview.

4. The earthquake caused heavy _____.

5. He fell into a state of profound _____ upon hearing the news of her death.

6. People who are _____ to pollen should not get close to flowers.

7. He thought that his reputation was_____ by the failure.

8. Over 500 people died during last year's flu _____.

9. She worked for the _____ of the underprivileged.

10.It's a common _____ that black cats are unlucky.

练习题答案

连线题答案

doomed	注定失败的	effluent	工业废水
repellent	令人反感的	diabetes	糖尿病
euphoria	极度愉快的心情	amnesia	健忘症
formidable	可怕的	notorious	臭名昭著的
aftermath	后果	arthritis	关节炎
odor	气味	frustrate	挫败
landfill	垃圾堆	convulsion	痉挛
catastrophe	灾难，灾祸	vindictive	报复性的
dismal	阴暗的；沮丧的	obesity	肥胖，过胖
stench	臭气，恶臭	hypertension	高血压
ailment	不适，小病	sunburn	晒伤
nightmare	噩梦	asthma	哮喘
trauma	心灵创伤	agitate	鼓动，煽动

选词填空答案

well-being	casualty	obsess	allergic	epidemic
aversion	contaminate	melancholy	superstition	blemish

1. They are（contaminating）the minds of our young people with these subversive ideas.
2. Miranda has been（obsessed）with some handsome lifeguard for months.
3. In spite of his（aversion）to publicity, he still accepts the interview.
4. The earthquake caused heavy（casualties）.
5. He fell into a state of profound (melancholy) upon hearing the news of her death.
6. People who are（allergic）to pollen should not get close to flowers.
7. He thought that his reputation was（blemished）by the failure.
8. Over 500 people died during last year's flu（epidemic）.
9. She worked for the（well-being）of the underprivileged.
10. It's a common（superstition）that black cats are unlucky.

Word List 19

音频

属性(一)

属性(一)

数 量

abundant [əˈbʌndənt] *adj.* 充裕的(sufficient)
【例】China is *abundant* with natural resources.
【派】abundance(*n.* 大量，充足)

adequate [ˈædɪkwət] *adj.* 足够的(sufficient)
【例】What you have given us is not *adequate*; you must find more.
【派】adequacy(*n.* 足够)

affluent [ˈæfluənt] *adj.* 富足的(wealthy)
【例】As people become more *affluent*, their standard and style of living improves.
【派】affluence(*n.* 富足)

aggregate [ˈæɡrɪɡət] *n* 合计，总计 (total amount) [ˈæɡrɪɡeɪt] *v.* 总计达…(amount to)
【例】The audiences *aggregated* a million people.
【派】aggregation(*n.*集合，群体)

altitude [ˈæltɪtuːd] *n.* (尤指海拔)高度，高处(海拔甚高的地方)

ample [ˈæmpl] *adj.* 富足的，充足的(sufficient, enough)
【例】There is *ample* evidence that climate patterns are changing.

cumulative [ˈkjuːmjəleɪtɪv] *adj.* 累计的，渐增的(increasing gradually by successive addition)
【例】Depression is often caused by the *cumulative* effects of stress and overwork.

deficient [dɪˈfɪʃnt] *adj.* 缺乏的，不足的(lacking, incomplete)
【例】A diet *deficient* in vitamin D may cause the disease rickets.
【派】deficiency(*n.* 缺乏，不足，短缺)

entirety [ɪnˈtaɪərəti] *n.* 全数，全体

enumerate [ɪˈnjuːməreɪt] *vt.* 枚举；计数(count; numerate)
【记】e(出) + numer(数字) + ate → 按数列出 → 枚举
【例】Sam can *enumerate* all the presidents of the United States.
【派】enumerator(*n.* 计数员) enumeration(*n.* 列举)

exodus [ˈeksədəs] *n.* 大批离去，成群外出

fecundity [fɪˈkʌndəti] *n.* 肥沃，多产（fertility, fruitfulness）

fertile [ˈfɜːrtl] *adj.* 肥沃的；多产的（fruitful; rich）
【记】fer（带来）+ tile → 能带来粮食 → 肥沃的
【例】The very *fertile* couple had six children in eight years.
【派】fertility（*n.* 肥沃；多产）

frequency [ˈfriːkwənsi] *n.* 频率，发生次数

fruitful [ˈfruːtfl] *adj.* 富有成效的；多产的，果实累累的
【例】It was a *fruitful* meeting; we made a lot of important decisions.

gauge [geɪdʒ] *vt.* 计量（calculate, measure）*n.* 厚度，直径；规格，尺度
【例】Tom *gauged* the distance to the river to be about a mile.

multitude [ˈmʌltɪtjuːd] *n.* 众多（host, mass）
【记】multi（多）+ tude → 众多

opulent [ˈɑːpjələnt] *adj.* 富裕的（very rich）；充足的；豪华的（luxurious）
【例】Europe's *opulent* elite
【派】opulence（*n.* 富裕）

prolific [prəˈlɪfɪk] *adj.* 多产的（productive）
【例】The *prolific* author published over 80 novels.
【派】prolifically（*adv.* 多产地）

quantitative [ˈkwɑːntəteɪtɪv] *adj.* 定量的
【记】quant（数量）+ itative → 定量的
【例】A *quantitative* analysis showed that he has grown 10 pounds fatter.
【派】quantitatively（*adv.* 数量上地）

segment [ˈsegmənt] *n.* 部分（part, section, portion, sector）；片段
【例】The Cultural Revolution in fact affected every *segment* of the nation.

solely [ˈsoʊlli] *adv.* 唯一地；仅仅（only）
【例】Scholarships are given *solely* on the basis of financial need.

solo [ˈsoʊloʊ] *n.* 独奏，独唱 *adj.* 独唱的，独奏的
【派】soloist（*n.* 独奏者，独唱者）

sprinkle [ˈsprɪŋkl] *n.* 少量（small amount）；小雨（rain）*v.* 撒，洒（spray, scatter）
【例】I *sprinkled* cocoa over my latte.
【派】sprinkling（*n.* 少量）

substantial [səbˈstænʃl] *adj.* 相当的(plentiful, considerable)

【例】Mary has a *substantial* amount of money in the bank.

【派】substantially(*adv.* 相当多地)

sufficient [səˈfɪʃnt] *adj.* 足够的，充分的(enough, adequate)

【例】We can only prosecute if there is *sufficient* evidence.

【派】sufficiency(*n.* 充足) suffice(*v.* 足够)

proportion [prəˈpɔːrʃn] *n.* 比例(percentage, ration)；部分

【记】比较portion(*n.* 部分)

附　属

accessory [əkˈsesəri] *n.* 附件（a supplementary part）；配饰（ornament）；同谋，帮凶（accomplice）*adj.* 附属的，辅助的；同谋的

ancillary [ˈænˈsɪləri] *adj.* 辅助的，附属的（subsidiary, auxiliary, supplementary）

【例】The complex includes offices, stables and other *ancillary* buildings of red brick.

auxiliary [ɔːɡˈzɪliəri] *adj.* 辅助的，补充的(subsidiary, supplementary)

【例】He holds an *auxiliary* position in the company.

derivative [dɪˈrɪvətɪv] *n.* 衍生物，引出物 *adj.* 衍生的，派生的

inherent [ɪnˈhɪrənt] *adj.* 固有的(innate, intrinsic)

【记】in(里面) + her(连) + ent → 天生(与身体内)连着 → 固有的

【例】I'm afraid the problems you mention are *inherent* in the system.

【派】inherently(*adv.* 天性地，固有地)

innate [ɪˈneɪt] *adj.* 天生的(inborn, inherent)

【记】in(进) + nate(生) → 与出生一起来 → 天生的

【例】The singer had an *innate* talent for music.

【派】innately(*adv.* 天生地)

intrinsic [ɪnˈtrɪnsɪk] *adj.* 固有的，内在的，本质的(being part of the nature or character of someone or something)

【例】There is nothing in the *intrinsic* nature of the work that makes it more suitable for women.

【派】intrinsically(*adv.* 内在地)

possessive [pəˈzesɪv] *adj.* 所有的；占有欲强的(wanting someone to love you and no one else)

【例】She was terribly *possessive* of our eldest son.

【派】possessively(*adv.*控制地) possessiveness(*n.* 自制力)

subordinate [sə'bɔːrdɪnət] *adj.* 次要的，附属的(inferior, secondary)

【记】sub(下面) + ordin(顺序) + ate → 下面的顺序 → 附属的

【例】Pleasure should be *subordinate* to duty.

【派】subordination(*n.* 次级)

相　邻

adjacent [ə'dʒeɪsnt] *adj.* 邻近的(adjoining, neighboring)

【例】Tom's house is *adjacent* to the park.

adjoining [ə'dʒɔɪnɪŋ] *adj.* 接近的，邻接的(adjacent, neighboring)

【例】We requested *adjoining* rooms at the hotel.

contiguous [kən'tɪgjuəs] *adj.* 接触的，临近的(next to)

【例】England is *contiguous* with Wales.

关　系

analogous [ə'næləgəs] *adj.* 相似的，可比拟的(similar, comparable)

【例】The report's findings are *analogous* with our own.

【派】analogue(*n.* 相似物) analogy(*n.* 类似；类推法)

antecedent [ˌænti'siːdnt] *adj.* 发生在前的，先行的（ preceding in time or order, prior ）*n.* 发生在之前的事，先例

【例】Those were events *antecedent* to the revolution.

antedate [ˌænti'deɪt] *v.* 先于，早于(precede)；(在信、文件上)写上较早的日期

【例】That event *antedated* World War Ⅱ.

applicable [ə'plɪkəbl] *adj.* 适当的，适用的（ appropriate, fitting, able to be applied ）

【例】These tax laws are not *applicable* to foreign companies.

【派】applicability(*n.* 适用性，适应性)

approximate [ə'prɑːksɪmət] *adj.* 近似的(proximate)

【记】ap + proxim(接近) + ate → 近似的

【例】What is the *approximate* travel time from your house to your job?

【派】approximately(*adv.* 近似地，大约)

bilateral [ˌbaɪ'lætərəl] *adj.* 双方的，双边的

【例】They have been negotiating a *bilateral* trade deal.

【派】unilateral(*adj.* 单边的)

binary ['baɪnəri] *adj.* 由两个东西组成的，双的（dual）

【例】Computers operate using *binary* system.

comparable ['kɑːmpərəbl] *adj.* 可比的（worthy of comparison）；类似的（similar）

【例】I suggested two *comparable* solutions to the problem.

comparative [kəm'pærətɪv] *adj.* 比较的；相比之下的，相对来说的

【例】Let's make a *comparative* study of the two languages. / After many hardships, he now lives in *comparative* ease.

compatible [kəm'pætəbl] *adj.* 兼容的（harmonious, congruous）

【例】Is this software *compatible* with my computer?

【派】compatibility（*n.* 兼容性）incompatible（*adj.* 不兼容的）

complement ['kɑːmplɪmənt] *n.* 互为补充的东西 ['kɑːmplɪment] *v.* 补充（to add to, make complete）

【例】The two suggestions *complement* each other.

complementary [ˌkɑːmplɪ'mentri] *adj.* 补充的（supplementary, subsidiary）

【例】The computer and the human mind have different but *complementary* abilities.

concurrent [kən'kɜːrənt] *adj.* 同时发生的（simultaneous）

【记】con + current（发生）→ 同时发生的

【例】There were several *concurrent* attempts to climb the mountain.

coordinate [koʊ'ɔːrdɪnət] *adj.* 同等的，并列的（equal, juxtaposed）*n.*【数】坐标 [koʊ'ɔːrdɪneɪt] *v.* 调和，使协调（harmonize）

【例】John only speaks to those who are *coordinate* with him in ranks. / Maybe we can *coordinate* the relation of them.

【派】coordination（*n.* 协调；和谐）

correlate ['kɔːrəleɪt] *vt.* 相关联（associate, relate）

【记】cor + relate（关联）→ 相关联

【例】The scientist could not *correlate* the data with his hypothesis.

【派】correlation（*n.* 关联，关系）correlative（*adj.* 相关的，关联的）

dichotomy [daɪ'kɑːtəmi] *n.* 两分，分裂（division into two parts）

disparate ['dɪspərət] *adj.* 根本不同的，不能比较的（utterly different or distinct in kind）

【例】Chalk and cheese are *disparate* substances.

【派】disparity（*n.* 不同，悬殊）

distinct [dɪˈstɪŋkt] *adj.* 截然不同的（totally different）；清晰的，明显的（clear, obvious）

【例】There is a *distinct* improvement in your spoken English.

distinguish [dɪˈstɪŋgwɪʃ] *v.* 辨别，区别（to differentiate）；扬名

【例】Can you *distinguish* the twins apart?

【派】distinguishing（*adj.* 有区别的）distinguished（*adj.* 卓越的，著名的）

diverse [daɪˈvɜːrs] *adj.* 不同的，种种的（different, various）

【例】Jane made a pretty bouquet of *diverse* flowers.

【派】diversity（*n.* 多样性）

diversify [daɪˈvɜːrsɪfaɪ] *vt.* 使多样化（vary）

【例】That factory has *diversified* its products.

【派】diversification（*n.* 变化，多样性）

egalitarian [iˌgælɪˈteriən] *adj.* 平等主义的 *n.* 平等主义者

【例】Clearly the *egalitarian* society remains a dream.

【派】egalitarianism（*n.* 平等主义）

equalize [ˈiːkwəlaɪz] *vt.* 使…相等（make equal or uniform）

【例】We have tried to *equalize* the workload between the different teachers.

equidistant [ˌiːkwɪˈdɪstənt] *adj.* 等距的

【记】equi(等) + distant(距) → 等距的

equilateral [ˌiːkwɪˈlætərəl] *adj.* 等边的

equivalent [ɪˈkwɪvələnt] *adj.* 等同的，相当的（equal, interchangeable）*n.* 等同品

【例】There is no exactly *equivalent* Chinese word to this English word.

【派】equivalence/equivalency（*n.* 等同，等价，等值）

heterogeneity [ˌhetərədʒəˈniːəti] *n.* 异类，不同

【派】heterogeneous（*adj.* 多种多样的）

homogeneity [ˌhɑːmədʒəˈniːəti] *n.* 同种，同质（heterogeneity的反义词）

homogeneous [ˌhoʊməˈdʒiːniəs] *adj.* 同类的，同性质的（uniform, same）

【记】homo(同) + gen(产生) + eous → 产生相同的 → 同类的

【例】The population of the small town was *homogeneous*, mostly merchants and laborers.

horizontal [ˌhɔːrəˈzɑːntl] *adj.* 水平的，与地平线平行的（level, flat）

【记】horizon(地平线) + tal → 水平的

【例】The lake has a *horizontal* surface.

identical [aɪˈdentɪkl] *adj.* 完全相同的(same)

【例】Bill and John have *identical* briefcases, and sometimes Bill picks up John's briefcase by mistake.

integral [ˈɪntɪɡrəl] *adj.* 组成的;完整的(complete, full)

【记】integr(完整) + al → 完整的

【例】Vegetables are an *integral* part of our diet.

【派】integrally(*adv.* 完整地;固有地)

irrelevant [ɪˈreləvənt] *adj.* 离题的;无关的(impertinent, extraneous)

【记】ir(无) + relevant(有关的) → 无关的

【例】Bob's comments about religion were *irrelevant* to our discussion about politics.

linkage [ˈlɪŋkɪdʒ] *n.* 连接;结合;联系(link)

【例】the *linkage* between wages and prices

mutual [ˈmjuːtʃuəl] *adj.* 相互的;共同的(reciprocal, joint)

【记】mut(变化) + ual → 你变我也变 → 相互的

【例】We signed the contract based on *mutual* benefit.

【派】mutually(*adv.* 共同地)

parallel [ˈpærəlel] *adj.* 平行的,类似的 *vt.* 匹敌(match, rival)

【例】His paintings *parallels* that of Qi Baishi.

pertain [pərˈteɪn] *vi.* 关于,有关(to relate directly to something)

【例】legislation *pertaining* to employment rights

relevant [ˈreləvənt] *adj.* 有关的(related, pertinent);贴切的

【例】What you say is not *relevant* with the matter in hand.

【派】relevance(*n.* 关联,切题) relevantly(*adv.* 贴切地)

resemble [rɪˈzembl] *vt.* 像,类似

【例】Mary *resembles* her mother in many ways.

similarity [ˌsɪməˈlærəti] *n.* 类似处,相似(affinity)

【记】similar(相似的) + ity → 相似

【例】The present crisis bears some *similarity* to the oil crisis of the 1970s.

affinity [əˈfɪnəti] *n.* 类似处(similarity);喜爱(liking, inclination)

【例】You can see the *affinity* in appearance between mother and daughter.

练 习 题

连线题

parallel	肥沃，多产	homogeneity	同时发生的
analogous	等同的，相当的	intrinsic	附件
dichotomy	全数，全体	bilateral	异类，不同
cumulative	相互的	sufficient	双方的，双边的
affluent	相似的，可比拟的	prolific	固有的，内在的
mutual	(海拔)高度	approximate	完全相同的
fecundity	分裂	comparable	足够的
entirety	不同的，种种的	solo	多产的
diverse	频率	auxiliary	可比的
frequency	富足的	concurrent	独奏，独唱
affinity	平行的	accessory	同种，同质
altitude	累计的	heterogeneity	辅助的，补充的
equivalent	类似处	identical	近似的

选词填空

aggregate	deficient	fruitful	sprinkle	inherent
adjacent	complement	distinguish	equalize	irrelevant

1. A diet _____ in vitamin D may cause the disease rickets.

2. I'm afraid the problems you mention are _____ in the system.

3. These young students live in _____rooms.

4. Please do not talk about matters _____ to our text in the class.

5. It was a _____ meeting; we made a lot of important decisions.

6. Sheila's earnings from all sources _____ 10,000 a month.

7. The priest _____ the baby with holy water.

8. His attorney argued that the plaintiff could not _____ between right and wrong.

9. The dark red walls _____ the red leather chairs.

10. A small adjustment would _____ the temperature in the two rooms.

练习题答案

连线题答案

parallel	平行的	homogeneity	同种, 同质
analogous	相似的, 可比拟的	intrinsic	固有的, 内在的
dichotomy	分裂	bilateral	双方的, 双边的
cumulative	累计的	sufficient	足够的
affluent	富足的	prolific	多产的
mutual	相互的	approximate	近似的
fecundity	肥沃, 多产	comparable	可比的
entirety	全数, 全体	solo	独奏, 独唱
diverse	不同的, 种种的	auxiliary	辅助的, 补充的
frequency	频率	concurrent	同时发生的
affinity	类似处	accessory	附件
altitude	(海拔)高度	heterogeneity	异类, 不同
equivalent	等同的, 相当的	identical	完全相同的

选词填空答案

aggregate	deficient	fruitful	sprinkle	inherent
adjacent	complement	distinguish	equalize	irrelevant

1. A diet（deficient）in vitamin D may cause the disease rickets.
2. I'm afraid the problems you mention are（inherent）in the system.
3. These young students live in （adjacent）rooms.
4. Please do not talk about matters（irrelevant）to our text in the class.
5. It was a （fruitful）meeting; we made a lot of important decisions.
6. Sheila's earnings from all sources（aggregated）10,000 a month.
7. The priest（sprinkled）the baby with holy water.
8. His attorney argued that the plaintiff could not（distinguish）between right and wrong.
9. The dark red walls（complement）the red leather chairs.
10. A small adjustment would （equalize）the temperature in the two rooms.

Word List 20

音频

属性（二）

属性(二)

新　旧

antiquated [ˈæntɪkweɪtɪd] *adj.* 过 时 的 ，陈 旧 的（ obsolete, outdated ）
【例】They attempted in vain to modernize these *antiquated* industries.

antique [ænˈtiːk] *n.* 古物，古董 *adj.* 古董的；古代的，古老的（ ancient, archaic ）
【例】Jacobs collects *antique* fountain pens.
【派】antiquity（ *n.* 古老；古物 ）

bygone [ˈbaɪɡɔːn] *adj.* 以 往 的 ，旧 时 的（ past, former ）*n.* 过去的事

cliché [kliːˈʃeɪ] *n.* 陈腔滥调

conventional [kənˈvenʃənl] *adj.* 传统的，习俗的（ traditional, customary ）
【例】Mary thought marriage and family was too *conventional* so she joined the army.

hoary [ˈhɔːri] *adj.*（ 毛发等 ）因年老而灰白的（ having grey or white hair ）；古老的，陈旧的
【例】All the grass in front was brittle and *hoary* white.

stale [steɪl] *adj.* 陈腐的（ smelly, musty, flat ）
【例】The *stale* bread was dry and hard.

stereotype [ˈsteriətaɪp] *n.* 陈规，老套 *vt.* 对…产生成见（ prejudice ）
【例】Homeless people are *stereotyped* as alcoholics or addicts.
【派】stereotyping（ *n.* 成见 ）stereotyped（ *adj.* 套用陈规的 ）

incipient [ɪnˈsɪpiənt] *adj.* 初期的（ just starting to be or happen ）
【例】an *incipient* disease

novice [ˈnɑːvɪs] *n.* 新信徒；生手（ beginner, tyro, layman ）
【记】nov（新）＋ ice（表示人）→ 生手

pristine [ˈprɪstiːn] *adj.* 纯洁的（ fresh or clean ）；质朴的；原有的
【例】The car has been restored to *pristine* condition.

秘　密

arcane [ɑːrˈkeɪn] *adj.* 鲜为人知的，神秘的(mysterious, esoteric)

【例】The language of the law is *arcane*.

mysterious [mɪˈstɪriəs] *adj.* 神秘的；难以理解的(cryptic, undecipherable)

【例】The police are investigating the *mysterious* deaths of children at the hospital.

【派】mysteriously(*adv.* 不可思议地)

mystic [ˈmɪstɪk] *adj.* 神秘的(mystical)；神秘主义的 *n.* 神秘主义者

cue [kjuː] *n.* 【戏】尾白，提示；暗示

furtive [ˈfɜːrtɪv] *adj.* 偷偷摸摸的，鬼鬼祟祟的

【例】The teacher was suspicious of the student's *furtive* behavior during the exam.

informant [ɪnˈfɔːrmənt] *n.* 报告者，告密者(informer)

prowl [praʊl] *v.* (野兽等)四处觅食；[喻]暗中来回寻觅

【例】Gangs of teenagers are *prowling* the streets.

secretary [ˈsekrəteri] *n.* 秘书

【派】secretarial(*adj.* 秘书的，书记的)

suggestive [səˈdʒestɪv] *adj.* 提示的，暗示的(implying, signifying)

【例】It was a huge sound, *suggestive* of whales calling each other.

【派】suggestiveness(*n.* 启发性)

真　实

authentic [ɔːˈθentɪk] *adj.* 可靠的，有根据的，真实的；真的(genuine, real)

【例】Is your diamond ring *authentic*?

【派】authenticity(*n.* 确实性，真实性) authenticate(*v.* 证实…是真实的)

factual [ˈfæktʃuəl] *adj.* 事实的，真实的(based on facts or relating to facts)

【例】This is a *factual* account of the war.

genuine [ˈdʒenjuɪn] *adj.* 真实的，真正的(authentic, real)

【例】My necklace is made with *genuine* pearls.

量 词

batch ［bætʃ］*n.* 一批，一组，一群

【例】Here comes a fresh *batch* of visitors.

bout ［baʊt］*n.* 一回，一场，一阵；回合，较量，比赛

bunch ［bʌntʃ］*n.*（一）球，束，串 *v.*（使）成捆（束，串）

【例】She *bunched* the cloth up and threw it away.

cluster ［ˈklʌstər］*n.*（果实、花、人等）串、簇、群、组

calorie ［ˈkæləri］*n.* 卡（热量单位）

centimeter ［ˈsentɪmiːtər］*n.* 厘米

pint ［paɪnt］*n.* 品脱（英美干量或液量名=1/2夸脱）

ration ［ˈræʃn］*n.* 定量配给（a fixed amount of something）

slice ［slaɪs］*n.* 薄片，切片（a thin flat piece）；部分（a part）

利 害

beneficial ［ˌbenɪˈfɪʃl］*adj.* 有益的（profitable, lucrative）

【例】Mary's college classes were *beneficial* to her career path.

edge ［edʒ］*n.* 优势，优越条件

【例】competitive *edge*

vantage ［ˈvæntɪdʒ］*n.* 优势，有利地位（good position）

【例】From my *vantage* point on the hill, I could see the whole procession.

necessitate ［nəˈsesɪteɪt］*vt.* 使⋯成为必要，需要（to make it necessary for you to do something）

【例】Lack of money *necessitated* a change of plan.

持 续

chronic ［ˈkrɑːnɪk］*adj.* 长期的；慢性的（recurring, periodic）

【记】chron（时间）+ic → 长时间的 → 长期的

【例】Mike said a *chronic* disease troubled John in his whole life.

coherent ［koʊˈhɪrənt］*adj.* 连贯的，一致的（logical, unified）

【例】The student had a *coherent* explanation for being late.

【派】coherence（*n.* 连贯性，一致性）incoherent（*adj.* 不连贯的，不一致的）

constant ['kɑːnstənt] *adj.* 不变的，持续的(invariable, continuous)

【例】The *constant* noise from the road crew gave Bill a headache.

【派】constancy(*n.* 不变)

continuation [kənˌtɪnjuˈeɪʃn] *n.* 连续，持续；延长部分(prolongation)

【例】He argued for a *continuation* of the search.

continuous [kənˈtɪnjuəs] *adj.* 连续的，没有中断的(uninterrupted, unceasing)

【例】The brain needs a *continuous* supply of blood.

durability [ˌdʊrəˈbɪləti] *n.* 耐久性(lastingness, enduringness, strength)

duration [duˈreɪʃn] *n.* 持续的时间，期间 (the length of time that something lasts or continues)

eternal [ɪˈtɜːrnl] *adj.* 永久的，永恒的(everlasting, perpetual)

【例】The bride and groom pledged their *eternal* love to each other.

longevity [lɔːnˈdʒevəti] *n.* 长寿，长命；持久 (long life or the long time that something lasts)

【例】The ancient Chinese claimed that garlic promoted *longevity*.

perennial [pəˈreniəl] *adj.* 长久的，永远的(permanent, long lasting)

【例】Teddy bears are a *perennial* favorite with children.

【记】per(全部) + enn(年) + ial → 长年的 → 长久的

【派】perennially(*adv.* 永久地)

periodic [ˌpɪriˈɑːdɪk] *adj.* 周期的，定期的(happening a number of times, usually at regular times)

【例】*periodic* home visits by nurses

【派】periodically(*adv.* 定期地) periodicity(*n.* 周期性)

permanent ['pɜːrmənənt] *adj.* 永久的(constant, continuous)

【例】Anne took a *permanent* position with the law firm.

【派】permanently(*adv.* 永久地)

perpetuate [pərˈpetʃueɪt] *vt.* 使…永恒，使…延续

【例】Every kind of plant has its own way to *perpetuate* itself.

【派】perpetuation(*n.* 永存，不朽)

persistent [pərˈsɪstənt] *adj.* 坚持不懈的(dogged)

【记】per(始终) + sist(坐) + ent → 始终坐着 → 坚持不懈的

【例】I told the *persistent* salesman to leave me alone.

【派】persistence(*n.* 坚持不懈)

progressive [prəˈɡresɪv] *adj.* 逐渐的；进步的；进行的 (gradual; advanced; continuous)

【例】Britain's *progressive* decline as a world power

【派】progressively(*adv.* 日益增加地) progressiveness(*n.* 进步)

successive [sək'sesɪv] *adj.* 连续的(consecutive)

【例】The baseball player hit four *successive* home runs.

【派】successively(*adv.* 接连地)

sustain [sə'steɪn] *vt.* 使继续；遭受(suffer)

【例】He *sustained* a fatal injury in the accident.

【派】sustainable(*adj.* 可持续的)

lease [liːs] *n.* 租约，租期 *v.* 出租(rent)

【例】The owner *leased* his spare houses to make a fortune.

【派】leasable(*adj.* 可出租的)

incoherent [ˌɪnkoʊ'hɪrənt] *adj.* 不连贯的(disconnected)

【记】in(不) + coherent(连贯的)→ 不连贯的

【例】Harris gave rambling, *incoherent* answers to questions about the case.

【派】incoherence(*n.* 不连贯；语无伦次)

inconsistent [ˌɪnkən'sɪstənt] *adj.* 不一致的，不协调的；易变的，不稳定的

【例】His dissolute life is *inconsistent* with his puritan upbringing.

intermittent [ˌɪntər'mɪtənt] *adj.* 断断续续的，间歇的（stopping and starting often and for short periods）

【例】The weather forecast is for sun, with *intermittent* showers.

【派】intermittently(*adv.* 间歇地)

temporary ['tempəreri] *adj.* 临时的(momentary)

【例】I'm living with my parents, but it's only *temporary*.

【派】temporarily(*adv.* 暂时地)

简　洁

brevity ['brevəti] *n.* 短暂(briefness)；简洁(conciseness)

compact ['kɑːmpækt] *adj.* 压缩的(packed)；密集的；小巧的

【记】com + pact(打包，压紧)→ 压缩的

【例】Jane has a *compact* kitchen with room for only one person.

sketchy ['sketʃi] *adj.* 概略的，粗略的(not thorough or complete)

【例】Details of the accident are still *sketchy*.

superficial [ˌsjuːpər'fɪʃl] *adj.* 表面的，肤浅的(seeming, apparent)

【记】super(上面) + fic(做) + ial → 表面的

【例】Susan prefers deep thinkers to people who are *superficial*.

【派】superficially(*adv.* 浅薄地)

succinct [səkˈsɪŋkt] *adj.* 简明的，简洁的（terse, concise）

【例】a *succinct* explanation

【派】succinctly（*adv.* 简洁地）succinctness（*n.* 简洁，简明）

复　杂

complex [ˈkɑːmpleks] *adj.* 复杂的（complicated, tangled）*n.* 综合体，结合体；【生】染色体组

【例】The student thought the algebraic formula was *complex*.

complexity [kəmˈpleksəti] *n.* 复杂性（the state or quality of being complex）；复杂的事物

【例】The *complexity* of the road map puzzled me.

convoluted [ˈkɑːnvəluːtɪd] *adj.* 旋绕的（twisted, coiled, rolled）；费解的（difficult to comprehend）

【例】The writer's meaning was obscured by his *convoluted* prose.

inexplicable [ˌɪnɪkˈsplɪkəbl] *adj.* 无法解释的（not capable of explanation; unexplainable）

【例】Her *inexplicable* absence worried me.

inextricable [ˌɪnɪkˈstrɪkəbl] *adj.* 无法摆脱的；解不开的，复杂的（entangled）

【例】There is an *inextricable* connection between language and culture.

【派】inextricably（*adv.* 逃不掉地；解不开地，解决不了地）

intricate [ˈɪntrɪkət] *adj.* 错综复杂的（complicated, entangled）；难懂的

【记】in（进入）+ tric（复杂）+ ate → 错综复杂的

【例】*intricate* patterns

【派】intricately（*adv.* 复杂地）

profound [prəˈfaʊnd] *adj.* 深奥的（deep）

【例】Dean is a *profound* thinker.

【派】profoundly（*adv.* 深刻地）

练 习 题

连线题

antiquated	有益的	coherent	耐久性
hoary	陈旧的	durability	长久的
incipient	陈腐的	eternal	连贯的
pristine	初期的	perennial	费解的
stale	原有的	perpetuate	永久的
arcane	四处觅食	permanent	简明的
furtive	暗示的	successive	临时的
prowl	神秘的	succinct	连续的
suggestive	偷偷摸摸的	inextricable	解不开的
factual	事实的	convoluted	错综复杂的
bout	回合	intricate	间歇的
ration	定量配给	temporary	使…永恒
beneficial	(因年老)灰白的	intermittent	永恒的

选词填空

longevity	conventional	authentic	secretary	mysterious
progressive	profound	necessitate	superficial	cluster

1. He is _____ in his approach to life.

2. Benson later disappeared in _____ circumstances.

3. My _____will fax you all the details.

4. Finally they arrived at a Chinese restaurant and found the _____ Chinese food.

5. A _____ of children stood around the ice cream van.

6. This would _____ interviewing all members of staff.

7. The worms have a _____ of about two years.

8. The Chinese government made_____ and forward-looking policies.

9. Naturally, such visits can allow only the most _____ understanding of prison life.

10.Tolstoy's experiences of war had a _____ effect on his work.

练习题答案

连线题答案

antiquated	陈旧的	coherent	连贯的
hoary	(因年老)灰白的	durability	耐久性
incipient	初期的	eternal	永恒的
pristine	原有的	perennial	长久的
stale	陈腐的	perpetuate	使…永恒
arcane	神秘的	permanent	永久的
furtive	偷偷摸摸的	successive	连续的
prowl	四处觅食	succinct	简明的
suggestive	暗示的	inextricable	解不开的
factual	事实的	convoluted	费解的
bout	回合	intricate	错综复杂的
ration	定量配给	temporary	临时的
beneficial	有益的	intermittent	间歇的

选词填空答案

longevity	conventional	authentic	secretary	mysterious
progressive	profound	necessitate	superficial	cluster

1. He is (conventional) in his approach to life.

2. Benson later disappeared in (mysterious) circumstances.

3. My (secretary) will fax you all the details.

4. Finally they arrived at a Chinese restaurant and found the (authentic) Chinese food.

5. A (cluster) of children stood around the ice cream van.

6. This would (necessitate) interviewing all members of staff.

7. The worms have a (longevity) of about two years.

8. The Chinese government made (progressive) and forward-looking policies.

9. Naturally, such visits can allow only the most (superficial) understanding of prison life.

10. Tolstoy's experiences of war had a (profound) effect on his work.

Word List 21

音频

属性(三)

属性(三)

重 要

consequence [ˈkɑːnsəkwəns] *n.* 结果，后果(results, outcome)；重要性，重大

【例】Nobody can tell what the *consequences* may be. / This matter is of great *consequence* to all of us.

crucial [ˈkruːʃl] *adj.* 严重的；极重要的(decisive, critical)

【例】Knowing first aid is *crucial* for saving lives.

dominant [ˈdɑːmɪnənt] *adj.* 占优势的，主导的(predominant, prevalent)

【例】The *dominant* color in the design is red.

【派】dominate(*v.* 统治，支配) domination(*n.* 控制，统治)

elite [eɪˈliːt] *n.* 精英，中坚分子(the best members of a group)

essential [ɪˈsenʃl] *adj.* 重要的，必需的(crucial, necessary, vital)；基本的，本质的(fundamental)

【例】Cells are an *essential* structure in living organisms.

far-reaching [ˈfɑːˈriːtʃɪŋ] *adj.* 影响深远的

【例】The government has made a lot of *far-reaching* decisions.

fatal [ˈfeɪtl] *adj.* 致命的

【例】I made the *fatal* mistake of letting her talk.

fatality [fəˈtæləti] *n.* 宿命；天数；命运

momentous [moʊˈmentəs] *adj.* 极重要的(important, critical)

【记】moment(时刻) + ous → 刻不容缓的 → 极重要的

【例】*Momentous* events are taking place in the U.S.

paramount [ˈpærəmaʊnt] *adj.* 最高权力的；决定性的，紧要关头的(more important than anything else)

【例】Women's role as mothers is of *paramount* importance to society.

【派】paramountcy(*n.* 最高权威)

pivotal [ˈpɪvətl] *adj.* 关键的；枢纽的

【例】Chairman of the board is the *pivotal* figure among the managing board.

primary [ˈpraɪmeri] *adj.* 重要的（crucial, vital）

【记】prim（最初的）+ ary → 最初的决定总是重要的 → 重要的

【例】Our *primary* concern is to provide the refugees with food and healthcare.

【派】primarily（*adv.* 首先，主要地）

signify [ˈsɪɡnɪfaɪ] *vt.* 表示，意味着（indicate, mean）

【例】Dark clouds *signify* that it will rain soon.

【派】signification（*n.* 含义）

substantive [ˈsʌbstəntɪv] *adj.* 实质性的（actual）

【例】An accident is just the appearance; a malicious murder is actually *substantive*.

【派】substantively（*adv.* 实质上）

elementary [ˌelɪˈmentri] *adj.* 基本的，初级的（fundamental, basic）；小学的

【例】I took a course in *elementary* chemistry. / *elementary* school

inconsequential [ɪnˌkɑːnsɪˈkwenʃl] *adj.* 不重要的，微不足道的（of no important consequences）

【例】Your objections are *inconsequential* and may be disregarded.

marginal [ˈmɑːrdʒɪnl] *adj.* 界限的；勉强够格的；很少的（too small to be important）

【例】a *marginal* increase in the unemployment figures

【派】marginally（*adv.* 少量地）

minuscule [ˈmɪnəskjuːl] *adj.* 极小的（extremely small, tiny）

【例】Her office is *minuscule*.

minute [maɪˈnjuːt] *adj.* 微小的，极小的（extremely small）

【例】You only need a *minute* amount.

negligible [ˈneɡlɪdʒəbl] *adj.* 可以忽略的，不予重视的（insignificant, minimal）

【例】The damage done to his property was *negligible*.

nuance [ˈnuːɑːns] *n.* 细微的差异

peripheral [pəˈrɪfərəl] *adj.* 非本质的，次要的（not as important as other things or people in a particular activity, idea, etc.）

【例】a diplomat who had a *peripheral* role in the negotiations / Her involvement in the case was *peripheral*.

【派】peripherally（*adv.* 外围地）

periphery	[pəˈrɪfəri] n. 外围（the edge of an area）; 不重要的部分

【例】a residential area on the *periphery* of the city

trivial	[ˈtrɪviəl] adj. 微不足道的（unimportant, trifling）

【例】I didn't bother Bob with my *trivial* concerns because he was busy.

unobtrusive	[ˌʌnəbˈtruːsɪv] adj. 不显眼的（not easily noticed）; 谦虚的; 不唐突的

【例】The staff are trained to be *unobtrusive*.

【派】unobtrusively（adv. 不显眼地）

外　表

configuration	[kənˌfɪgjəˈreɪʃn] n. 构造，形状，轮廓（the arrangement of the parts of something）
contour	[ˈkɑːntʊr] n. 轮廓（shape of the outer edges）; 海岸线（outline, profile）
exterior	[ɪkˈstɪriər] adj. 外部的（external）n. 外面，外貌，外表

【例】The *exterior* walls need a new coat of paint.

【派】interior（adj. 内部的）

ostensible	[ɑːˈstensəbl] adj. 表面上的; 伪装的（faking）

【例】The *ostensible* reason for his resignation was ill health.

【派】ostensibly（adv. 表面上）

profile	[ˈproʊfaɪl] n. 外形，轮廓（outline, contour, sketch）

【记】pro（前）+ file（线条）→ 前面的线条 → 轮廓

crinkle	[ˈkrɪŋkl] n.（布或纸的）皱纹

笨　重

cumbersome	[ˈkʌmbərsəm] adj. 笨重的（burdensome, clumsy）

【例】It's rather *cumbersome* having to carry all these cases around.

178
178

unwieldy [ʌnˈwiːldi] *adj.* 笨重的，不易移动的；难驾驭的（big, heavy; difficult to move or control）

【例】*unwieldy* bureaucracy

【派】unwieldiness（*n.* 笨拙）

underweight [ˌʌndərˈweɪt] *n./adj.* 重量不足(的)（weigh less than usual）

【例】Women who smoke risk giving birth to *underweight* babies.

先　后

hitherto [ˌhɪðərˈtuː] *adv.* 到目前为止

【例】*Hitherto* he had experienced no great success in his attempt.

delay [dɪˈleɪ] *vt.* 推迟，耽搁，延误（detain, postpone）*n.* 延迟

【例】Today I will *delay* this matter till I can decide what I should do.

ensue [ɪnˈsuː] *vi.* 接着发生，因而发生（to happen after or as a result of something）

【例】I objected to what he had just said and a heated argument then *ensued*.

eventual [ɪˈventʃuəl] *adj.* 最后的，最终的（final, ultimate）

【例】Owning a restaurant is Bill's *eventual* goal, but now he is just an assistant chef.

【派】eventually（*adv.* 终于，最后）

posthumous [ˈpɒstjuməs] *adj.* 死后获得的（happening, printed, etc. after someone's death）

【例】a *posthumous* collection of his articles

【派】posthumously（*adv.* 于死后）

postpone [poʊˈspoʊn] *vt.* 延迟（delay, put off）

【记】post(后) + pone → 推后 → 延迟

【例】The meeting was *postponed* by one day because my boss was sick.

subsequent [ˈsʌbsɪkwənt] *adj.* 随后的，后来的（following, later）

【记】sub(下面) + sequent(随着的) → 随后的

【例】*Subsequent* events proved the man to be right.

【派】subsequence（*n.* 随后）

ultimate [ˈʌltɪmət] *adj.* 最后的(final, eventual)

【记】ultim(最远) + ate → 最后的

【例】*Ultimate* success can be only achieved by those who hang on.

【派】ultimately(*adv.* 最后)

simultaneously [ˌsaɪmlˈteɪniəsli] *adv.* 同时地(at the same time, concurrently)

【例】The two balls, big and little, hit the ground *simultaneously*.

synchronize [ˈsɪŋkrənaɪz] *vt.* 同时发生(concur)

【记】syn(共同) + chron(时间) + ize → 同时发生

【例】They *synchronized* their steps.

【派】synchronized(*adj.* 同步的)

sequence [ˈsiːkwəns] *n.* 序列(procession, progression)

【记】sequ(跟随) + ence → 跟随着 → 序列

【派】sequential(*adj.* 连续的)

imminent [ˈɪmɪnənt] *adj.* 即将来临的(impending, approaching)

【记】im(进) + min(伸) + ent → 伸进来 → 即将来临的

【例】The *imminent* storm gives us a sign that the day is turning bad.

【派】imminence(*n.* 迫切,急迫)

instantaneous [ˌɪnstənˈteɪniəs] *adj.* 瞬间的,即刻的(ephemeral)

【记】instant(马上) + aneous → 瞬间的

【例】modern methods of *instantaneous* communication

【派】instantaneously(*adv.* 即刻)

precaution [prɪˈkɔːʃn] *n.* 预防措施

【例】Fire *precautions* were neglected.

precede [prɪˈsiːd] *vt.* 先于 *vi.* 领先(come before)

【记】pre(前) + cede(走) → 领先

【例】An informal meeting will *precede* the conference.

predate [prɪˈdeɪt] *v.* 提早日期,居先(to happen or exist earlier)

【例】The kingdom *predates* other African cultures by over 3,000 years.

predecessor [ˈpriːdɪsesər] *n.* 前辈,前任者;(被取代的)原有事物

preliminary [prɪˈlɪmɪneri] *adj.* 初步的,预备的 (happening before something more important)

【例】the *preliminary* stages of the competition

previous [ˈpriːviəs] *adj.* 以前的(preceding, foregoing)

【记】pre(预先) + vious → 以前的

【例】I've met him before on two *previous* occasions.

【派】previously(*adv.* 先前,以前)

primitive [ˈprɪmətɪv] *adj.* 原始的，最初的(crude, original, primordial)
【例】a *primitive* society
【派】primitively(*adv.* 最初地) primitiveness(*n.* 原始)

primordial [praɪˈmɔːrdiəl] *adj.* 初生的，初发的，原始的(existing at the beginning of time, ancient)
【例】the *primordial* matter

proactive [ˌproʊˈæktɪv] *adj.* 积极主动的，先发制人的 (make things happen)
【例】a *proactive* approach to staffing requirements

prompt [prɑːmpt] *adj.* 迅速的(quick)
【例】*Prompt* action must be taken.
【派】promptness(*n.* 迅速)

unprecedented [ʌnˈpresɪdentɪd] *adj.* 前所未有的，空前的(never have happened)
【例】Crime has increased on an *unprecedented* scale.
【派】unprecedentedly(*adv.* 空前地)

疏　密

dense [dens] *adj.* 密集的(thick, close)
【例】The airport was closed because of the *dense* fog.

intimate [ˈɪntɪmət] *adj.* 亲密的；内部的，私人的
vt. 宣布，通知；暗示
【例】 "*Intimate* friend" was usually used as written form of "close friend", which is more popular in oral English.
【派】intimacy(*n.* 熟悉；亲近)

replete [rɪˈpliːt] *adj.* 饱满的，塞满的(full)
【例】Literature is *replete* with tales of power.

程　度

drastic [ˈdræstɪk] *adj.* 激烈的(violent)；(法律)极端的，严厉的
【例】The emergency called for *drastic* measure. / The principal felt that the cheater's punishment should be *drastic*.

emergent [iˈmɜːrdʒənt] *adj.* 紧急的(urgent)；出现的(coming into being or notice)

enormous [ɪˈnɔːrməs] *adj.* 巨大的 (huge, vast, immense, tremendous)

【记】e(出) + norm(正常) + ous → 超出了正常状态 → 巨大的

【例】We prepared an *enormous* dinner because we were very hungry.

exaggerate [ɪɡˈzædʒəreɪt] *v.* 夸大，夸张(overstate, overemphasize)

【例】Bill *exaggerates* every story he tells his friends.

excessive [ɪkˈsesɪv] *adj.* 过多的，极度的(overabundant, inordinate)

【例】You must curb your *excessive* spending, or you will become penniless.

exhaustive [ɪɡˈzɔːstɪv] *adj.* 无遗漏的；彻底的；广泛的(comprehensive, thorough)

【例】The real estate agent gave the prospective buyers an *exhaustive* tour of the new house.

exorbitant [ɪɡˈzɔːrbɪtənt] *adj.* 过分的，过度的(excessive, unreasonable)

【例】I will not pay such an *exorbitant* price for these shoes!

immoderate [ɪˈmɑːdərət] *adj.* 无节制的(excessive)

【例】*immoderate* drinking

extremely [ɪkˈstriːmli] *adv.* 极端地，非常地(exceptionally, intensely)

【例】That is *extremely* interesting.

radical [ˈrædɪkl] *adj.* 根本的(fundamental)；激进的

【例】The American Revolution is not a *radical* one, but a gradual evolution.

【派】radically〔*adv.* 根本上地(basically)〕

rudimentary [ˌruːdɪˈmentri] *adj.* 根本的；低级的 (undeveloped, elementary, primitive, unsophisticated)

【记】rudi(无知的) + ment + ary → 无知的 → 低级的

【例】I took a *rudimentary* cooking class in high school.

thorough [ˈθɜːroʊ] *adj.* 彻底的，详尽的(detailed, careful)

【例】The doctor gave him a *thorough* check-up.

【派】thoroughly(*adv.* 彻底地)

ingrained [ɪnˈɡreɪnd] *adj.* 根深蒂固的 (attitudes or behaviors firmly established and difficult to change)

【例】The idea of doing our duty is deeply *ingrained* in most people.

underlying [ˌʌndərˈlaɪɪŋ] *adj.* 根本的 (fundamental)；隐含的；下层的

【例】There is an *underlying* assumption that younger workers are easier to train.

intact [ɪnˈtækt] *adj.* 完整的，未动过的 (not broken, damaged, or spoiled)

【例】Only the medieval tower had remained *intact*.

moderate [ˈmɑːdərət] *adj.* 温和的；适度的 (average, reasonable)

【记】moder=mod (方式) + ate → 方式正确 → 适度的

【例】Even *moderate* amounts of alcohol can be dangerous.

permissive [pərˈmɪsɪv] *adj.* 许可的 (allowable)；过分纵容的 (indulgent)

【例】His *permissive* answer cheered the students up.

【派】permissively (*adv.* 自由地)

pertinent [ˈpɜːrtnənt] *adj.* 适当的；切题的 (relevant)

【例】He asked me a lot of very *pertinent* questions.

【派】pertinently (*adv.* 适当地)

immature [ˌɪməˈtʃʊr] *adj.* 发育未完全的；不成熟的

mature [məˈtʃʊr] *v.* 成熟；到期 (to become fully grown or developed) *adj.* 成熟的

【例】She has *matured* into a fine writer.

【派】maturation (*n.* 成熟)

premature [ˈpremətʃə(r)] *adj.* 早熟的，不成熟的；过早的 (done too early or too soon)

【例】a *premature* order to attack / Any talk of a deal is *premature*.

练 习 题

连线题

elementary	决定性的	posthumous	积极主动的
essential	即将来临的	instantaneous	瞬间的
marginal	必需的	proactive	提早日期
negligible	不显眼的	predate	同时地
paramount	勉强够格的	simultaneously	彻底的
peripheral	可以忽略的	subsequent	最后的
pivotal	初级的	ultimate	饱满的
momentous	构造	replete	过分的
unobtrusive	关键的	unprecedented	随后的
configuration	极重要的	exhaustive	过多的
cumbersome	接着发生	excessive	适当的
imminent	次要的	exorbitant	死后获得的
ensue	笨重的	pertinent	前所未有的

选词填空

rudimentary	intimate	substantive	hitherto	precede
crucial	postpone	synchronize	ostensible	ingrained

1. This aid money is _____ to the government's economic policies.

2. The State Department reported that _____ discussions had taken place with Beijing.

3. The _____ purpose of the war was to liberate a small nation from tyranny.

4. The printing press made books available to people _____ unable to afford them.

5. They've decided to _____ having a family for a while.

6. Lunch will be _____ by a short speech from the chairman.

7. Gradually, I acquired a _____ knowledge of music.

8. He has an _____ prejudice against all foreigners.

9. Businesses must _____ their production choices with consumer choices.

10. She's on _____ terms with important people in the government.

练习题答案

连线题答案

elementary	初级的	posthumous	死后获得的
essential	必需的	instantaneous	瞬间的
marginal	勉强够格的	proactive	积极主动的
negligible	可以忽略的	predate	提早日期
paramount	决定性的	simultaneously	同时地
peripheral	次要的	subsequent	随后的
pivotal	关键的	ultimate	最后的
momentous	极重要的	replete	饱满的
unobtrusive	不显眼的	unprecedented	前所未有的
configuration	构造	exhaustive	彻底的
cumbersome	构造笨重的	excessive	过多的
imminent	即将来临的	exorbitant	过分的
ensue	接着发生	pertinent	适当的

选词填空答案

rudimentary	intimate	substantive	hitherto	precede
crucial	postpone	synchronize	ostensible	ingrained

1. This aid money is (crucial) to the government's economic policies.
2. The State Department reported that (substantive) discussions had taken place with Beijing.
3. The (ostensible) purpose of the war was to liberate a small nation from tyranny.
4. The printing press made books available to people (hitherto) unable to afford them.
5. They've decided to (postpone) having a family for a while.
6. Lunch will be (preceded) by a short speech from the chairman.
7. Gradually, I acquired a (rudimentary) knowledge of music.
8. He has an (ingrained) prejudice against all foreigners.
9. Businesses must (synchronize) their production choices with consumer choices.
10. She's on (intimate) terms with important people in the government.

Word List 22

音频

属性（四）

属性(四)

范　围

coverage [ˈkʌvərɪdʒ] *n.* 覆盖范围（the amount or extent to which something is covered）；新闻报道（reportage）

extent [ɪkˈstent] *n.* 长度，面积，范围（scope）；程度（degree）

incidence [ˈɪnsɪdəns] *n.* 发生率，影响范围（degree, extent, or frequency of occurrence）
【例】This area has a high *incidence* of crime, disease, unemployment, etc.

span [spæn] *n.* 跨度 *vt.* 跨越（cover, reach across）
【例】The Mongol Empire *spanned* much of Central Asia.

extensive [ɪkˈstensɪv] *adj.* 大量的；广泛的（comprehensive; thorough）
【例】The editor made *extensive* changes in the article.
【派】extensively（*adv.* 广泛地）

pervasive [pərˈveɪsɪv] *adj.* 无处不在的，遍布的（existing everywhere）
【例】the *pervasive* influence of television
【派】pervasiveness（*n.*【医】渗透性）

universal [ˌjuːnɪˈvɜːrsl] *adj.* 普遍的（suitable in every situation）；宇宙的
【例】a topic of *universal* interest
【派】universality（*n.* 普遍性，一般性）

widespread [ˈwaɪdspred] *adj.* 分布广的；普遍的，广泛的（general, extensive）
【例】There was *widespread* support for the war.

endemic [enˈdemɪk] *adj.* 地方性的（native, local）
【例】This disease is *endemic* to the Southerners, and will not spread in the cold North.

in-house [ɪnˈhaʊs] *adj.* 起源于机构内部的；机构内部的（working within a company or organization）
【例】We have an *in-house* training unit.

residential [ˌrezɪˈdenʃl] *adj.* 住宅的（relating to homes）

【例】a quiet *residential* neighborhood

phase [feɪz] *n.* 阶段 (stage, period); 状态

【例】The three *phases* of matter are solid, liquid and gas.

exception [ɪkˈsepʃn] *n.* 例外

【例】This is considered an *exception* to the rule.

【派】exceptional (*adj.* 例外的)

方　位

external [ɪkˈstɜːrnl] *adj.* 外部的 (exterior)

【例】The crab's *external* shell must be removed before you eat the meat inside.

【派】internal (*adj.* 内部的)

extrinsic [eksˈtrɪnsɪk] *adj.* 外部的，非固有的 (coming from outside or not directly related)

【例】That's something *extrinsic* to the subject.

outermost [ˈaʊtərmoʊst] *adj.* 最外层的 (furthest from the middle)

【例】the *outermost* stars

outmost [ˈaʊtmoʊst] *adj.* 最外面的，远离中心的 (the furthest)

without [wɪˈðaʊt] *n.* 外面，外部

【例】from *without*

frontal [ˈfrʌntl] *adj.* 前面的，正面的 (in the front)

【例】The enemy made a *frontal* attack on our troops.

interior [ɪnˈtɪriər] *n.* 内部 (inside, inner)

【记】比较exterior (*n.* 外部)

【例】The building's *interior* needed to be repaired.

lateral [ˈlætərəl] *adj.* 边的 (relating to the sides of something)

【例】The wall is weak and requires *lateral* support.

【派】laterally (*adv.* 旁边地)

unilateral [ˌjuːnɪˈlætrəl] *adj.* 单方面的，单边的

【例】a *unilateral* declaration of independence

【派】unilaterally (*adv.* 单方面地) unilateralism (*n.* 单方)

verge [vɜːrdʒ] *n.* 边缘 (edge)

wayside [ˈweɪsaɪd] *n.* 路边 (the side of a road) *adj.* 路边的

proximity [prɑːkˈsɪməti] *n.* 接近，邻近(nearness)

【记】proxim(接近) + ity → 接近

【例】He looked around the *proximity* for his lost dog.

vicinity [vəˈsɪnəti] *n.* 接近，附近(area around)

【例】The stolen car was found in the *vicinity* of the station.

outskirts [ˈaʊtskɜːrts] *n.* 郊区，市郊(the parts of a city that are far from the center)

【例】They live on the *outskirts* of Paris.

suburban [səˈbɜːrbən] *adj.* 城郊的(relating to a suburb)

【例】narrow-minded, *suburban* attitudes

interstate [ˈɪntərsteɪt] *adj.* (美)州与州间的，州际的(involving different states, especially in the U.S.)

【例】*interstate* commerce

underlie [ˌʌndərˈlaɪ] *vt.* 位于或存在于(某物)之下，引起(cause)

【例】the one basic principle that *underlies* all of the party's policies

【派】underlying(*adj.* 潜在的)

颜　色

colorize [ˈkʌləraɪz] *vt.* 使…变成彩色

【派】coloration(*n.* 染色，着色)

hue [hjuː] *n.* 形式，样子；颜色，色彩

monochrome [ˈmɑːnəkroʊm] *n.* 单色，单色照片 *adj.* 单色的(in shades of only one color)

【例】We looked out over the grey, *monochrome* landscape.

大　小

immense [ɪˈmens] *adj.* 巨大的 (unusually large, huge, vast)；无限的

【记】im(不) + mense(测量) → 不能测量 → 无限的

【例】They made an *immense* improvement in English.

【派】immensity(*n.* 巨大，无限)

jumbo [ˈdʒʌmboʊ] *adj.* 庞大的，巨大的 (larger than other things of the same type)

【例】*jumbo*-sized hot dogs

metropolitan ［ˌmetrə'pɑːlɪtən］ *adj.* 首都的，主要都市的，大城市的(relating or belonging to a very large city)

【例】a *metropolitan* area of South Australia

prodigious ［prə'dɪdʒəs］ *adj.* 巨大的(colossal, enormous)

【记】prodig(巨大) + ious → 巨大的

【例】I have a *prodigious* amount of work to do before I leave.

【派】prodigy(*n.* 奇事；天才)

sensational ［sen'seɪʃənl］ *adj.* 耸人听闻的，轰动的(interesting, exciting, and surprising)

【例】a *sensational* discovery

【派】sensationally(*adv.* 耸人听闻地)

titanic ［taɪ'tænɪk］ *adj.* 巨大有力的(huge, immense)

【记】美国影片《泰坦尼克号》的英文名

【例】The politician tried to reduce the *titanic* deficit.

tremendous ［trə'mendəs］ *adj.* 巨大的，惊人的(huge, great)

【例】She was making a *tremendous* effort to appear calm.

【派】tremendously(*adv.* 极大地)

peerless ［'pɪrləs］ *adj.* 无与伦比的(matchless, unparalleled)

【记】peer(同等) + less → 无相提并论者 → 无与伦比的

【例】the *peerless* blues musician B.B. King

unparalleled ［ʌn'pærəleld］ *adj.* 无比的，无双的，空前未有的(incomparable)

【例】an achievement *unparalleled* in sporting history

predominate ［prɪ'dɑːmɪneɪt］ *vt.* 占优势，支配(prevail)

【记】pre + domin(统治) + ate → 占优势

【例】Cheap and inferior commodities often *predominate* the morning market.

【派】predominant(*adj.* 占优势的) predominantly(*adv.* 显著地)

miniature ［'mɪnətʃər］ *adj.* 小型的，微小的(much smaller than normal) *n.* 微小模型

【例】He looked like a *miniature* version of his father.

公　正

dispassionate ［dɪs'pæʃənət］ *adj.* 平心静气的(uninfluenced by emotion)；公正的(impartial)

【例】Weber's report provides a *dispassionate* analysis of the conflict.

equitable ['ekwɪtəbl] *adj.* 公平的，公正的（fair, just）

【例】Twenty dollars is an *equitable* price for this lamp.

impartial [ɪm'pɑːrʃl] *adj.* 公正的，无偏见的（fair, unbiased）

【例】The judge should make his appraisal *impartial*.

impartiality [ˌɪmpɑːrʃi'æləti] *n.* 公平，无私

impersonal [ɪm'pɜːrsənl] *adj.* 冷淡的，不受个人情感影响的，客观的

【例】Business letters do not have to be *impersonal* and formal.

soundness ['saʊndnəs] *n.* 坚固；公正；稳固（rightness; stability）

neutral ['nuːtrəl] *adj.* 中性的；中立的（nonaligned）

【记】neutr(中) + al → 中性的

【例】The British government acted as a *neutral* observer during the talks.

【派】neutrally（*adv.* 中立地）

结　　构

procedure [prə'siːdʒər] *n.* 程序，手续，步骤（process）

【例】What's the *procedure* for applying for a visa?

constitute ['kɑːnstətuːt] *vt.* 构成，组成（form, compose, make up）

【例】We must redefine what *constitutes* a family.

【派】constitution（*n.* 构造；宪法，法规）

formation [fɔːr'meɪʃn] *n.* 形成，构成；形成物

【记】form(形成) + ation → 形成

frame [freɪm] *n.* 框架，构架 *vt.* 给…加框；表达；构造

【例】He *framed* his life according to a noble pattern.

framework ['freɪmwɜːrk] *n.* 构架，框架（structure, skeleton）

platform ['plætfɔːrm] *n.* 纲领；平台，站台 （the main ideas and aims of a political party; a raised place）

scenario [sə'nærioʊ] *n.* 脚本，方案，纲要（written description, plan）

skeleton ['skelɪtn] *n.* 骨架，框架，提纲（bones, structure）

形　状

inflection　[ɪnˈflekʃn] *n.* 向内弯曲；【音】变音，变调
【派】inflectional(*adj.* 抑扬的)

live　[laɪv] *adj.* 实况播送的，参加实况播送的
【例】There will be *live* TV coverage of tonight's big match.

retention　[rɪˈtenʃn] *n.* 保持力；滞留(keeping)
【例】The UN will vote on the *retention* of sanctions against Iraq.

static　[ˈstætɪk] *adj.* 静的，静态的(changeless, stagnant)；坚固的
【例】*Static* air pressure indicates that the weather will not change soon.

stationary　[ˈsteɪʃəneri] *adj.* 固定的(fixed, immobile, static)
【例】I think your arm is broken. Try to keep it *stationary* until we get to the hospital.

status quo　现状(current situation)

status quo ante　原状，以前的状态(previous situation)

servitude　[ˈsɜːrvətuːd] *n.* 奴役(状况)(slavery)
【例】They may grant you power, honor, and riches but afflict you with *servitude*, infamy, and poverty.

stiff　[stɪf] *adj.* 硬的，僵直的
【例】Her legs were *stiff* from kneeling.
【派】stiffly(*adv.* 僵硬地) stiffness(*n.* 生硬)

lamellar　[ləˈmelər] *adj.* 薄片状的，薄层状的

oval　[ˈoʊvl] *adj.* 卵形的
【例】an *oval* mirror

plumb　[plʌm] *adj.* 垂直的(straight, vertical) *vt.* 探究，探索(to succeed in understanding something completely)
【例】Psychologists try to *plumb* the deepest mysteries of the human psyche.

spiny　[ˈspaɪni] *adj.* 多刺的，带刺的
【例】*spiny* bushes

stubby　[ˈstʌbi] *adj.* 短而粗的(short and thick or fat)
【例】*stubby* fingers

wedge-shaped [ˈwedʒˌʃeɪpt] *adj.* 楔形的

速　度

rapidity [rəˈpɪdəti] *n.* 快速(fast); 险峻

【例】Their debts mounted with alarming *rapidity*.

tempo [ˈtempoʊ] *n.* (动作、生活的)步调, 速度(speed)

【例】the easy *tempo* of island life

hasty [ˈheɪsti] *adj.* 匆忙的(rushed); 草率的

【例】You will have time for a *hasty* snack before the train leaves.

The man who has made up his mind to win will never say "impossible".
凡是决心取得胜利的人是从来不说"不可能的"。
　　　　　　　　　——法国皇帝 拿破仑(*Bonaparte Napoleon, French emperor*)

练 习 题

连线题

endemic	内部	tremendous	固定的
residential	巨大的	unparalleled	惊人的
universal	住宅的	dispassionate	单色
extrinsic	地方性的	equitable	公平的
interior	最外层的	scenario	脚本
outermost	轰动的	stationary	保持力
proximity	单边的	retention	匆忙的
unilateral	附近	lamellar	薄片状的
vicinity	形式	stubby	平心静气的
hue	邻近	hasty	步调
immense	无限的	tempo	弯曲
prodigious	外部的	inflection	短而粗的
sensational	普遍的	monochrome	无比的

选词填空

exceptional	constitute	extensive	pervasive	impartial
predominate	metropolitan	plumb	peerless	underlying

1. The exhibition has received _____ coverage in the national press.
2. There is _____ mood of apathy in the city.
3. Richard is an _____ student.
4. We need to find out the _____ causes of her depression.
5. Jenny is in the Los Angeles _____ area.
6. Their _____ performances in ice dancing won applause from the audience.
7. In this type of case, the rights of the parent _____.
8. We offer _____ advice on tax and insurance.
9. The rise in crime _____ a threat to society.
10. When his wife left him, Matt _____ the very depths of despair.

连线题答案

endemic	地方性的	tremendous	惊人的
residential	住宅的	unparalleled	无比的
universal	普遍的	dispassionate	平心静气的
extrinsic	外部的	equitable	公平的
interior	内部	scenario	脚本
outermost	最外层的	stationary	固定的
proximity	邻近	retention	保持力
unilateral	单边的	lamellar	薄片状的
vicinity	附近	stubby	短而粗的
hue	形式	hasty	匆忙的
immense	无限的	tempo	步调
prodigious	巨大的	inflection	弯曲
sensational	轰动的	monochrome	单色

选词填空答案

exceptional	constitute	extensive	pervasive	impartial
predominate	metropolitan	plumb	peerless	underlying

1. The exhibition has received (extensive) coverage in the national press.
2. There is (pervasive) mood of apathy in the city.
3. Richard is an (exceptional) student.
4. We need to find out the (underlying) causes of her depression.
5. Jenny is in the Los Angeles (metropolitan) area.
6. Their (peerless) performances in ice dancing won applause from the audience.
7. In this type of case, the rights of the parent (predominate).
8. We offer (impartial) advice on tax and insurance.
9. The rise in crime (constitutes) a threat to society.
10. When his wife left him, Matt (plumbed) the very depths of despair.

Word List 23

音频

状态变化

状态变化

减少/减轻/缩小

abridge [ə'brɪdʒ] *vt.* 缩短，删节(to shorten, condense, abbreviate)
【记】a + bridge (桥)→ 桥使路程变短 → 缩短
【例】The rights of citizens must not be *abridged*.
【派】abridged(*adj.* 缩短的，删减的) abridgment(*n.* 删节)

alleviate [ə'liːvɪeɪt] *vt.* 缓和，减轻 (to mitigate, relieve)
【例】The doctor gave her an injection to *alleviate* the pain.

curtail [kɜːr'teɪl] *vt.* 缩减，截断 (cut back, reduce)
【记】cur + tail(尾巴)→ 尾巴短了 → 缩减
【例】The discussions were *curtailed* when the fire alarm went off.

cutback ['kʌtbæk] *n.* 削减，减少(decrease or reduction)

decelerate [ˌdiː'seləreɪt] *v.* (使)减速(decrease the speed of)
【例】Many countries are seeking measures to *decelerate* the arms buildup.
【派】accelerate(*v.* 加速)

deduct [dɪ'dʌkt] *vt.* 扣除，减去(to subtract)
【例】My employer *deducted* ten pounds from my wages this week.

deduction [dɪ'dʌkʃn] *n.* 扣除，扣除之量；推论，演绎法

diminish [dɪ'mɪnɪʃ] *vt.* 减少；缩小(decrease, dwindle)
【记】di(向下) + mini(小) + sh → 小下去 → 缩小
【例】Unexpected expenses *diminished* the size of my bank account.

diminution [ˌdɪmɪ'nuːʃn] *n.* 减少，缩减(reduction, decrease)

reduction [rɪ'dʌkʃn] *n.* 减少，缩小；降价(a decrease in the size, price etc.)

dwindle ['dwɪndl] *v.* 日渐减少，变小(diminish, decrease)
【例】The stream will continue to *dwindle* if it doesn't rain.

minimize ['mɪnɪmaɪz] *vt.* 使最小化(to reduce something to the smallest possible amount or degree)
【例】Every effort is being made to *minimize* civilian casualties.
【派】minimum(*n.* 最小值)

debilitate [dɪ'bɪlɪteɪt] *vt.* 使(人或人的身体)非常虚弱(to make feeble)

【例】Heat *debilitates* many people.

【派】debilitation(*n.*【医】虚弱，乏力)

disarm [dɪs'ɑːrm] *vt.* 缴械；使人消除敌意

【记】dis(取消) + arm(武装) → 缴械

【例】Her words *disarmed* him at once.

ease [iːz] *v.* (使)减轻，舒缓，使宽慰(to sooth, relieve, allay)

【例】The news that her child was safe *eased* her mind.

mitigate ['mɪtɪgeɪt] *vt.* 缓和，减轻(alleviate, relieve)

【记】miti(小) + gate(做) → 往小做 → 缓和

【例】Nothing could *mitigate* the cruelty with which she had treated him.

【派】mitigation(*n.* 缓解)

subdue [səb'duː] *vt.* 征服，压制；减轻(defeat, control)

【例】Napoleon *subdued* much of Europe.

【派】subdued(*adj.* 缓和的)

sap [sæp] *n.* 树液；活力 *vt.* 削弱，耗尽(weaken)

【例】Her long illness was gradually *sapping* Charlotte's strength.

discount ['dɪskaʊnt] *n./vt.* (打)折扣(reduction)

【例】Mary gets an employee *discount* at the department store.

downsizing ['daʊnsaɪzɪŋ] *n.* 减小规模；精简，裁员

relegate ['relɪgeɪt] *vt.* 使降级，使降职(give a less important job etc.)

【例】Women tended to be *relegated* to typing and filing jobs.

【派】relegated(*adj.* 降级的)

impair [ɪm'per] *vt.* 损害(harm, damage)

【记】im(进入) + pair(坏) → 使…坏 → 损害

【例】His misdeeds greatly *impaired* our friendship.

【派】impairment(*n.* 损害，损伤)

retard [rɪ'tɑːrd] *vt.* 延迟(detain)

【记】re(使) + tard(迟缓) → 延迟

【例】The heavy winds *retarded* the plane's speed.

regressive [rɪ'gresɪv] *adj.* 税率递减的；回归的；退化的(returning to a less advanced state)

【例】Many considered the changes to the welfare laws a *regressive* step.

steep [stiːp] *adj.* 极高的；陡峭的；急剧下降的(increase or decrease quickly)

【例】The road became rocky and *steep*.

【派】steeply(*adv.* 险峻地) steepness(*n.* 险峻)

增加/加重/扩大

accelerate [əkˈseləreɪt] *vt.* 加速 *vi.* 增速, 进行(expedite, speed)

【记】ac + cele + rate(速度)→ 加速

【例】The car *accelerated* as it went downhill.

【派】acceleration(*n.* 加速度)

accretion [əˈkriːʃn] *n.* 增长(gradual increase, addition)

accrue [əˈkruː] *v.* 增长, 增加(to increase)

【例】Interest will *accrue* until payment is made.

additional [əˈdɪʃənl] *adj.* 增加的, 额外的(extra)

【例】Passengers have to pay *additional* charges for their extra luggage.

enhance [ɪnˈhæns] *vt.* 增加, 增强 (raise, improve, heighten)

【例】You can *enhance* your appearance with makeup.

upgrade [ˌʌpˈgreɪd] *vt.* 使升级, 改良(improve)

[ˈʌpgreɪd] *n.* 升级, 增加

【例】You'll need to *upgrade* your hard drive to 4MB before running this software.

upsurge [ˈʌpsɜːrdʒ] *n./v.* 增长, 高涨(sudden increase)

【例】There was an *upsurge* in violence during June and July.

upturn [ˈʌptɜːrn] *n.* (情况)好转; (价格)提高; 向上的趋势(an increase in level)

【例】an economic *upturn*

zoom [zuːm] *vi.* 急速上升, (价格)猛增(increase, escalate)

【例】Inflation *zoomed* to 123%.

boom [buːm] *v.* 激增, 猛涨; 兴隆(increase, flourish, thrive)

【例】Business is *booming*.

maximize [ˈmæksɪmaɪz] *vt.* 使增至最大限度(to increase something as much as possible)

【例】The company's main function is to *maximize* profit.

【派】maximum(*n.* 最大值)

burgeon [ˈbɜːrdʒən] *v.* 迅速成长, 发展(to develop fast)

【例】Our company's business is *burgeoning* now.

aggravate [ˈæɡrəveɪt] *v.* 加重，恶化(worsen)；激怒(infuriate)

【例】The lack of rain *aggravated* the already serious lack of food.

exacerbate [ɪɡˈzæsərbeɪt] *vt.* 使恶化，使加重(to worsen)

【例】The drugs they gave her only *exacerbated* the pain.

consolidate [kənˈsɑːlɪdeɪt] *vt.* 巩固，加强(to enhance, strengthen)；合并(to combine, merge)

【例】The company has *consolidated* its position as the country's leading gas supplier.

fortify [ˈfɔːrtɪfaɪ] *vt.* 加强(strengthen, reinforce)

【记】fort(强) + ify → 加强

【例】We *fortified* the bridge with extra supports.

【派】fortification(*n.* 防御工事，要塞)

intensify [ɪnˈtensɪfaɪ] *vt.* 加强(enhance, strengthen)

【例】The general *intensified* the defense of the northern border by sending more troops there.

【派】intensity(*n.* 强度)

reinforce [ˌriːɪnˈfɔːrs] *vt.* 加强，加固(increase, strengthen)

【记】re(再次) + in + force(力量) → 再次增加力量 → 加强

【例】The Congress passed a bill on *reinforcing* information technology in the coming decade.

strengthen [ˈstreŋθn] *v.* 加强，巩固(reinforce)

【例】Our enemy has greatly *strengthened* during the truce talks.

substantiate [səbˈstænʃieɪt] *vt.* 加强，证实(corroborate, verify)

【例】Evidences *substantiated* that he was the murderer.

【派】substantiation(*n.* 证实)

additive [ˈædətɪv] *adj.* 添加的，附加的；【数】加法的 *n.* 添加剂

agglomeration [əˌɡlɑːməˈreɪʃn] *n.* 结块，凝聚

【派】agglomerate(*v.* 使成块，使凝聚 *adj.* 成块的)

amass [əˈmæs] *v.* 积聚

【例】They have *amassed* a fortune in just a few years.

amplify [ˈæmplɪfaɪ] *v.* 放大，扩大；增强(to augment, enlarge, expand, increase)

【例】The new manager wants to *amplify* the company.

【派】amplifier(*n.* 扩音器，放大器) amplification(*n.* 扩增，扩大)

broaden [ˈbrɔːdn] *v.* 放宽，变阔

【记】broad(宽) + en → 放宽

【例】The city *broadened* the road at the dangerous turn.

bulge [bʌldʒ] *n./v.* 肿胀，鼓起（to stick out in a rounded shape）

【例】His pockets were *bulging* with candy.

enrich [ɪnˈrɪtʃ] *vt.* 使富裕，使丰富（make rich, enhance）

【记】en + rich(富)→ 使富裕

【例】I *enriched* my coffee with cream and sugar.

escalate [ˈeskəleɪt] *vt.* 使…升级，扩大，增高（to increase, intensify）

【例】The government *escalated* the war by starting to bomb enemy cities.

【派】escalator(*n.* 自动扶梯) escalation(*n.* 扩大，增加)

expand [ɪkˈspænd] *vi.* 扩张（outspread）

【记】ex + pand(分散)→ 分散出去 → 扩张

【例】The balloon *expanded* slowly.

【派】expansion(*n.* 扩张，膨胀)

swell [swel] *v.* 膨胀（expand, inflate）

【例】My ankle began to *swell* when I injured.

【派】swelling(*n.* 膨胀)

prolong [prəˈlɔːŋ] *vt.* 拖长，延长（extend, lengthen）

【记】pro(向前) + long(长)→ 延长

【例】His journey to China was *prolonged* because there is too much to see.

【派】prolongation(*n.* 延伸)

expedite [ˈekspədaɪt] *vt.* 加速（speed up, hasten）

【记】ex + ped(脚) + ite → 脚跨出去 → 加速

【例】The person I talked to on the phone promised to *expedite* the shipment of the book I ordered.

改 变

adaptation [ˌædæpˈteɪʃn] *n.* 改写，改编（revision, rewriting）；适应，顺应（adjustment）

【例】The book described the *adaptation* of desert species to the hot conditions.

【派】adapt(*v.* 适应；改编) adaptable(*adj.* 可适应的；可改编的)

amend [əˈmend] *v.* 修改，修订（change, emend）；改良（improve）

【记】a + mend(修补)→ 修改

【例】The law was *amended* to include women.

【派】amendment(*n.* 修改，修正案)

revise [rɪˈvaɪz] *vt.* 修订 (amend, emend, edit)

【记】re(再) + vise(看) → 重新审查 → 修订

【例】The student *revised* his paper carefully, following the professor's suggestions.

【派】revision(*n.* 修订) revisionist(*n.* 修订主义者)

adjust [əˈdʒʌst] *vt.* 调节；使适于 (to adapt)

【记】ad + just(合适的) → 使适于

【例】Mary *adjusted* the TV to get a clearer picture.

【派】adjusted(*adj.* 调整过的) adjustment(*n.* 调整)

convert [kənˈvɜːrt] *vt.* 转换 (change, transform)；使皈依宗教 [ˈkɑːnvɜːrt] *n.* 皈依宗教者

【例】I *converted* the spare bedroom into a reading room.

【派】conversion(*n.* 转变；皈依)

diversion [daɪˈvɜːrʒn] *n.* 转移，转向(the act of diverting)；分散注意力

【例】High tariffs often cause a *diversion* of trade from one country to another.

distract [dɪˈstrækt] *vt.* 分散(心思)，打扰(divert)

【记】dis + tract(拉) → 心被拉开 → 分散

【例】The school students were *distracted* by the noise outside the classroom.

【派】distraction(*n.* 使人分心的事) distractive(*adj.* 分散注意力的，扰乱的)

distort [dɪˈstɔːrt] *vt.* 歪曲(misrepresent, twist)

【例】An electrical disturbance *distorted* the picture on the television set.

【派】distortion(*n.* 曲解)

fluctuate [ˈflʌktʃueɪt] *v.* 波动(waver, alternate, move up and down)

【例】The stock prices *fluctuated* wildly.

【派】fluctuation(*n.* 波动，起伏)

innovation [ˌɪnəˈveɪʃn] *n.* 改革，革新(reformation)

【记】innovat(e)(革新) + ion → 革新

【例】Susan's design *innovations* saved the company a great deal of money.

metamorphose [ˌmetəˈmɔːrfoʊz] *vt.* 使变成，使变质 (to change completely and become something different)

【例】From an easy-going young girl, she had *metamorphosed* into a neurotic middle-aged woman.

mutation [mjuːˈteɪʃn] *n.* 变化(transformation)

【记】mut(变) + ation → 变化

【例】A little frog was transformed into a monster due to a *mutation* aroused by nuclear emission.

perversion [pərˈvɜːrʒn] *n.* 堕落；曲解；变态

【例】a *perversion* of the true meaning of democracy

renovate [ˈrenəveɪt] *vt.* 革新；修复(renew, restore)

【记】re(重新) + nov(新) + ate → 重新翻新 → 革新

【派】renovation(*n.* 翻新，整修)

switch [swɪtʃ] *v.* 转换，转变(change)

【例】He worked as a librarian before *switching* to journalism.

【派】switching(*n.* 转换；开关)

transform [trænsˈfɔːrm] *vt.* 变换(change, transmute)

【记】trans(变) + form(形) → 变形 → 变换

【例】A fresh coat of paint can *transform* a room.

【派】transformation(*n.* 变换)

upheaval [ʌpˈhiːvl] *n.* 动乱，大变动(unrest, turmoil)

variation [ˌveriˈeɪʃn] *n.* 变化(alteration, change)

【记】vari(变化) + ation → 变化

【例】The global warming trend has made considerable *variation* of temperature.

variety [vəˈraɪəti] *n.* 品种(type)；变化，多样化

【例】Artista offers a wide *variety* of sandwiches.

volatile [ˈvɑːlətl] *adj.* 反复无常的(changeable)；挥发性的

【例】an increasingly *volatile* political situation

【派】volatility(*n.* 反复无常)

impressionable [ɪmˈpreʃənəbl] *adj.* 易受影响的(easily influenced)

【例】The child is at an *impressionable* age.

invariable [ɪnˈveriəbl] *adj.* 恒定的，不变的，始终如一的(never changing)

【例】His *invariable* answer was "Wait and see."

【派】invariably(*adv.* 始终不变地)

decent [ˈdiːsnt] *adj.* 正派的；体面的(proper)

【例】The house was in *decent* shape when we bought it.

【派】decency(*n.* 正派，体面，端庄)

malleable [ˈmæliəbl] *adj.* 有延展性的(pliable)；可锻的

【记】malle(锤子) + able → 用锤子打 → 可锻的

练 习 题

连线题

abridge	截断	amplify	放大
curtail	精简	escalate	使恶化
debilitate	删节	exacerbate	加速
decelerate	增长	expedite	使变质
deduct	使虚弱	fluctuation	波动
downsizing	减速	zoom	迅速成长
diminution	结块	distract	急速上升
regressive	使降级	volatile	肿胀
relegate	减少	impressionable	分散
accelerate	加速	metamorphose	易受影响的
accretion	退化的	burgeon	延长
additive	扣除	prolong	反复无常的
agglomeration	添加的	bulge	使…升级

选词填空

upsurge	aggravate	impair	mitigate	distort
fortify	retard	consolidate	alleviate	subdue

1. This is a new medicine to _____ the symptoms of flu.
2. The illness had _____ his ability to think and concentrate.
3. Measures need to be taken to _____ the environmental effects of burning more coal.
4. Cold weather _____ the growth of many plants.
5. Police managed to _____ the angry crowd.
6. Building the new road will only _____ the situation.
7. The team _____ their lead with a third goal.
8. Her position was _____ by election successes and economic recovery.
9. There was a genuine _____ of religious feeling.
10. His account was badly _____ by the press.

练习题答案

连线题答案

abridge	删节	amplify	放大
curtail	截断	escalate	使…升级
debilitate	使虚弱	exacerbate	使恶化
decelerate	减速	expedite	加速
deduct	扣除	fluctuation	波动
downsizing	精简	zoom	急速上升
diminution	减少	distract	分散
regressive	退化的	volatile	反复无常的
relegate	使降级	impressionable	易受影响的
accelerate	加速	metamorphose	使变质
accretion	增长	burgeon	迅速成长
additive	添加的	prolong	延长
agglomeration	结块	bulge	肿胀

选词填空答案

upsurge	aggravate	impair	mitigate	distort
fortify	retard	consolidate	alleviate	subdue

1. This is a new medicine to（alleviate）the symptoms of flu.
2. The illness had（impaired）his ability to think and concentrate.
3. Measures need to be taken to（mitigate）the environmental effects of burning more coal.
4. Cold weather（retards）the growth of many plants.
5. Police managed to（subdue）the angry crowd.
6. Building the new road will only（aggravate）the situation.
7. The team（consolidated）their lead with a third goal.
8. Her position was（fortified）by election successes and economic recovery.
9. There was a genuine（upsurge）of religious feeling.
10. His account was badly（distorted）by the press.

Word List 24

音频

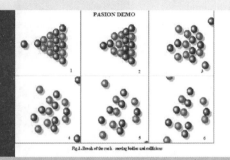

物体行为（一）

物体行为(一)

躲 避

absenteeism [ˌæbsən'tiːɪzəm] *n.* 旷课,旷工
【派】absentee(*n.* 缺席者)

avoidance [ə'vɔɪdəns] *n.* 回避,避开(keeping away from, dodging)

circumvent [ˌsɜːrkəm'vent] *vt.* 回避,设法克服或避免(to avoid, evade or go around)
【例】They opened an office abroad in order to *circumvent* the tax laws.
【派】circumvention(*n.* 规避;陷害,欺骗)

elude [i'luːd] *vt.* 躲避(escape, evade)
【记】e(出) + lude(玩) → 出去玩 → 躲避
【例】The gangster *eluded* the police.
【派】elusion(*n.* 逃避,规避)

elusive [i'luːsɪv] *adj.* 躲避的,躲闪的
【例】We got a glimpse of the *elusive* movie star as he entered his private car.

eschew [ɪs'tʃuː] *vt.* 避开;远离(avoid; shun)
【例】Jane *eschews* both alcohol and tobacco.

indispensable [ˌɪndɪ'spensəbl] *adj.* 不可缺少的,绝对必要的(essential, vital)
【例】This is an *indispensable* book.

inevitable [ɪn'evɪtəbl] *adj.* 不可避免的,必然的(unavoidable, certain)
【例】Death is the *inevitable* ending of life.
【派】inevitability(*n.* 必然性)

sidestep ['saɪdstep] *n.* (侧面)台阶;(拳击等)横跨一步躲避打击;[喻]回避(困难)*v.* 回避,躲避(avoid dealing with difficulties)
【例】The report *sidesteps* the environmental issues.

促 进

activate ['æktɪveɪt] *v.* 激励,触发(to make active);【化】使活化,使激活;

【原】使产生放射性(to make radioactive)

【例】We must *activate* the youth to study.

【派】activation(*n.*激活;【化】活化作用) activator(*n.*催化剂)

actuate ['æktʃueɪt] *vt.* 开动(机器);激励,驱使(to motivate, put into action)

【例】The pump is *actuated* by a belt driven by an electric motor.

boost [buːst] *vt.* 提高,促进;支援;(用广告)吹捧

【例】These changes will help to *boost* share prices.

impetus ['ɪmpɪtəs] *n.* 推动力(urge, momentum)

【记】im(进入) + pet(追求) + us → 追求力 → 推动力

【例】His longing for another kind of life is a major *impetus* for his hard working.

incentive [ɪn'sentɪv] *n.* 刺激;动机(motivation)

【例】People doubt about her *incentive* to marry that rich old fellow.

promote [prə'moʊt] *vt.* 升职;促进

【记】pro(前) + mote(动) → 促进

【例】You're so happy. Are you *promoted*?

【派】promotion(*n.* 升职)

trigger ['trɪgər] *n.* (枪)扳机 *v.* 引发,引起(cause, bring about)

【例】The assassination *triggered* off a wave of rioting.

spur [spɜːr] *vt.* 刺激,鞭策(stimulate, provoke, urge)

【例】*Spurred* by his students, the teacher started to talk about his first love.

stimulate ['stɪmjuleɪt] *vt.* 刺激,激励,激发(motivate, encourage, incite, actuate)

【记】stimul(刺激) + ate → 刺激

【例】The mass was *stimulated* by his words and burned Caesar's house.

【派】stimulation(*n.* 刺激) stimulus(*n.* 刺激物)

breakthrough ['breɪkθruː] *n.*突破

【例】Scientists have made a *breakthrough* in their treatment of that disease.

impulse ['ɪmpʌls] *n.* 一时冲动;刺激,推动力 *v.* 推动(urge)

【记】比较pulse(*n.* 脉搏,跳动)

【例】On seeing the poor little girl, he has an *impulse* to adopt her.

【派】impulsive(*adj.* 易冲动的)

groundbreaking ['graʊndbreɪkɪŋ] *adj.*开创性的,突破性的(innovative, innovational)

【例】The *groundbreaking* study in this area was conducted by a female scientist.

预　知

anticipate [ænˈtɪsɪpeɪt] v. 预感，预见，期望（to expect, foresee）

【例】I *anticipate* deriving much instruction from the lecture.

【派】anticipated（*adj.* 预期的）anticipation（*n.* 预期，期盼）

expectation [ˌekspekˈteɪʃn] n. 预料，期望

forecast [ˈfɔːrkæst] n./v. 预测，预报（to predict）

【例】Now scientists can *forecast* the weather accurately.

【派】forecaster（*n.* 预报员）

foresee [fɔːrˈsiː] vt. 预知（foreshadow, predict）

【记】fore（前）+ see（看）→ 预先看到 → 预知

【例】Those who can *foresee* difficulties on their way to success may keep calm when they really appear.

inspiration [ˌɪnspəˈreɪʃn] n. 灵感，鼓舞人心的人或事物（a good idea about what you should do, write etc., especially one which you get suddenly）

【例】He raised his eyes to the altar as if seeking *inspiration*.

omen [ˈoʊmən] n. 征兆，预兆（a sign of what will happen in the future）

【例】The car won't start. Do you think it's an *omen*?

portend [pɔːrˈtend] vt. 预兆，预示（to be a sign that something is going to happen）

【例】strange events that *portend* disaster

precursor [priːˈkɜːrsər] n. 先兆；先驱（sign; forerunner, pioneer, ancestor）

【记】pre（提前）+ curs（跑）+ or → 提前跑到事情的前面 → 先兆

【例】Dark clouds are often treated as *precursor* of a storm.

prediction [prɪˈdɪkʃn] n. 预言，预报（forecast, prophecy）

symptom [ˈsɪmptəm] n. 症状；征候，征兆（sign, indication）

【例】One *symptom* of the disease is a high fever.

【派】symptomatic（*adj.* 有症状的）

estimate [ˈestɪmeɪt] vt. 估计（gauge, compute）

【例】I *estimate* that Tom will be promoted to department manager.

prescient [ˈpresiənt] adj. 有预知能力的，有先见之明的（knowing what will happen）

【例】extraordinarily *prescient* memorandum

【派】prescience（*n.* 预知）

prospective [prəˈspektɪv] *adj.* 预期的(forthcoming)
【例】the *prospective* costs of providing pensions

假　设

assumption [əˈsʌmpʃn] *n.* 假设(supposition, hypothesis)
【例】A lot of people make the *assumption* that poverty only exists in the Third World.

extrapolate [ɪkˈstræpəleɪt] *vt.* 推断，推算(to infer)
【例】It is possible to *extrapolate* future developments from current trends.
【派】extrapolation(*n.* 推断，预测)

hypothesis [haɪˈpɑːθəsɪs] *n.* 假设，前提，假说(assumption)
【记】hypo(下，次) + thesis(论点) → 次论点 → 非正式论点 → 假设

hypothesize [haɪˈpɑːθəsaɪz] *v.* 假设，猜测(to suppose, assume)
【例】Scientists *hypothesize* that the dinosaurs were killed by a giant meteor.
【派】hypothetical(*adj.* 假设的，假定的)

postulate [ˈpɒstjʊlət]/[ˈpɑːstʃəleɪt] *n./v.* 假设，假定 (to suggest that something might have happened or be true)
【例】It has been *postulated* that the condition is inherited.
【派】postulation(*n.* 假定)

presume [prɪˈzuːm] *vt.* 假定，假设(suppose, imagine, assume)
【例】We cannot *presume* the existence of life on other planets.
【派】presumption(*n.* 推定，猜想) presumably(*adv.* 大概，可能)

压　缩

compile [kəmˈpaɪl] *vt.* 收集；编纂(collect, put together)
【记】com + pile(堆) → 有序地堆 → 编纂
【例】The scientists *compiled* a great amount of data to help develop their theory.
【派】compilation(*n.* 编写；编辑物)

compress [kəmˈpres] *v.* 压紧，压缩(to squeeze, compact, condense)
【记】com(共同) + press(压) → 压紧

【例】In her anger she *compressed* her lips so tightly that they went white.

【派】compressor(*n.* 压缩机) compression(*n.* 挤压，压缩)

condense [kən'dens] *v.* (使)浓缩；精简

【记】con + dense(密度大的) → 密度变大，相对面积减少 → 精简

【例】Steam *condenses* to water when it touches a cold surface.

【派】condensation(*n.* 冷凝；浓缩；缩写，精简)

encapsulate [ɪn'kæpsjuleɪt] *v.* 装入胶囊，压缩；总结，囊括(to sum up)

【例】The words of the song neatly *encapsulate* the mood of the country at that time.

epitome [ɪ'pɪtəmi] *n.* 缩影，典型的人或事，典范

【例】He was the very *epitome* of evil.

【派】epitomize(*v.* 成为某事物的缩影)

腐　蚀

caustic ['kɔːstɪk] *adj.* 刻薄的(acrid, unkind)；腐蚀性的(abrasive, corrosive)

【例】The *caustic* remark caused the candidate to lose the election.

corrode [kə'roʊd] *v.* 腐蚀(erode, eat away)

【例】Battery acid *corroded* the inside of the camera.

【派】corrosion(*n.* 腐蚀) corrosive(*adj.* 腐蚀性的)

erode [ɪ'roʊd] *vt.* 蚀，腐蚀(corrode, wear away)

【例】A constant stream of water *eroded* the rock mountain.

【派】erosion(*n.* 腐蚀，磨损) erosive(*adj.* 腐蚀性的)

分　裂

crack [kræk] *v.* 爆裂(to break)；(健康、精神)衰退 *n.* 裂缝

【例】Don't put boiling water in the glass or it will *crack*.

debacle [deɪ'bɑːkl] *n.* 崩溃，溃败(a sudden disastrous collapse or defeat, a complete failure)

dismember [dɪs'membər] *vt.* 割下(动物的)肢，肢解；割裂，瓜分

【例】Mr. Corry might have to *dismember* the company more than he wants to.

fracture ['fræktʃər] *n./v.* (使)折断，断裂(break)

【例】Her leg *fractured* in two places.

rupture ['rʌptʃər] *n./v.* 破裂，决裂(burst, breach)

【记】rupt(断) + ure → 破裂

【例】Water streamed from the *rupture* in the pipe.

scatter ['skætər] *vt.* 使分散(disperse, spread)

【例】Farmer *scattered* the corn in the yard for the hens.

segregate ['segrɪgeɪt] *vt.* 隔离，分离(alienate, separate)

【记】se(分开) + greg(群体) + ate → 和群体分开 → 隔离

【例】Solid and liquid are *segregated* and then mixed again in the experiment.

【派】segregation(*n.* 隔离)

fissure ['fɪʃər] *n.* 狭长的裂缝或裂隙

fragment ['frægmənt] *n.* 碎片，破片(piece, scrap)

fragmentary ['frægmənteri] *adj.* 碎片的；不连续的(discontinuous, disconnected)

【例】I have only a *fragmentary* recollection of the house where I grew up.

【派】fragmentation(*n.* 分裂，破碎)

partially ['pɑːrʃəli] *adv.* 部分地(not completely, partly)

【例】The operation was only *partially* successful.

respective [rɪ'spektɪv] *adj.* 分别的，各自的(individual)

【例】The applicants received *respective* interviews.

【派】respectively(*adv.* 分别地)

crumple ['krʌmpl] *vt.* 压皱(rumple, wrinkle)

【例】Anne *crumpled* the letter and threw it away.

粉　碎

crumble ['krʌmbl] *v.* 粉碎，崩溃(collapse, crash)；把…弄成碎屑

【记】crumb(碎屑) + le → 把…弄成碎屑

【例】His last hope *crumbled* to nothing.

debris [də'briː] *n.* 碎片，残骸(fragments or remnants of something destroyed or broken)

demolish [dɪ'mɑːlɪʃ] *vt.* 推翻，摧毁(destroy, raze)

【例】The car was *demolished* in the accident.

【派】demolition(*n.* 破坏,拆除)

disintegration [dɪsˌɪntɪ'greɪʃn] n. 瓦解，崩溃（decomposition, dissolution）

【例】This defeat led to the *disintegration* of the empire.

fragile ['frædʒl] adj. 脆的（breakable, brittle）

【记】frag(碎) + ile → 易碎的 → 脆的

【例】You must cushion *fragile* objects carefully when you pack them.

【派】fragility(n. 脆弱，虚弱)

衰　落

decay [dɪ'keɪ] v. (使)腐败（rot, decompose）；衰退，衰落（decline）

【例】The vegetables have begun to *decay*.

degenerate [dɪ'dʒenərət] adj. 堕落的 [dɪ'dʒenəreɪt] vi. 退步（degrade, deteriorate）

【记】de(坏) + gener(产生) + ate → 往坏产生 → 堕落的

【例】I was shocked by the lack of morals in the *degenerate* book.

【派】degeneration(n. 退化；恶化；变质)

degrade [dɪ'greɪd] vt. 使降级；使堕落（degenerate, lower）

【记】de(向下) + grade(级) → 使降级

【例】He *degrade* himself by cheating and telling lies.

【派】degrading (adj. 丢脸的, 有辱人格的) degradation (n. 降级, 降格；退化)

deteriorate [dɪ'tɪriəreɪt] vi. 恶化，变坏（to become worse, decay）

【例】Ethel's health has *deteriorated*.

【派】deterioration(n. 衰退；恶化)

练 习 题

连线题

absenteeism	回避	postulate	破裂
circumvent	预测	compile	收集
eschew	远离	compress	压紧
activate	一时冲动	encapsulate	装入胶囊
impetus	激励	epitome	粉碎
incentive	假设	caustic	缩影
stimulate	动机	fragmentary	不连续的
groundbreaking	刺激	fracture	恶化
impulse	开创性的	debacle	假定
anticipate	预感	rupture	折断
forecast	旷课	deteriorate	崩溃
precursor	推动力	degenerate	退步
hypothesize	先兆	crumble	刻薄的

选词填空

indispensable	elude	boost	demolish	estimate
erode	inevitable	foresee	segregate	trigger

1. He managed to _____ his pursuers by escaping into a river.

2. Meat is not _____ for maintaining a healthy diet.

3. It is _____ that doctors will make the occasional mistake.

4. The new resort area has _____ tourism.

5. Certain forms of mental illness can be _____ by food allergies.

6. Organizers _____ the crowd at 50,000.

7. I've put your name on the list and I don't _____ any problems.

8. The cliffs are being constantly _____ by heavy seas.

9. Blacks were _____ from whites in schools.

10. He _____ my argument in minutes.

练习题答案

连线题答案

absenteeism	旷课	postulate	假定
circumvent	回避	compile	收集
eschew	远离	compress	压紧
activate	激励	encapsulate	装入胶囊
impetus	推动力	epitome	缩影
incentive	动机	caustic	刻薄的
stimulate	刺激	fragmentary	不连续的
groundbreaking	开创性的	fracture	折断
impulse	一时冲动	debacle	崩溃
anticipate	预感	rupture	破裂
forecast	预测	deteriorate	恶化
precursor	先兆	degenerate	退步
hypothesize	假设	crumble	粉碎

选词填空答案

indispensable	elude	boost	demolish	estimate
erode	inevitable	foresee	segregate	trigger

1. He managed to (elude) his pursuers by escaping into a river.
2. Meat is not (indispensable) for maintaining a healthy diet.
3. It is (inevitable) that doctors will make the occasional mistake.
4. The new resort area has (boosted) tourism.
5. Certain forms of mental illness can be (triggered) by food allergies.
6. Organizers (estimated) the crowd at 50,000.
7. I've put your name on the list and I don't (foresee) any problems.
8. The cliffs are being constantly (eroded) by heavy seas.
9. Blacks were (segregated) from whites in schools.
10. He (demolished) my argument in minutes.

Word List 25

音频

物体行为(二)

物体行为(二)

描　述

delineate [dɪˈlɪnieɪt] *vt.* 刻画；记述(depict, portray)
【记】de(加强) + line(线) + ate → 用力画线 → 刻画
【例】He *delineated* his plan in this notebook.

depict [dɪˈpɪkt] *vt.* 描写，叙述(delineate, describe, portray)
【例】The poet tried to *depict* the splendor of the setting sun in his poem.
【派】depiction(*n.* 描写，叙述)

elaborate [ɪˈlæbəreɪt] *vt.* 详细阐述(to explain in detail) [ɪˈlæbərət] *adj.* 精心构思的(carefully planned)
【例】We ask Mary to *elaborate* her trip to Tibet.

embody [ɪmˈbɑːdi] *vt.* 包含(to include, incorporate)；(作品等)表达，体现，象征(to symbolize, present)
【记】em + body(身体，主体) → 体现
【例】The new edition *embodies* many improvements. / The heroic deeds of him *embodied* the glorious tradition of the troops.
【派】embodiment(*n.* 体现，化身)

narrator [nəˈreɪtər] *n.* 讲述者，叙述者(the person who tells the story in a book or a play)

portray [pɔːrˈtreɪ] *vt.* 绘制(delineate, depict)
【例】His work *portrays* the beautiful view of his hometown.
【派】portrayal(*n.* 画像；扮演)

sketch [sketʃ] *n.* 草图(drawing, chart) *vt.* 勾画(compose, outline)
【例】He *sketched* out a plan for his inferiors to execute.

specify [ˈspesɪfaɪ] *vt.* 详述(define)
【例】The student *specified* several reasons for his being late.
【派】specification(*n.* 详述)

reiterate [riˈɪtəreɪt] *vt.* 重述(restate)
【记】re(反复) + iterate(重申) → 重述
【例】The spokesman *reiterated* the policy of the government.
【派】reiteration(*n.* 重复，反复)

underscore [ˌʌndərˈskɔːr] *vt.* 强调，在…下画线 (underline)
[ˈʌndərskɔːr] *n.* 底线，下方画线

excerpt [ˈeksɜːrpt] *n.* 摘录，节录；引用

quotation [kwoʊˈteɪʃn] *n.* 引用，引述 (a sentence from books, etc.)

过　失

delinquent [dɪˈlɪŋkwənt] *adj.* 违法的，有过失的 (guilty)；失职的 (failing in or neglectful of duty or obligation) *n.* 少年犯
【例】Jail is not a good place to rehabilitate *delinquent* youths.
【派】delinquency (*n.* 过失，罪过；少年犯罪)

erroneous [ɪˈroʊniəs] *adj.* 错误的 (incorrect, mistaken)
【例】The so-called facts you gave me were totally *erroneous*.

flawed [flɔːd] *adj.* 有瑕疵的，有缺陷的
【例】The research behind this report is seriously *flawed*.

fallacy [ˈfæləsi] *n.* 谬误，谬见，谬论
【派】fallacious (*adj.* 谬误的)

fault [fɔːlt] *n.* 【地】断层；缺点；故障；过失

malfunction [ˌmælˈfʌŋkʃn] *vi.* 失灵，发生故障 *n.* 故障 (a fault in the way a machine or part of someone's body works)
【例】A warning light seems to have *malfunctioned*.

mishap [ˈmɪshæp] *n.* 灾祸，不幸 (mischance, accident)
【记】mis (坏) + hap (运气) → 不幸
【例】The fisherman drowned in a boating *mishap*.

mismatch [ˈmɪsmætʃ] *vt.* 使配错，使配合不当 *n.* 错配
【例】the *mismatch* between the demand of health care and supply
【派】mismatched (*adj.* 配错的)

disregard [ˌdɪsrɪˈɡɑːrd] *vt.* 不理会，无视 (to give little or no attention to; to ignore) *n.* 漠视，忽视
【记】dis (不) + regard (注视，注重) → 无视
【例】She completely *disregarded* all our objections.

negligence [ˈneɡlɪdʒəns] *n.* 过失，疏忽 (failure to take enough care over something that you are responsible for)
【例】The bridge's architect was sued for criminal *negligence*.

oversight [ˈoʊvərsaɪt] *n.* 疏忽，忽略，失察 (a mistake in which you forget or do not notice something)
【例】I assure you that this was purely an *oversight* on my part.

液体及相关行为

drain [dreɪn] *vt.* 排水(to draw off water); 喝干 *vi.* 水流掉, 消耗 *n.* 排水沟; 流尽, 用光
【例】It was not easy to *drain* the flooded mine.
【派】drainage(*n.* 排水系统; 排水; 污水)

drift [drɪft] *n./v.* 漂流(move aimlessly)
【例】The piece of wood was *drifting* down the river.

drizzle [ˈdrɪzl] *vi.* 下毛毛雨 *n.* 毛毛雨
【例】It *drizzled* off and on all day.

eject [iˈdʒekt] *vt.* 喷出(emit, ejaculate); 逐出
【记】e(出) + ject(扔) → 扔出 → 喷出
【例】The machine *ejected* finished parts faster than we could count them.
【派】ejection(*n.* 喷出, 排出物)

spill [spɪl] *v.* 溢出, 泼出, 涌出(pour)
【例】Katie almost *spilled* her milk.

instill [ɪnˈstɪl] *vt.* 滴注; 逐渐灌输
【记】in(进入) + still(滴) → 灌输
【例】Courtesy must be *instilled* in childhood.

irrigate [ˈɪrɪgeɪt] *vt.* 灌溉; 修水利
【例】They *irrigated* the land in order to increase the produce.
【派】irrigation(*n.* 灌溉)

implant [ɪmˈplænt] *v.* 注入, 灌输 (to establish firmly, inculcate, instil); (器官等)移植
【例】Early experiences can *implant* fears in the subconscious.
【派】implantation(*n.* 灌输; 移植)

influx [ˈɪnflʌks] *n.* 流入, 汇集; 河口
【记】in(进入) + flux(流入) → 流入
【例】a large *influx* of tourists in the summer

spray [spreɪ] *n./v.* 喷雾(sprinkle, shower)
【例】John *sprayed* insecticide on the plants.

inundate [ˈɪnʌndeɪt] *vt.* 淹没(swamp); (洪水般地)涌来, 充满; 使难以应付
【例】After the broadcast, we were *inundated* with requests for more information.
【派】inundation(*n.* 洪水; 淹没)

submerge [səb'mɜːrdʒ] *vt.* 浸没，淹没 *vi.* 潜水

【记】sub(下面) + merge(沉) → 沉到下面 → 淹没

【例】I *submerged* my head in the water completely. / The submarine *submerged* to avoid enemy ships.

saturate ['sætʃəreɪt] *vt.* 浸透(soak, imbue)

【例】His shoes were *saturated* after the rain.

【派】saturated(*adj.* 湿透的)

rinse [rɪns] *vt.* 冲洗，冲刷(wash)

【例】Let me just *rinse* my hands.

scour ['skaʊər] *vt.* 四处搜索(search carefully)；擦洗，擦亮

【例】Her family began to *scour* the countryside for a suitable house.

scrub [skrʌb] *v.* 刷洗(rub to clean)；取消(cancel)

【例】He *scrubbed* the dirt off his boots.

defrost [ˌdiː'frɔːst] *v.* (给…)化霜，(使…)解冻(unfreeze, dissolve, thaw)

【例】Don't let the meat *defrost* too quickly.

dip [dɪp] *v.* 浸，蘸，沾(immerse in) *n.* 倾斜；下沉；溶液

【例】She *dipped* her finger into the liquid and tasted it.

evaporate [ɪ'væpəreɪt] *v.* 蒸发(vaporize)；消失(disappear)

【例】His hopes *evaporated*.

【派】evaporation(*n.* 蒸发作用)

moisture ['mɔɪstʃər] *n.* 潮湿，湿气(small amounts of water that are present in the air, in a substance, or on a surface)

purify ['pjʊrɪfaɪ] *vt.* 净化，提纯(clean, make something pure)

【例】They prayed to God to *purify* them.

【派】purification(*n.* 净化)

launder ['lɔːndər] *v.* 洗烫(衣服等)；洗(黑钱)

【例】The law is designed to prevent money *laundering*.

secrete [sɪ'kriːt] *vt.* 分泌(discharge, release)

【例】The stomach begins to *secrete* a certain type of enzyme when food reaches it.

【派】secretion(*n.* 分泌物)

solvent ['sɑːlvənt] *adj.* 溶解的；有偿付能力的 (able to pay back)；有溶解力的 *n.* 溶媒，溶剂

【例】I don't know how we managed to remain *solvent*.

【派】solvency(*n.* 溶解力；偿付能力)

leakage ['liːkɪdʒ] *n.* 漏，漏出，漏出物

【例】*leakages* of confidential information

mobility [moʊˈbɪləti] *n.* 流动能力(the ability to move easily from one job, area, or social class to another)

【例】social *mobility*

osmosis [ɑːzˈmoʊsɪs] *n.* 潜移默化，耳濡目染(gradually learn them by hearing them often)

【例】Children learn new languages by *osmosis*.

【派】osmotic(*adj.* 渗透的，渗透性的)

气体及相关行为

emanate [ˈeməneɪt] *vi.* (气体等)从…传出

【例】Do you know where these rumors *emanated* from?

【派】emanation(*n.* 散发；发射)

emit [iˈmɪt] *vt.* 发出，放射(discharge, give off)

【例】All the cars that *emit* poisonous gas have been called back.

【派】emission(*n.* 放射，排放)

exhale [eksˈheɪl] *vt.* 呼出(breathe out, respire)；发出；散发

【记】ex + hale(气)→ 呼出气 → 呼出

【例】Bill inhaled the cigarette smoke and then *exhaled* deeply.

inhale [ɪnˈheɪl] *v.* 吸入，吸气(to breathe in air, smoke, or gas)

【例】It is dangerous to *inhale* ammonia fumes.

【派】inhalation(*n.* 吸入，吸入物)

fume [fjuːm] *n.* 烟雾；气味

fumigate [ˈfjuːmɪgeɪt] *vt.* 用化学品熏(以杀虫或消毒)(to treat with fumes or smoke)

【派】fumigation(*n.* 烟熏)

vent [vent] *vt.* 开孔；发泄(情绪)(express feelings)

【例】If he's had a bad day, Paul *vents* his anger on the family.

光及相关动作

fluorescent [ˌflɔːˈresnt] *adj.* 荧光的，发光的

【例】This shop sells *fluorescent* paint.

luminous [ˈluːmɪnəs] *adj.* 发光的，光亮的(glowing, bright)

【记】lumin(光)+ ous → 发光的

【例】The astronomer gazed at the *luminous* star.

【派】luminosity(*n.* 发光体) luminescence(*n.* 发光)

nocturnal [nɑːkˈtɜːrnl] *adj.* 夜间的(nighttime, nightly)

【记】noct(夜) + urnal → 夜间的

【例】An owl is an *nocturnal* bird, while a sparrow is diurnal.

【派】nocturnally(*adv.* 在夜里)

luminous [ˈluːmɪnəs] *adj.* 发光的;光亮的(glowing; bright)

【记】lumin(光) + ous → 发光的

【例】The astronomer gazed at the *luminous* star.

optical [ˈɑːptɪkl] *adj.* 眼的,视力的;光学的

【例】*optical* fiber

illuminate [ɪˈluːmɪneɪt] *vt.* 照明,照亮(to light);说明,阐释(to explain)

【记】il(一再) + lumin(光明) + ate → 给予光明 → 照亮

【例】Could you please illuminate your theory with a little more explanation?

【派】illumination(*n.* 照明;灯饰)

irradiate [ɪˈreɪdieɪt] *vt.* 照亮(lighten);使生辉;用X射线等治疗

【例】His little face was *irradiated* by happiness.

【派】irradiation(*n.* 放射,照射)

radiate [ˈreɪdieɪt] *v.* 射出(emit, give off)

【例】Heat *radiated* from the stove.

【派】radiation(*n.* 放射)

rekindle [ˌriːˈkɪndl] *vt.* 重新点燃;重新激起(have a particular feeling again)

【例】The trial has *rekindled* painful memories of the war.

spectrum [ˈspektrəm] *n.* 光,光谱,型谱,频谱

火及相关动作

campfire [ˈkæmpfaɪər] *n.* 营火,篝火

combustible [kəmˈbʌstəbl] *n.* 易燃物 *adj.* 易燃的,可燃的(capable of igniting and burning)

【例】Don't smoke near *combustible* materials.

【派】combustion(*n.* 燃烧,焚毁)

ignite [ɪgˈnaɪt] *vt.* 使燃烧(inflame, kindle)

【例】A smoldering cigarette *ignited* the newspapers.

ignition [ɪgˈnɪʃn] *n.* 点火，着火

【例】an *ignition* point

incinerate [ɪnˈsɪnəreɪt] *vt.* 把…烧成灰烬（to burn up completely）

【例】All the infected clothing was *incinerated*.

【派】incineration（*n.* 烧成灰，焚化）

sear [sɪr] *vt.* 烧灼

【例】The hot iron *seared* the trousers.

weld [weld] *vt.* 焊接，熔接；结合（join）

【例】The new handle will have to be *welded* on.

We often hear of people breaking down from overwork, but in nine cases out of ten they are really suffering from worry or anxiety.

我们常常听人说，人们因工作过度而垮下来，但是实际上十有八九是因为饱受担忧或焦虑的折磨。

——英国银行家 卢伯克. *J.*（*John Lubbock, British banker*）

练 习 题

连线题

delineate	下毛毛雨	osmosis	易燃的
excerpt	摘录	rinse	冲洗
reiterate	重述	secrete	溶解的
underscore	强调	solvent	荧光的
delinquent	蒸发	fumigate	用化学品熏
erroneous	刻画	exhale	滴注
mishap	违法的	luminous	发光的
negligence	灾祸	nocturnal	潜移默化
defrost	错误的	incinerate	分泌
drizzle	(给⋯)化霜	combustible	夜间的
eject	淹没	irradiate	把⋯烧成灰烬
evaporate	喷出	fluorescent	照亮
inundate	过失	instill	呼出

选词填空

illuminate	elaborate	disregard	weld	influx
scour	submerge	emanate	embody	radiate

1. McDonald refused to _____ on his reasons for resigning.
2. She _____ everything I admire in a teacher.
3. Mark totally _____ my advice.
4. A sudden _____ of cash happened.
5. The police _____ the whole place for the child.
6. Wonderful smells are _____ from the kitchen.
7. The report _____ the difficult issues at the heart of science policy.
8. The tunnel entrance was _____ by rising sea water.
9. Kindness _____ from her.
10. His job is now to _____ the players into a single team.

连线题答案

delineate	刻画	osmosis	潜移默化
excerpt	摘录	rinse	冲洗
reiterate	重述	secrete	分泌
underscore	强调	solvent	溶解的
delinquent	违法的	fumigate	用化学品熏
erroneous	错误的	exhale	呼出
mishap	灾祸	luminous	发光的
negligence	过失	nocturnal	夜间的
defrost	(给…)化霜	incinerate	把…烧成灰烬
drizzle	下毛毛雨	combustible	易燃的
eject	喷出	irradiate	照亮
evaporate	蒸发	fluorescent	荧光的
inundate	淹没	instill	滴注

选词填空答案

illuminate	elaborate	disregard	weld	influx
scour	submerge	emanate	embody	radiate

1. McDonald refused to (elaborate) on his reasons for resigning.
2. She (embodies) everything I admire in a teacher.
3. Mark totally (disregarded) my advice.
4. A sudden (influx) of cash happened.
5. The police (scoured) the whole place for the child.
6. Wonderful smells are (emanating) from the kitchen.
7. The report (illuminated) the difficult issues at the heart of science policy.
8. The tunnel entrance was (submerged) by rising sea water.
9. Kindness (radiated) from her.
10. His job is now to (weld) the players into a single team.

Word List 26

音频

自身行为（一）

自身行为(一)

废　除

abolish [əˈbɑːlɪʃ] *vt.* 废除，取消(abandon, annul, terminate)
【例】Slavery was *abolished* in the U.S. in the 19th century.
【派】abolition(*n.* 废除) abolitionism(*n.* 废除主义) abolitionist(*n.* 废除主义者)

abrogation [ˌæbrəˈɡeɪʃn] *n.* 废除，废止(cancel)
【派】abrogate(*vt.* 废除)

obsolescence [ˌɑːbsəˈlesns] *n.* 废弃，陈旧过时(old-fashioned and no longer useful)

obsolete [ˌɑːbsəˈliːt] *adj.* 过时的(disused, outmoded)；偶然的
【记】ob(不) + solete(使用)→过时的
【例】This new computer rendered my *obsolete* one.

repeal [rɪˈpiːl] *vt.* 废除，废止(officially ends)
【例】*repeal* a law

rescind [rɪˈsɪnd] *vt.* 废除，取消(end a law, or change a decision)
【例】*rescind* a contract

摩　擦

abrasion [əˈbreɪʒn] *n.* 磨损，擦伤(friction, erosion)
【例】*abrasion* resistance
【派】abrasive(*adj.* 有磨损作用的；粗鲁的)

attrition [əˈtrɪʃn] *n.* 磨损(wear and tear)；消耗
【例】They're trying to stop the *attrition* of their rights.

breakage [ˈbreɪkɪdʒ] *n.* 破坏，破损，破损量(the act or result of breaking)

breakdown [ˈbreɪkdaʊn] *n.* 损坏，故障；破裂；衰竭，衰弱
【例】Our car had a *breakdown* on the motorway. / His remarks led to the *breakdown* of talks between the staff and the management. / She suffered a nervous *breakdown*.

friction [ˈfrɪkʃn] *n.* 摩擦，摩擦力；冲突，不和
【例】Oil can reduce *friction*.

熟　悉

accomplished [əˈkɑːmplɪʃt] *adj.* 熟练的(experienced, skillful)

【例】Bill is the most *accomplished* musician I have ever known.

【派】accomplishment(*n.* 技能，才艺；完成)

adept [əˈdept] *adj.* 擅长的(adroit, apt)

【例】Mary is very *adept* at tuning pianos.

adroit [əˈdrɔɪt] *adj.* 机敏的；熟练的(skillful, adept, deft)

【记】a + droit(灵巧)→ 机敏的

【例】The elderly man couldn't walk, but he was still *adroit* with his hands.

deft [deft] *adj.* 灵巧的，熟练的(skillful, adroit)

【例】The pianist's *deft* fingers were delightful to watch.

dexterous [ˈdekstrəs] *adj.* 灵巧的(adroit, skillful)

【记】dexter(右边的) + ous → 右手 → 灵巧的

【例】She's very *dexterous* with the knitting needles.

【派】dexterity(*n.* 灵巧，敏捷)

acquaintance [əˈkweɪntəns] *n.* 相识的人 (a person who you know but is not a close friend)；了解；认识 (knowledge or experience of a particular subject)

【例】At the hotel, I made the *acquaintance* of a young American actor.

familiarity [fəˌmiliˈærəti] *n.* 熟悉，通晓；亲近

familiarize [fəˈmɪliəraɪz] *vt.* 使熟悉

【记】familiar(熟悉的) + ize(动词后缀)→ 使熟悉

【例】It is important to *familiarize* yourself with a foreign language nowadays.

认　可

accord [əˈkɔːrd] *vt.* 给予 *vi.* 符合，一致(match, agree with)

【例】His story *accords* with what I saw.

accordingly [əˈkɔːrdɪŋli] *adv.* 因此，因而(therefore)；照着，相应地

【例】He was told to speak briefly. *Accordingly* he cut short his remarks.

approbation [ˌæprəˈbeɪʃn] *n.* 赞成，同意(official praise or approval)

【例】The manager surveyed her report with *approbation*.

connive [kə'naɪv] *v.* 默许(to acquiesce); 共谋(to plot together, conspire)

【例】The guards were suspected of *conniving* at the prisoner's escape.

【派】connivance(*n.* 纵容，默许)

endorse [ɪn'dɔːrs] *vt.* 确认; 赞同，支持(certify; support, ratify)

【例】The labor union *endorsed* the democratic candidate for president.

【派】endorsement(*n.* 赞同，支持)

ratify ['rætɪfaɪ] *vt.* 批准(approve, endorse)

【例】The government *ratified* the treaty.

【派】ratification(*n.* 批准，认可)

sanction ['sæŋkʃn] *n.* 认可，批准(official permission); 制裁

【例】take *sanctions* against

unanimous [ju'nænɪməs] *adj.* 意见一致的(uniform)

【例】My friends and I made a *unanimous* decision to order pizza.

【派】unanimity(*n.* 全体一致)

教 育

academic [ˌækə'demɪk] *adj.* 学院的(collegiate); 理论的(theoretical); 学术的 *n.* 学者(scholar)

【例】John was invited to give an *academic* address at a conference.

extracurricular [ˌekstrəkə'rɪkjələr] *adj.* 学校课程以外的

【记】extra(额外) + curricular(课程的) → 学校课程以外的

【例】Most of the students in the class took an active part in *extra-curricular* activities.

pedagogical [ˌpedə'gɑːdʒɪkl] *adj.* 教育的，教学法的(relating to teaching methods)

【派】pedagogically(*adv.* 受教育地)

didactic [daɪ'dæktɪk] *adj.* 教诲的，说教的(instructive)

【例】He started to know the real meaning of life from a *didactic* speech given by a celebrity.

curriculum [kə'rɪkjələm] *n.* 课程

elective [ɪ'lektɪv] *n.* 选修课 *adj.* 由选举产生的; 有选举权的; (课程等)选修的,可选的; (手术等)可做可不做的

【例】They discussed whether patients should have to pay for all *elective* surgery.

discourse ['dɪskɔːrs] *n.* 演讲(lecture); 论文(disquisition) [dɪs'kɔːrs] *vi.* 讲述, 著述(to speak or write formally)

【例】He went on to *discourse* on the nature of fat.

doctorate ['dɑːktərət] *n.* 博士学位

expertise [ˌekspɜːr'tiːz] *n.* 专门知识或技能

lore [lɔːr] *n.* 知识; 全部传说(unwritten knowledge or information)

【例】According to local *lore*, a ghost still haunts the castle.

grade school <美> 小学

primer ['praɪmər] *n.* 启蒙书, 识字课本 (a book containing basic information)

qualification [ˌkwɑːlɪfɪ'kɪʃn] *n.* 学历, 资历; 合格

【例】Applicants should have an EFL *qualification* and a year's teaching experience.

seminar ['semɪnɑːr] *n.* 研讨会, 培训会(class on particular subjects)

apprentice [ə'prentɪs] *n.* 学徒, 初学者 *v.* 当学徒

【派】apprenticeship(*n.* 学徒的身份或年限)

proctor ['prɑːktər] *n.* 代理人; 学监 (someone watching students in case they cheat in examinations)

principal ['prɪnsəpl] *n.* 校长(head, headmaster) *adj.* 主要的(main); 负责人的

【例】His *principal* reason for making the journey was to visit his family.

【派】principally(*adv.* 主要地)

sophomore ['sɑːfəmɔːr] *n.* 大二年级学生(second year students at colleges or universities); 自以为样样都懂而实际上幼稚的人

adopt [ə'dɑːpt] *v.* 收养(take in and bring up); 采用, 采纳(to choose, use, approve)

【例】The factories have *adopted* the newest modern technology.

【派】adoption(*n.* 收养; 采用)

envision [ɪn'vɪʒn] *vt.* 想象, 预想(to envisage, foresee, imagine)

【记】en(使) + vision(眼力) → 想象

【例】As a young teacher, I *envisioned* a future of educational excellence.

experimental [ɪkˌsperɪ'mentl] *adj.* 实验的(used for, relating to, or resulting from experiments)

【例】A hypothesis is tested by finding *experimental* evidence for it.

qualify ['kwɑːlɪfaɪ] *vt.* 使合格(equip someone to have knowledge); 限制

【例】Fluency in three languages *qualifies* her for work in the European Parliament.

【派】qualified(*adj.* 合格的)

tuition [tuˈɪʃn] *n.* 学费; 课程讲授(teaching)

【例】I had to have extra *tuition* in maths.

获 得

access ['ækses] *n.* 通路, 途径(outlet); 接近或取得的方式(the act of approaching or entering)

【例】You can easily get *access* to her.

accessible [əkˈsesəbl] *adj.* 容易接近、取得的(easy to reach, obtain or use)

【例】Medicine should not be kept where it is *accessible* to children.

【派】accessiblity(*n.* 可接近性)

inaccessible [ˌɪnækˈsesəbl] *adj.* 达不到的, 不可及的(not accessible, unapproachable)

【例】The top of Mount Everest is the most *inaccessible* place in the world.

acquire [əˈkwaɪər] *vt.* 获得(obtain, attain)

【例】Susan *acquired* an appreciation of classical music.

【派】acquisition(*n.* 获得)

acquired [əˈkwaɪərd] *adj.* 后天习得的(not inborn)

【例】*Acquired* characteristics, such as a broken nose, cannot be passed on to future generations.

obtainable [əbˈteɪnəbl] *adj.* 可获得的; 可取得的(able to be gotten)

【例】The form is *obtainable* at your local post office.

procure [prəˈkjʊr] *vt.* 采购, 获得, 取得(acquire, obtain)

【例】He swears he will *procure* a solution to this difficult problem.

【派】procurement(*n.* 采购)

reclaim [rɪˈkleɪm] *vt.* 取回, 拿回(get back); 废料回收

【例】You can *reclaim* old boards and use them as shelves.

【派】reclamation(*n.* 开拓; 改造)

secure [səˈkjʊr] *vt.* 获得(get, achieve)

【例】Boyd's goal *secured* his team's place in the Cup Final.

爱 好

addiction [ə'dɪkʃn] *n.* 毒瘾；沉溺，癖好（strong desire to have something regularly）

【例】His *addiction* to drugs propelled him towards a life of crime.

【派】addict(*v.* 对…有瘾) addicted(*adj.* 沉溺的，上瘾的) addictive (*adj.* 使上瘾的)

amateur ['æmətər] *n.* 业余爱好者

appetite ['æpɪtaɪt] *n.* 胃口，食欲；欲望（a desire or liking for something）

【例】She has an amazing *appetite* for knowledge.

【派】appetizer(*n.* 开胃品)

philanthropy [fɪ'lænθrəpi] *n.* 博爱，慈善事业（the practice of giving money and help to people who are poor or in trouble）

predisposition [ˌpriːdɪspə'zɪʃn] *n.* 事先安排；倾向（a tendency to behave in a particular way）

【例】a *predisposition* towards alcoholism

preference ['prefrəns] *n.* 优先，优先权（privilege）；偏爱（inclination）

【记】prefer(喜欢) + ence → 偏爱

【例】The king showed *preference* to his eldest son.

【派】preferential(*adj.* 优惠的) preferentially(*adv.* 优先地)

propensity [prə'pensəti] *n.* 倾向（inclination）

【例】Anne has a *propensity* for eating when she's nervous.

劝 告

admonition [ˌædmə'nɪʃn] *n.* 告诫，劝告（warning, expression of disapproval）

advisory [əd'vaɪzəri] *adj.* 劝告的；咨询的（giving advice）

【例】He was appointed to the *Advisory* Committee last month.

dissuade [dɪ'sweɪd] *vt.* 劝阻（to persuade not to do）

【例】I tried to *dissuade* her from getting married.

lobby ['lɑːbi] *v.* 向…进行游说（try to persuade）

【例】The group is *lobbying* for a reduction in defence spending.

【派】lobbyist(*n.* 说客)

recommend [ˌrekə'mend] vt. 劝告；推荐(suggest)

【例】She *recommended* the book to her students.

【派】recommendation(n. 推荐)

分 离

alien ['eɪliən] adj. 外国的(foreign)；陌生的 n. 外国人，外星人

【例】He quickly adjusts to the *alien* environment.

alienate ['eɪliəneɪt] vt. 使疏远(to estrange)；转让，让渡财产

【例】The Prime Minister's policy *alienated* many of her followers.

【派】alienation(n. 疏远；转让) alienated(adj. 疏离的)

differentiate [ˌdɪfə'renʃieɪt] v. 区分，辨别(to tell apart, distinguish)

【例】It's wrong to *differentiate* between boys and girls.

【派】differentiation(n. 区别，分化)

discrepant [dɪs'krepənt] adj. 差异的(inconsistent, conflicting, at variance)

【派】discrepancy(n. 差异，不一致之处)

discrete [dɪ'skriːt] adj. 不相关联的，分离的(distinct, separate)

【例】A computer can perform millions of *discrete* functions per second.

discrimination [dɪˌskrɪmɪ'neɪʃn] n. 歧视(prejudice)

【记】dis + crimin(罪行) + ation → 歧视是一种罪行 → 歧视

【例】Different groups of people in many countries of the world face *discrimination*.

【派】discriminate(v. 歧视；辨别)

displace [dɪs'pleɪs] vt. 迫使离开家(或祖国)

【例】*displaced* person

diverge [daɪ'vɜːrdʒ] v. 分叉；分歧，相异(differ, deviate)

【记】di + verge(转) → 转开 → 分歧

【例】I'm afraid our opinions *diverge* from each other on the direction of investment.

【派】divergent(adj. 分叉的；分歧的) divergence(n. 分歧)

estrange [ɪ'streɪndʒ] vt. 使疏远(to alienate)

【例】The argument *estranged* him from his brother.

expatriate [ˌeks'peɪtriət] n. 侨民，放弃本国国籍的人 [ˌeks'peɪtrieɪt] v. 驱逐出国，脱离国籍

insulate ['ɪnsəleɪt] vt. 使绝缘；使隔离

【例】The royal family tried to *insulate* him from the prying eyes of the

234

media.

【派】insulation(*n.* 隔离，绝缘)

isolation [ˌaɪsəˈleɪʃn] *n.* 隔离，隔绝；孤独(separation)

【例】The political prisoner had been held in complete *isolation*.

partition [pɑːrˈtɪʃn] *n./v.* 分开，隔开 (to divide a country, building, or room into two or more parts)

【例】She *partitioned* off part of the living room to make a study.

polarity [pəˈlærəti] *n.* 极端性，两级分化 (a state in which people, ideas, etc. are completely opposite to each other)

【例】the *polarity* between the intellect and the emotions

split [splɪt] *v.* (使)裂开，(使)破裂(separate, break, tear)

【例】The war has *split* the nation in two.

Victory won't come to me unless I go to it.

胜利是不会向我走来的，我必须自己走向胜利。

——美国女诗人 穆尔(*M. Moore, American poetess*)

练 习 题

连线题

abrogation	博士学位	envision	教育的
obsolescence	废弃	experimental	想象
obsolete	磨损	pedagogical	倾向
abrasion	赞成	procure	实验的
friction	废除	philanthropy	博爱
acquaintance	相识的人	propensity	告诫
adept	擅长的	admonition	使绝缘
adroit	使疏远	diverge	采购
dexterous	过时的	discrepant	区别
approbation	机敏的	polarity	差异的
didactic	教诲的	insulate	极端性
doctorate	灵巧的	expatriate	分歧
estrange	摩擦	differentiate	侨民

选词填空

familiarize	abolish	connive	endorse	unanimous
lobby	reclaim	alienate	secure	accomplished

1. That *Act* was _____ in 1964.
2. You may be entitled to _____ some tax.
3. Jason is a highly _____ designer.
4. Employees must _____ themselves with the health and safety manual.
5. He would not be the first politician to _____ at a shady business deal.
6. The Prime Minister is unlikely to _____ this view.
7. The decision to appoint Matt was almost _____.
8. The company recently _____ a $20 million contract with Ford.
9. We've been _____ our state representative to support the new health plan.
10. The latest tax proposals will _____ many voters.

练习题答案

连线题答案

abrogation	废除	envision	想象
obsolescence	废弃	experimental	实验的
obsolete	过时的	pedagogical	教育的
abrasion	磨损	procure	采购
friction	摩擦	philanthropy	博爱
acquaintance	相识的人	propensity	倾向
adept	擅长的	admonition	告诫
adroit	机敏的	diverge	分歧
dexterous	灵巧的	discrepant	差异的
approbation	赞成	polarity	极端性
didactic	教诲的	insulate	使绝缘
doctorate	博士学位	expatriate	侨民
estrange	使疏远	differentiate	区别

选词填空答案

familiarize	abolish	connive	endorse	unanimous
lobby	reclaim	alienate	secure	accomplished

1. That *Act* was（abolished）in 1964.
2. You may be entitled to（reclaim）some tax.
3. Jason is a highly（accomplished）designer.
4. Employees must（familiarize）themselves with the health and safety manual.
5. He would not be the first politician to（connive）at a shady business deal.
6. The Prime Minister is unlikely to（endorse）this view.
7. The decision to appoint Matt was almost（unanimous）.
8. The company recently（secured）a $20 million contract with Ford.
9. We've been（lobbying）our state representative to support the new health plan.
10. The latest tax proposals will（alienate）many voters.

Word List 27

音频

自身行为(二)

自身行为（二）

服　从

amenable [əˈmiːnəbl] *adj.* 顺从的（obedient, docile）；易控制的；愿接受的（willing to accept）

【例】Young people are more *amenable* than older citizens to the idea of immigration.

comply [kəmˈplaɪ] *vi.* 顺从，遵循（obey）

【例】A good citizen *complies* with the laws of the country.

【派】compliance（*n.* 顺从，听从）

compromise [ˈkɑːmprəmaɪz] *v.* 妥协；危害

conform [kənˈfɔːrm] *vi.* 遵守；符合；顺应（to comply）

【例】The building does not *conform* to safety regulations.

【派】conformity（*n.* 遵从；符合；一致）

obedience [əˈbiːdiəns] *n.* 服从，顺从（deference, submission）

【例】I was pleased by my dog's *obedience* to my commands.

submission [səbˈmɪʃn] *n.* 屈服，服从

【记】sub（下面）+ miss（放）+ ion → 放在下面 → 屈服

succumb [səˈkʌm] *vi.* 屈服（submit, yield）

【例】The country *succumbed* after only a short siege.

yield [jiːld] *v.* 生产；屈服；让出（produce; give in）

【例】Our research has only recently begun to *yield* important results.

【派】yielding（*adj.* 顺服的；生产的）

deferential [ˌdefəˈrenʃl] *adj.* 充满敬意的（respectful, dutiful）

【例】A teacher should not act too *deferential* to the students.

ductile [ˈdʌktaɪl] *adj.* 有延展性的（malleable）；顺从的，易受影响的（docile）

【例】Steel in this class is tough, *ductile* and easily machined.

pliant [ˈplaɪənt] *adj.* 易弯的；柔软的（soft and moving easily）

【例】Isabel was *pliant* in his arms.

【派】pliantly（*adv.* 委婉地）pliancy（*n.* 柔软）

disobey [ˌdɪsəˈbeɪ] *v.* 不顺从，不服从（to refuse to obey）

【例】It was unfair of the teacher to make us stay after school, but no one dared *disobey*.

sturdy [ˈstɜːrdi] *adj.* 不屈的，顽强的(strong, stout)

【例】The *sturdy* bridge withstood the shaking of the earthquake.

【派】sturdily(*adv.* 坚强地) sturdiness(*n.* 坚固)

tenacious [təˈneɪʃəs] *adj.* 抓住不放的；顽强的(stubborn, resolute)

【记】ten(拿) + acious → 拿住 → 抓住不放的

【例】The *tenacious* applicant soon got the job.

【派】tenaciously(*adv.* 坚持地)

供 给

bestow [bɪˈstoʊ] *vt.* 把…赠予，授予

【例】He was *bestowed* the honor of "Hero Citizen".

confer [kənˈfɜːr] *v.* 协商 (discuss)；授予，赋予 (to grant or bestow)

【例】I *conferred* with my friends about what we should eat for dinner. / An honorary degree was *conferred* on him by the university.

donate [dəˈneɪt] *vt.* 捐赠(to contribute, give as a charity)

【例】Steve *donated* the old couch to charity.

【派】donation(*n.* 捐赠；捐赠物)

enfranchise [ɪnˈfræntʃaɪz] *vt.* 给予投票权(to give the right to vote)

impart [ɪmˈpɑːrt] *vt.* 给予；传递；告诉(inform, disseminate)

【记】im(进入) + part(部分) → 成为(信息的)一部分 → 传递

【例】A teacher's job is mainly *imparting* knowledge to students.

oversupply [ˈoʊvərsəplaɪ]/[ˌoʊvərsəˈplaɪ] *n./v.* 过度供给(the state of having more of something than you need)

provenance [ˈprɑːvənəns] *n.* 起源，出处，原产地(source)

【例】The *provenance* of the paintings is unknown.

provision [prəˈvɪʒn] *n.* 供应(supply, furnishing)

stockpile [ˈstɑːkpaɪl] *n.* (堆在路边为修路用的)料堆；贮存(store) *vt.* 积聚(accumulate)

【例】An enormous volume of explosives was *stockpiled* inside one of the buildings.

storage [ˈstɔːrɪdʒ] *n.* 贮存，贮藏；仓库（warehouse）

【例】the *storage* of radioactive material

限　制

circumscribe [ˈsɜːrkəmskraɪb] *vt.* 划界限（encompass, encircle）；限制

【记】circum（绕圈）+ scribe（画）→ 画圈 → 限制

【例】The moves you can make in a chess game are *circumscribed* by the rules of the game.

【派】circumference（*n.* 周围；圆周）circumferential（*adj.* 周围的，环绕的；圆周的）

confine [kənˈfaɪn] *vt.* 限制（to keep within bounds, limit, restrict）

【例】Bill *confined* his dog to the house all day.

【派】confinement（*n.* 限制，禁闭）

constraint [kənˈstreɪnt] *n.* 限制（limit）；强制，强迫（compulsion, force）

【例】*Constraints* on spending have forced the company to rethink its plans.

impose [ɪmˈpoʊz] *vt.* 强加，迫使（to enforce, inflict）

【例】Overcrowding *imposes* mental strains.

【派】imposition（*n.* 征税，强加）

imprisonment [ɪmˈprɪznmənt] *n.* 监禁，关押（the state of being in prison）

incarcerate [ɪnˈkɑːrsəreɪt] *vt.* 监禁，禁闭（to confine or imprison）

【例】He spent nearly half his life *incarcerated* in prison.

【派】incarceration（*n.* 幽闭）

restrain [rɪˈstreɪn] *vt.* 限制（restrict, limit）

【记】re + strain（拉紧）→ 限制

【例】The alcoholist tried his best to *restrain* himself from alcohol.

restriction [rɪˈstrɪkʃn] *n.* 约束，局限（a rule or law that limits what people do）

regulate [ˈregjuleɪt] *vt.* 控制，管理；调整（control; adjust）

【例】People sweat to *regulate* their body heat.

【派】regulation（*n.* 管理，规章）regulatory（*adj.* 监管的）

interfere [ˌɪntərˈfɪr] *vi.* 干涉，干预（intervene, meddle）；妨碍

【例】Please stop *interfering*. This is none of your business.

【派】interference（*n.* 干涉，干预）

intervene [ˌɪntərˈviːn] *vi.* 干涉(interfere, influence)

【记】inter(中间) + vene(来) → 来到中间 → 干涉

【例】The brothers wouldn't stop arguing until their mother *intervened*.

【派】intervention(*n.* 介入，干涉)

optional [ˈɑːpʃənl] *adj.* 可选择的，非强制的(not compulsory)

【例】The other excursions are *optional*.

分　类

category [ˈkætəgɔːri] *n.* 类别，种类

【派】categorize(*v.* 分类，归类)

classify [ˈklæsɪfaɪ] *v.* 分类，归类(to arrange or order by classes, to categorize)

【例】Librarians spend a lot of time *classifying* books.

【派】classification(*n.* 分类；类别)

zone [zoʊn] *n.* 带(region, area)

【例】time *zone*

【派】zoning(*n.* 分区制)

偿　赎

compensate [ˈkɑːmpenseɪt] *v.* 补偿(to make amends, make up for)

【例】Nothing can *compensate* for losing my husband.

【派】compensation(*n.* 补偿)

countervail [ˈkaʊntərveɪl] *v.* 补偿，抵消(to counteract, counterbalance)

liquidation [ˌlɪkwɪˈdeɪʃn] *n.* 清算(the act of paying a debt)；清仓；了结

【例】Hundreds of small businesses went into *liquidation*.

【派】liquidator(*n.* 清算人)

offset [ˈɔːfset] *vt.* 抵消，补偿(neutralize)

【例】Cuts in prices for milk, butter, and cheese will be *offset* by direct payments to farmers.

ransom [ˈrænsəm] *n.* 赔偿金(payment, redemption) *vt.* 赎回，解救(pay to set someone free)

【例】They were all *ransomed* and returned unharmed.

refund [rɪˈfʌnd] *vt.* 退还，偿还(repay, pay back)

【记】re(重新) + fund(钱) → 重新还回钱 → 退还

【例】I will *refund* you the full of your fare.

reimburse [ˌriːɪmˈbɜːrs] *vt.* 偿还(pay back, refund)

【记】re(重新) + im=in(进入) + burse(钱包) → 偿还

【例】You should *reimburse* the taxi fee those strangers paid to get you to hospital.

【派】reimbursement(*n.* 偿还)

repayment [rɪˈpeɪmənt] *n.* 偿还,偿付(pay back)

【例】the *repayment* of debt

replenish [rɪˈplenɪʃ] *vt.* 补充,填满(fill up, refill)

【记】re(重新) + plen=plenty(多) + ish → 重新变多 → 补充

【例】The music will *replenish* my weary soul.

【派】replenishment(*n.* 补给)

restitution [ˌrestɪˈtuːʃn] *n.* 归还(compensation, giving back);复职

supplement [ˈsʌplɪmənt]/[ˈsʌplɪment] *n./v.* 增补,补充(add)

【例】Kia *supplements* her regular salary by tutoring in the evenings.

【派】supplementation(*n.* 增补)

命　令

compulsory [kəmˈpʌlsəri] *adj.* 义务的(obligatory, mandatory, required);必修的

【记】com + puls (推,冲) + ory → 向前冲 → 义务的

【例】The use of seat belts is *compulsory* in many states; failure to wear them may result in fines. / A composition class is *compulsory* for all college students.

embargo [ɪmˈbɑːrɡoʊ] *n.* 禁运令,封港令

imperative [ɪmˈperətɪv] *adj.* 急需的(necessary, urgent);命令的

【记】imper(命令) + ative → 命令的

【例】The man is dying; an immediate operation is *imperative*. / Don't talk in an *imperative* tone of voice.

injunction [ɪnˈdʒʌŋkʃn] *n.* 命令;【律】指令,禁令

【例】They failed to obtain an *injunction*.

mandate [ˈmændeɪt] *n.* 命令;要求(command)

【记】mand(命令) + ate → 命令

【派】mandatory(*adj.* 强制的)

承 认

commitment [kəˈmɪtmənt] *n.* 承诺，保证（promise）；投身，献身（dedication, devotion）；承担的任务（task undertaken）

concede [kənˈsiːd] *v.* 让步；承认（to admit or acknowledge）
【记】con + cede(让) → 让步
【例】I *conceded* that I had made a mistake.
【派】concession(*n.* 妥协，让步；承认) concessive(*adj.* 有妥协性的，让步的)

recognize [ˈrekəɡnaɪz] *vt.* 认识，认出；承认（acknowledge）
【例】I *recognized* Peter although I hadn't seen him for 10 years.
【派】recognition(*n.* 认识；承认)

testify [ˈtestɪfaɪ] *vt.* 证明，证实；作证（give evidence, verify）
【例】Her tears *testified* her grief.
【派】testimony(*n.* 证言)

disavow [ˌdɪsəˈvaʊ] *vt.* 不承认，抵赖；拒绝对…承担责任（to deny knowledge of, connection with, or responsibility for）
【例】The bus drivers' union has *disavowed* any involvement in the violence.
【派】disavowal(*n.* 不承认，否定)

生 养

conceive [kənˈsiːv] *v.* 想象（devise, visualize）；怀孕（to be pregnant）
【例】The inventor *conceived* a new gadget.
【派】conception(*n.* 观念；设想；怀孕)

pregnant [ˈpreɡnənt] *adj.* 怀孕的，孕育的
【派】pregnancy(*n.* 怀孕)

proliferate [prəˈlɪfəreɪt] *v.* 繁衍（multiply, increase）
【记】pro(前) + lifer(后代) + ate → 有了后代 → 繁衍
【例】Autumn is the best season for crab to *proliferate*.

reproduce [ˌriːprəˈduːs] *v.* 繁殖，再生
【例】Birds *reproduce* by laying eggs.
【派】reproduction(*n.* 复制；繁殖)

breeding [ˈbriːdɪŋ] *n.* 饲养（feeding）；教养（upbringing, nurture, cultivation）

foster [ˈfɔːstər] *v.* 养育（to uprear, bring up）；培养，促进（to cultivate, promote)

【例】*Fostering* a teenager is obviously different from *fostering* a small child. / *foster*-child / *foster*-parents

rear [rɪr] *vt.* 抚养，饲养(raise, look after)；栽种

【例】It's a good place to *rear* young children.

hatch [hætʃ] *v.* 孵出，孵(卵)(incubate, breed, emerge from the egg)

【例】Don't count your chickens before they are *hatched*.

incubation [ˌɪŋkjuˈbeɪʃn] *n.* 孵卵，孵化；（传染病的)潜伏期

livelihood [ˈlaɪvlihʊd] *n.* 生计，谋生（the way you earn money in order to live)

【例】Fishing is the main source of *livelihood* for many people in the area.

sojourn [ˈsoʊdʒɜːrn] *vi.* 逗留(stay)；寄居

【例】The explorers *sojourned* at the old castle expecting for a new find.

subsist [səbˈsɪst] *vi.* 生存(live, survive)

【例】The poor farmer's family *subsisted* on potatoes.

【派】subsistence(*n.* 生存)

survive [sərˈvaɪv] *vt.* 幸免于… *vi.* 活下来(outlive, remain)

【例】Those who *survived* rebuilt the city.

【派】survival(*n.* 幸存)

sterile [ˈsterəl] *adj.* 消过毒的(sanitary)；不孕的(infertile)

【例】Rinse the eye with *sterile* water.

【派】sterility(*n.* 不孕)

unviable [ˌʌnˈvaɪəbl] *adj.* 不能生存的；行不通的(impractical, unworkable)

【例】form an *unviable* opinion

wither [ˈwɪðər] *v.* 枯萎，凋零

【例】The flower *withered*.

【派】withered(*adj.* 枯萎的)

练 习 题

连线题

amenable	有延展性的	incarcerate	监禁
compromise	易弯的	intervene	补偿
conform	妥协	compensate	繁衍
deferential	遵守	countervail	命令
ductile	给予投票权	liquidation	枯萎
obedience	充满敬意的	imperative	抵消
sturdy	划界限	injunction	干涉
tenacious	服从	disavow	孵卵
pliant	限制	incubation	不能生存的
enfranchise	不屈的	proliferate	逗留
provenance	起源	unviable	急需的
circumscribe	抓住不放的	sojourn	清仓
constraint	顺从的	wither	抵赖

选词填空

succumb	comply	confer	regulate	reimburse
replenish	conceive	impose	testify	interfere

1. Failure to _____ with the regulations will result in prosecution.

2. Gina _____ to temptation and had a second serving of cake.

3. Franklin leant over and _____ with his attorneys.

4. It's not the church's job to _____ in politics.

5. Strict rules _____ the use of chemicals in food.

6. The company will_____ you for travel expenses.

7. More vaccines are needed to _____ our stocks.

8. The government _____ a ban on the sale of ivory.

9. Mr. Molto has agreed to _____ at the trial.

10.I can hardly _____ what it must be like here in winter.

练习题答案

连线题答案

amenable	顺从的	incarcerate	监禁
compromise	妥协	intervene	干涉
conform	遵守	compensate	补偿
deferential	充满敬意的	countervail	抵消
ductile	有延展性的	liquidation	清仓
obedience	服从	imperative	急需的
sturdy	不屈的	injunction	命令
tenacious	抓住不放的	disavow	抵赖
pliant	易弯的	incubation	孵卵
enfranchise	给予投票权	proliferate	繁衍
provenance	起源	unviable	不能生存的
circumscribe	划界限	sojourn	逗留
constraint	限制	wither	枯萎

选词填空答案

succumb	comply	confer	regulate	reimburse
replenish	conceive	impose	testify	interfere

1. Failure to（comply）with the regulations will result in prosecution.
2. Gina（succumbed）to temptation and had a second serving of cake.
3. Franklin leant over and（conferred）with his attorneys.
4. It's not the church's job to（interfere）in politics.
5. Strict rules（regulate）the use of chemicals in food.
6. The company will（reimburse）you for travel expenses.
7. More vaccines are needed to（replenish）our stocks.
8. The government（imposed）a ban on the sale of ivory.
9. Mr. Molto has agreed to（testify）at the trial.
10. I can hardly（conceive）what it must be like here in winter.

Word List 28

音频

自身行为（三）

自身行为(三)

感　觉

conscious [ˈkɑːnʃəs] *adj.* 有知觉的（alert and awake）；注意到的（conscious of = aware of）

【例】I fainted briefly but was *conscious* again in a few seconds.

perceptible [pərˈseptəbl] *adj.* 可感觉到的（something that can be noticed, although it is very small）；可理解的

【例】small but *perceptible* change

【派】perceptibly（*adv.* 可理解地）

sensory [ˈsensəri] *adj.* 感觉的（relating to senses）

【例】*sensory* stimuli such as music

sentient [ˈsenʃənt] *adj.* 有感觉能力的，有感觉的（able to experience through senses）

【例】Man is a *sentient* being.

hypersensitive [ˌhaɪpərˈsensətɪv] *adj.* 过分敏感的

【记】hyper（超过）+ sensitive（敏感）→ 过分敏感的

【例】She's *hypersensitive* to any form of criticism.

imperceptible [ˌɪmpərˈseptəbl] *adj.* 感觉不到的（too slight or gradual to be perceived）；细微的，逐渐的（slight, gradual）

【例】Such changes are *imperceptible* to even the best-trained eye.

【派】imperceptibly（*adv.* 察觉不到地，细微地）

unwitting [ʌnˈwɪtɪŋ] *adj.* 不知不觉的（unknowing）

【派】unwittingly（*adv.* 不知不觉地）

intuition [ˌɪntuˈɪʃn] *n.* 直觉（instinct）

【例】feminine *intuition* / *Intuition* told her it was unwise to argue.

【派】intuitive（*adj.* 凭直觉获知的）

olfactory [ɑːlˈfæktəri] *adj.* 嗅觉的（connected with the sense of smell）

【例】the *olfactory* cells in the nose

tactile [ˈtæktl] *adj.* 触觉的；触觉感知的（relating to your sense of touch）

【例】*tactile* sensations

sensual [ˈsenʃuəl] *adj.* （肉体上）享乐的（relating to body）

【例】the *sensual* pleasure of good food

【派】sensuality(*n.* 耽于声色) sensually(*adv.* 好色地)

seductive [sɪˈdʌktɪv] *adj.* 诱人的，有魅力的(attractive)

【例】She used all of her *seductive* charm to try and persuade him.

【派】seductively(*adv.* 诱惑地)

nostalgia [nɑːˈstældʒə] *n.* 思乡，怀旧

【记】nost(家) + alg(痛) + ia(病) → 思乡

【例】The old man remembered his college days with *nostalgia*.

morale [məˈræl] *n.* 民心；士气

【记】比较moral(*n.* 道德)

【例】With no food and water, the soldiers are in low *morale*.

psyche [ˈsaɪki] *n.* 心智，精神（mind, deepest feelings）

【例】Freud's account of the human *psyche*

计　划

conspire [kənˈspaɪər] *vi.* 阴谋，密谋(intrigue, plot)

【例】The bank tellers *conspired* to rob the bank.

【派】conspiracy(*n.* 阴谋)

intrigue [ɪnˈtriːg] *v.* 密谋；引起极大兴趣 *n.* 密谋策划，阴谋

【例】Other people's houses always *intrigued* her.

【派】intrigued(*adj.* 好奇的) intriguing(*adj.* 引人入胜的)

project [prəˈdʒekt] *vt.* 设计，规划(calculate)；突出(stick out)

【例】The company *projected* an annual growth rate of 3%.

【派】projected(*adj.* 规划中的) projection(*n.* 设想)

思　考

comprehend [ˌkɑːmprɪˈhend] *vt.* 理解(understand)；包含，包括(include)

【例】I could not *comprehend* the instructions for operating the computer.

【派】comprehensive(*adj.* 广泛的；综合的；有理解力的) comprehension (*n.* 理解，理解力；包括；综合)

deem [diːm] *v.* 认为（think, consider）

【例】He *deems* highly of this plan.

contemplate [ˈkɑːntəmpleɪt] *vt.* 凝视；沉思（muse, ponder）

【例】Philosophers *contemplate* the existence of humankind.

【派】contemplation（*n.* 沉思）

speculate [ˈspekjuleɪt] *v.* 推测；沉思（hypothesize, conjecture）

【例】He *speculated* there will be a comet visiting the Earth this May, but failed.

【派】speculation（*n.* 思索；投机）

recall [rɪˈkɔːl] *vt.* 忆起，记忆（recollect, remember）

【例】The victim was asked to *recall* what happened to him the day when he was robbed.

reminiscence [ˌremɪˈnɪsns] *n.* 回忆，缅怀往事（memoir）

【例】*reminiscences* of the war

reflective [rɪˈflektɪv] *adj.* 深思熟虑的（thinking quietly about）；反光的

【例】She was in a *reflective* mood.

speculative [ˈspekjələtɪv] *adj.* 思索的，推测出的；投机的；好奇的（curious; based on guessing）

【例】*speculative* fever

【派】speculatively（*adv.* 投机地）

subconscious [ˌsʌbˈkɑːnʃəs] *adj.* 下意识的，潜意识的（feelings hidden in mind）

【例】a *subconscious* fear of failure

【派】subconsciously（*adv.* 潜意识地）

probe [proʊb] *vi.* 探索，探查（investigate, inspect）

【例】The detective *probed* into the circumstances of the murder.

revert [rɪˈvɜːrt] *vi.* 回复（come back, return）

【例】After her divorce she *reverted* to using her maiden name.

处　理

filtration [fɪlˈtreɪʃn] *n.* 过滤，筛选

deal [diːl] *vi.* 处理（handle）；交易（do business）*n.* 交易

【例】You need to learn how to *deal* with problems like this.

dispose [dɪˈspoʊz] *vi.* 处理（deal with）；丢掉（get rid of）

【例】Man proposes, God *disposes*.

【派】disposal（*n.* 处理；清除）

disposable [dɪˈspoʊzəbl] *adj.* 一次性的；可自由使用的

【例】*disposable* chopsticks

装　饰

decorate [ˈdekəreɪt] *vt.* 装饰，修饰（embellish, adorn）

【例】My mother likes to *decorate* rooms.

【派】decorative（*adj.* 装饰性的）decoration（*n.* 装潢，装饰品）

embellish [ɪmˈbelɪʃ] *vt.* 装饰，修饰（decorate, adorn）；润色（作品）

【记】em + bell(美) + ish → 使美 → 装饰

【例】Anne *embellished* the shirt collar with lace.

intersperse [ˌɪntərˈspɜːrs] *vt.* 散布，散置；点缀

【例】sunny periods *interspersed* with showers

motif [moʊˈtiːf] *n.* 装饰图案；主题，主旨（theme）

【例】The theme of creation is a recurrent *motif* in Celtic mythology.

ornament [ˈɔːrnəmənt] *n.* 装饰物（decoration, embellishment）；装修

【记】orn(装饰) + ament → 装饰物

【派】ornamentation（*n.* 装饰）

ornate [ɔːrˈneɪt] *adj.* 装饰华丽的（covered with a lot of decoration）

【例】an *ornate* gold mirror

【派】ornately（*adv.* 装饰华丽地）

spruce [spruːs] *v.* 打扮，收拾整洁（clean, dress up）*adj.* 漂亮的（neat and clean）

【例】Paul went upstairs to *spruce* up before dinner.

【派】sprucely（*adv.* 整洁地）

inscribe [ɪnˈskraɪb] *vt.* 写；刻（to carefully cut, print, or write words on something）

【例】Inside the cover someone had *inscribed* the words "To Thomas, with love".

【派】inscription（*n.* 题词，献词）

collar ['kɑ:lər] *n.* 衣领

偏 离

depart [dɪ'pɑ:rt] *vi.* 离开，出发(leave, set off)

【记】de + part(离开) → 离开

【例】What time does the train *depart*?

detach [dɪ'tætʃ] *vt.* 分开；分离(to remove, separate)

【例】Sally *detached* the spray nozzle from the hose.

detached [dɪ'tætʃt] *adj.* 分离的(separated, disconnected)；超然的；公平的

【例】The house has a *detached* garage rather than an adjoining one.

deviate ['di:vieɪt] *v.* 偏离，越轨(deflect, diverge)

【记】de + via(路) + te → 离开正路 → 越轨

【例】I do not like to *deviate* from the set schedule.

【派】deviation(*n.* 偏离)

放 弃

dump [dʌmp] *vt.* 丢弃，倾倒(discarded, discharge)；倾销 *n.* 垃圾场

【例】They launched a campaign to stop cheap European beef being *dumped* in West Africa.

discard [dɪs'kɑ:rd] *vt.* 丢弃(reject)

【例】I tried to *discard* the old toys, but the children found them and put them back in the toy box.

jettison ['dʒetɪsn] *v.* 向外抛弃 *n.* 抛弃的货物

relinquish [rɪ'lɪŋkwɪʃ] *vt.* 放弃(abandon, give up, quit)

【记】re(再次) + linqu(离开) + ish → 再次离开 → 放弃

【例】The soldiers had to *relinquish* some unwieldy equipment to their enemies during their retreat.

resign [rɪ'zaɪn] *n./v.* 辞职

【例】Being so depressed, he *resigned* from a board of directors.

【派】resignation(*n.* 辞职)

retirement [rɪ'taɪərmənt] *n.* 退休，退役(stop working)

暴 露

divulge [daɪ'vʌldʒ] *vt.* 泄露(disclose, reveal)

【例】The president asked the managers not to *divulge* the news of the merger.

exposure [ɪk'spouʒər] *n.* 暴露,显露(disclosure, uncovering)

【例】Because of the reporter's *exposure* of fraud, the bank president was sentenced to prison.

play off 使暴露弱点,使出丑

【例】The two musicians *played off* each other in a piece of inspired improvisation.

reveal [rɪ'viːl] *vt.* 展现,揭露(exhibit, expose, disclose)

【例】The doctor didn't *reveal* the truth to him.

【派】revelation(*n.* 显示,揭露)

surface ['sɜːrfɪs] *vi.* 浮上水面,显露(pop up)

【例】Rumors about the killings have begun to *surface* in the press.

怀 疑

dubious ['duːbiəs] *adj.* 怀疑的(doubtful);不可靠的(unreliable)

【例】The *dubious* employees shook their heads as they carried out the order.

questionable ['kwestʃənəbl] *adj.* 可疑的,有疑问的(doubtful)

【例】The statistics are highly *questionable*.

skeptical ['skeptɪkl] *adj.* 怀疑的(dubious, incredulous)

【例】The *skeptical* student refused to accept the theory of evolution.

【派】skeptically(*adv.* 怀疑地) skepticism(*n.* 怀疑主义)

skeptic ['skeptɪk] *n.* 怀疑者

【例】*Skeptics* argued that the rise in prices was temporary.

得 出

derive [dɪ'raɪv] *v.* 得到,源于(to get something from something)

【例】Many students *derived* enormous satisfaction from the course.

elicit [ɪˈlɪsɪt] *vt.* 得出，引出（to give rise to, to evoke）

【例】Short questions are more likely to *elicit* a response.

genesis [ˈdʒenəsɪs] *n.* 创始，起源（[G-] 圣经《创世纪》）

traceable [ˈtreɪsəbl] *adj.* 可追踪的（derivable）

超　越

emulate [ˈemjuleɪt] *vt.* 努力赶上或超过

【例】I tried to *emulate* Mary's skill at playing the piano.

exceed [ɪkˈsiːd] *vt.* 超过，超越（to surpass）

【例】The demand for fish this month *exceeds* the supply.

outgrow [ˌaʊtˈɡroʊ] *vt.* 发展得超过…的范围（grow out of）

【例】They *outgrow* their clothes so quickly.

【派】outgrowth（*n.* 长出）

outnumber [ˌaʊtˈnʌmbər] *vt.* 在数量上超过（to be more in number than another group）

【例】Flats *outnumber* houses in this area.

pursue [pərˈsuː] *vt.* 追赶，追求（run after, court）

【例】Students should *pursue* their own interests.

【派】pursuit（*n.* 追赶，追求）

surpass [sərˈpæs] *vt.* 超过，超越，胜过（exceed, surmount）

【记】比较pass（*n.* 通过）

【例】The excellent runner *surpassed* all previous records.

崇　拜

enshrine [ɪnˈʃraɪn] *vt.* （作为神圣的东西）放置或保存（to hold as sacred）

【例】The right of free speech is *enshrined* in the *Constitution*.

esteem [ɪˈstiːm] *n./vt.* 尊敬（respect）

【例】I have a great deal of *esteem* for my parents.

lionize [ˈlaɪənaɪz] *vt.* 崇拜；看重（to treat someone as being very important）

【例】He wanted to be loved, not *lionized*.

obeisance [oʊˈbiːsns] *n.* 鞠躬，敬礼（respect and obedience shown by bending the upper part

of your body）

【例】They made *obeisance* to the sultan.

revere ［rɪˈvɪr］ *vt.* 尊敬（respect, worship）

【例】The political leader was *revered* by the people of his country.

【派】reverence（*n.* 尊敬）

venerable ［ˈvenərəbl］ *adj.* 值得尊敬的，年高德劭的（respected）；古老的

【例】the *venerable* guitarist Pat Martino

【派】venerably（*adv.* 尊敬地）

放　出

contagious ［kənˈteɪdʒəs］ *adj.* 传染的（catching, infectious）；有感染力的

【记】con + tag（接触）+ ious → 传染的

【例】Cancer is not *contagious*, so you shouldn't be afraid to touch someone with cancer.

【派】contagion（*n.* 传染）

transmit ［trænsˈmɪt］ *vt.* 传播（send out）；传染 *vi.* 发射，播送（broadcast）

【例】The system *transmits* information over digital phone lines.

【派】transmitter（*n.* 话筒，传送者）

transpire ［trænˈspaɪər］ *vt.* 发散；排出（exhale, send out）

【例】It was *transpired* that the king was already dead.

【派】transpiration（*n.* 散发）

emancipate ［ɪˈmænsɪpeɪt］ *vt.* 解放（奴隶、妇女等）

【例】Lincoln *emancipated* the slaves from their bondage.

【派】emancipation（*n.* 释放，解脱，解放）emancipatory（*adj.* 解放的，有助于解放的）

erupt ［ɪˈrʌpt］ *vi.* 爆发（explode, burst out）

【例】We feared that the volcano would *erupt* again.

【派】eruption（*n.* 喷发，爆发）

popularity ［ˌpɑːpjuˈlærəti］ *n.* 普遍，流行；有声望（liked or supported by a lot of people）

popularize ［ˈpɑːpjələraɪz］ *vt.* 使受欢迎（to make something well known and liked）；普及，推广

【例】Bob Marley *popularized* reggae music in the 1970s.

【派】popularizer（*n.* 大众化的人）

propaganda [ˌprɑːpə'gændə] *n.* 宣传(publicity)

【例】They have mounted a *propaganda* campaign against Western governments.

【派】propagandize(*v.* 宣传) propagandist(*n.* 宣传员)

propagate ['prɑːpəgeɪt] *vt.* 宣传

【例】Missionaries went far afield to *propagate* their faith.

【派】propagation(*n.* 传播)

publicity [pʌb'lɪsəti] *n.* 公开(性);(公众的)注意(attention);宣传(promotion)

【例】Standards in education have received much *publicity* over the last few years.

release [rɪ'liːs] *n./vt.* 发行

【例】The republisher *released* 500 new books last year.

render ['rendər] *vt.* 提供(provide)

【例】The passengers are not satisfied with the service *rendered* by the driver.

Few things are impossible in themselves; and it is often for want of will, rather than of means, that man fails to succeed.

事情很少有根本做不成的;其所以做不成,与其说是条件不够,不如说是由于决心不够。

——法国作家 罗切福考尔德(*La Rocheforcauld, French writer*)

练 习 题

连线题

hypersensitive	有感觉的	intersperse	向外抛弃
imperceptible	过分敏感的	spruce	散布
olfactory	感觉的	deviate	普及
perceptible	装饰	jettison	放置
sensory	民心	divulge	打扮
sentient	嗅觉的	dubious	偏离
unwitting	装饰华丽的	genesis	泄露
morale	回忆	obeisance	发散
intrigue	不知不觉的	enshrine	创始
reminiscence	投机的	emancipate	怀疑的
speculative	密谋	contagious	鞠躬
embellish	可感觉到的	transpire	解放
ornate	感觉不到的	popularize	有感染力的

选词填空

nostalgia	exceed	reveal	conspire	intrigue
contemplate	relinquish	dispose	propagate	speculate

1. He looked back on his university days with a certain amount of _____.
2. All six men admitted _____ to steal cars.
3. While King Richard was abroad, the barons had been _____ against him.
4. Did you ever _____ resigning?
5. Jones refused to _____ about what might happen.
6. Your idea at least _____ of the immediate problem.
7. Stultz _____ control to his subordinate.
8. He may be prosecuted for _____ secrets about the security agency.
9. His performance _____ our expectations.
10. The group launched a website to _____ its ideas.

练习题答案

连线题答案

hypersensitive	过分敏感的	intersperse	散布
imperceptible	感觉不到的	spruce	打扮
olfactory	嗅觉的	deviate	偏离
perceptible	可感觉到的	jettison	向外抛弃
sensory	感觉的	divulge	泄露
sentient	有感觉的	dubious	怀疑的
unwitting	不知不觉的	genesis	创始
morale	民心	obeisance	鞠躬
intrigue	密谋	enshrine	放置
reminiscence	回忆	emancipate	解放
speculative	投机的	contagious	有感染力的
embellish	装饰	transpire	发散
ornate	装饰华丽的	popularize	普及

选词填空答案

nostalgia	exceed	reveal	conspire	intrigue
contemplate	relinquish	dispose	propagate	speculate

1. He looked back on his university days with a certain amount of（nostalgia）.
2. All six men admitted（conspiring）to steal cars.
3. While King Richard was abroad, the barons had been（intriguing）against him.
4. Did you ever（contemplate）resigning?
5. Jones refused to（speculate）about what might happen.
6. Your idea at least（disposes）of the immediate problem.
7. Stultz（relinquished）control to his subordinate.
8. He may be prosecuted for（revealing）secrets about the security agency.
9. His performance（exceeded）our expectations.
10. The group launched a website to（propagate）its ideas.

Word List 29

音频

自身行为（四）

自身行为(四)

制 造

customize [ˈkʌstəmaɪz] v. 定制，定做（to modify according to a customer's individual requirements）

fabricate [ˈfæbrɪkeɪt] vt. 制造（make）；伪造（forge, coin）
【记】fabric(结构) + ate → 使出现结构 → 制造
【例】Jane *fabricated* the story that she was late because she was caught in traffic.
【派】fabrication(n. 制作；伪造)

forge [fɔːrdʒ] vt. 锻造（to create, make）；锻炼；伪造（feign, fabricate）n. 铁匠店；锻炉
【例】The blacksmith is *forging* the horseshoe.
【派】forgery(n. 伪造；伪造的东西)

generate [ˈdʒenəreɪt] vt. 造成（produce, give rise to）
【记】gener(产生) + ate → 造成
【例】His improper behavior *generates* a good deal of suspicion.

manufacture [ˌmænjuˈfæktʃər] vt. 制造（produce）
【记】manu(手) + fact(做) + ure → 用手做 → 制造
【例】His books seem to have been *manufactured* rather than composed.
【派】manufacturing(n. 制造 adj. 制造业的)

mold [moʊld] vt. 塑造（shape）
【例】The sculptor *molded* the clay into a flowerpot.

spurious [ˈspjʊriəs] adj. 伪造的，假的，谬误的（fake, incorrect, insincere）
【例】He demolished the opposition's *spurious* arguments.
【派】spuriously(adv. 伪造地)

模 仿

duplicate [ˈduːplɪkeɪt] vt. 复制（to copy）[ˈduːplɪkət] adj. 复制的 n. 复制品
【例】The manager asks the secretary to *duplicate* the document.
【派】duplication(n. 复制)

| **repetition** | [ˌrepə'tɪʃn] *n.* 重复，反复（doing the same thing many times）；复制品 |
| **phony** | ['founi] *adj.* [口]假的，欺骗的（fake, not real）*n.* 赝品；骗子 |

【例】a *phony* American accent

replacement	[rɪ'pleɪsmənt] *n.* 替换，替代品
replica	['replɪkə] *n.* 复制品，副本（an exact copy）
replicate	['replɪkeɪt] *v.* 重复，复制（redo）

【例】There is a need for further research to *replicate* these findings.

【派】replication（*n.* 复制）

| **substitute** | ['sʌbstɪtuːt] *n.* 替代品（replacement）*v.* 替代 |

【例】Fantasies are more than *substitutes* for unpleasant reality.

【派】substitution（*n.* 代替）

| **supersede** | [ˌsuːpər'siːd] *vt.* 替代（replace, substitute） |

【记】super(上面) + sede(坐) → 坐上 → 替代

【例】The use of robots will someday *supersede* manual labor.

| **imitate** | ['ɪmɪteɪt] *vt.* 模仿（copy, mimic） |

【例】Anne *imitated* the famous artist's style in her own paintings.

【派】imitation（*n.* 模仿，仿造物）imitator（*n.* 模仿者，仿效者）

| **mimic** | ['mɪmɪk] *vt.* 模仿（imitate）*n.* 模仿名人言行的娱乐演员 |

【例】He could *mimic* all the teachers' accents.

【派】mimicry（*n.* 模仿）

| **paradigm** | ['pærədaɪm] *n.* 典范，范例（a model or example that shows how something works or is produced） |

【例】He remained the *paradigm* of what a pope should be.

| **prototype** | ['proʊtətaɪp] *n.* 原型，典型；样品 |

【例】a working *prototype* of the new car

指　示

| **implicit** | [ɪm'plɪsɪt] *adj.* 暗示的（inferred, implied）；内含的 |

【记】im(进入) + plic(重叠) + it → 进入重叠层次状态中 → 内含的

【例】Her silence gave *implicit* consent.

| **indicate** | ['ɪndɪkeɪt] *vt.* 指示；表示（show, suggest, hint） |

【记】in + dic(言，说) + ate → 表示

【例】The smile on the old man's face *indicated* that he appreciated my help very much.

【派】indication(*n.* 指示；表示；象征，迹象)

prescribe [prɪˈskraɪb] *vt.* 指示(dictate)；规定

【例】The law *prescribes* what should be done.

propose [prəˈpoʊz] *v.* 提出，提议(suggest)

【例】Man *proposes*, God disposes.

【派】proposal(*n.* 提案，建议)

propound [prəˈpaʊnd] *vt.* 提出，建议

【例】The theory of natural selection was first *propounded* by Charles Darwin.

referent [ˈrefrənt] *n.* 指示物(pointer)

token [ˈtoʊkən] *n.* 象征 *adj.* 象征性的，作为标志的

【例】The government thinks it can get away with *token* gestures on environmental issues.

typify [ˈtɪpɪfaɪ] *vt.* 代表，象征(stand for)

【例】The long complicated sentences *typify* legal documents.

移　动

invert [ɪnˈvɜːrt] *vt.* 倒转(overturn, reverse)

【例】I *inverted* the glasses so the water would drain out of them.

rotate [ˈroʊteɪt] *v.* (使)旋转；轮换(turn, alternate)

【例】The coach *rotates* her players frequently near the end of the game.

rotation [roʊˈteɪʃn] *n.* 旋转(roll, spin)；轮流

【例】the *rotation* of the Earth on its axis

【派】rotational(*adj.* 转动的；轮流的)

whirl [wɜːrl] *v.* (使)旋转，转动(spin, turn)

【例】We watched the seagulls *whirling* and shrieking over the harbor.

locomotion [ˌloʊkəˈmoʊʃn] *n.* 运动；运动力 (movement or the ability to move)

migrate [ˈmaɪgreɪt] *vi.* 迁徙；迁移，移居

【例】Some birds *migrate* to find warmer weather.

【派】migration(*n.* 迁移) migrant(*n.* 移民)

remove [rɪ'muːv] *vt.* 移动，搬开；脱掉

【记】re(再次) + move(动) → 移动

【例】Please *remove* the dishes from the table.

【派】removal(*n.* 免职；移开)

shift [ʃɪft] *n./v.* 转移；替换(change; alteration)

【例】Workers in this factory work on 3 *shifts*.

transfer [træns'fɜːr] *v.* 转移，迁移(move)；转让

【例】He *transferred* from MI6 to the Security Service.

【派】transference(*n.* 转让)

transplant ['trænsplænt] *n.* 移植 [træns'plænt] *vt.* 移植；移居(migrate)

【例】*transplant* the mother's kidney to her son

【派】transplantation(*n.* 移植；移民)

jar [dʒɑːr] *vt.* 震动(shake)

【例】Her announcement really *jarred* me. I was shocked!

【派】jarring(*adj.* 不和谐的)

wiggle ['wɪgl] *v.* 摆动，起伏，摇动(move, shake)

【例】Henry *wiggled* his toes.

stagger ['stægər] *v.* (使)蹒跚

【例】The wounded man *staggered* along.

【派】staggering(*adj.* 令人吃惊的)

发　生

encounter [ɪn'kaʊntər] *n./v.* 遇到，碰到

【例】They *encountered* serious problems when two members of the expedition were injured.

incur [ɪn'kɜːr] *vt.* 招致，引起(arouse, provoke)

【记】in(进入) + cur(跑) → 跑进来 → 招致

【例】His arrogant attitude has *incurred* many people's discontent.

occurrence [ə'kɜːrəns] *n.* 发生，出现；事件(something that happens)

【例】Laughter was a rare *occurrence* in his classroom.

onset ['ɑːnset] *n.* 开始(beginning)

【记】来自set on(攻击)

【例】He had a sudden *onset* of conscious loss and then fell down in the supermarket.

originate [ə'rɪdʒɪneɪt] *vi.* 发源于(initiate, start)

【例】Compass *originated* from China.

【派】origination（*n.* 发源）

pop [pɑːp] *v.* 突然爆开；意外发生（to come suddenly out of something）

【例】The top button *popped* off my shirt.

prevail [prɪˈveɪl] *vi.* 流行，盛行（dominate）

【例】Justice will *prevail*.

【派】prevalence（*n.* 盛行）

spark [spɑːrk] *vt.* 发动；激发感情；鼓舞（cause, provoke）

【例】The police's response *sparked* outrage in the community.

spontaneous [spɑːnˈteɪniəs] *adj.* 自发的，本能的（impulsive, involuntary）

【记】spont（自然）+ aneous → 自然的 → 自发的

【例】There was *spontaneous* applause at the end of Mary's speech.

【派】spontaneously（*adv.* 自发地）

stage [steɪdʒ] *vt.* 举行，上演（organize）

【例】Activists *staged* a protest outside the parliament.

thrive [θraɪv] *vi.* 繁荣，旺盛（flourish）

【例】The wild deer that *throve* here are no more visible due to deforestation.

【派】thriving（*adj.* 兴旺的）

循　环

anew [əˈnuː] *adv.* 再，重新（over again, afresh）

【例】He's determined to begin his life *anew*.

aperiodic [ˌeɪpiəriˈɑːdɪk] *adj.* 非周期的（non-periodic）

circulation [ˌsɜːrkjəˈleɪʃn] *n.* 循环；（货币、消息等）流通；传播；发行；销路

【派】circulatory（*adj.* 循环的）

recapture [ˌriːˈkæptʃər] *vt.* 重获，收复（retake, bring back）；再经历

【例】The film really *recaptures* the atmosphere of those days.

retrieve [rɪˈtriːv] *v.* 重新找回（recover, save）

【记】re（重新）+ trieve（找到）→ 重新找回

【例】Jane *retrieved* the lost document from the garbage can.

【派】retrievable（*adj.* 可重新获取的）

regain [rɪˈɡeɪn] *vt.* 复得，赢回（get back）

【例】The family never quite *regained* its former influence.

recur [rɪˈkɜːr] *vi.* 复发，重来（repeat, return）

【例】Really scared by SARS, the world is thrilled at the news that it is *recurring* this spring.

rehash [ˌriːˈhæʃ] *vt.* 以新形式处理；改头换面地重复（to use the same ideas again in a new form）

【例】He simply *rehashed* the same story.

recast [ˌriːˈkæst] *vt.* 重新铸造（give something a new shape, etc.）；彻底改动

【例】an attempt to *recast* the statement in less formal language

rehabilitate [ˌriːəˈbɪlɪteɪt] *vt.* 恢复（restore）

【记】reh（重新）+ abili（能力）+ tate → 重新获得能力 → 恢复

【例】After World War II, many factories were *rehabilitated* rather than bulldozed.

【派】rehabilitation（*n.* 复兴；修复）

resurgence [rɪˈsɜːrdʒəns] *n.* 复兴，复活（reappearance and growth of something）

【例】a *resurgence* in the popularity of 60's music

revitalize [ˌriːˈvaɪtəlaɪz] *vt.* 使恢复元气，使有新的活力（put into new strength）

【例】They hope to *revitalize* the neighborhood by providing better housing.

【派】revitalization（*n.* 复兴）

revive [rɪˈvaɪv] *v.* 复兴，复苏（revitalize）

【记】re（重新）+ vive（活）→ 复苏

【例】The fresh air soon *revived* him.

【派】revival（*n.* 复苏）

retail [ˈriːteɪl] *n.* 零售

【例】We are looking for more *retail* outlets for our products.

出　现

advent [ˈædvent] *n.* 出现，到来（arrival, coming）

【例】Since the *advent* of atomic power, there have been great changes in industry.

emerge [iˈmɜːrdʒ] *vi.* 出现（appear, come into prominence）

【例】The divers *emerged* from the water.

【派】emergence（*n.* 出现）

germinate [ˈdʒɜːrmɪneɪt] *v.* 发芽（sprout）

【记】germ（幼芽）+ inate → 发芽

【例】After the seeds *germinated*, I transplanted them to a larger pot.

【派】germination(*n.* 发生；萌芽)

选 择

indiscriminate [ˌɪndɪˈskrɪmɪnət] *adj.* 不加选择的(lacking discrimination or careful choice)

【例】She disapproved of her son's *indiscriminate* television viewing.

alternative [ɔːlˈtɜːrnətɪv] *n.* 选择，取舍（option, choice, substitute）*adj.* 供选择的，供替代的

【例】Have you any *alternative* suggestions?

【派】alternate(*v.* 交替，轮换 *adj.* 轮流的；代替的)

preferable [ˈprefrəbl] *adj.* 可取的(advisable)；更好的

【记】prefer(喜欢) + able → 更好的

【例】A *preferable* option is to store the food in a refrigerator rather than throw them away.

【派】preferably(*adv.* 更好地)

reluctant [rɪˈlʌktənt] *adj.* 不情愿的，勉强的(unwilling)

【例】Jane seems *reluctant* to marry Jim.

【派】reluctantly(*adv.* 勉强地)

selective [sɪˈlektɪv] *adj.* 精挑细选的，选择的(careful about what to choose)

【例】We're very *selective* about what we let the children watch.

【派】selectively(*adv.* 不普遍地) selectivity(*n.* 选择性)

停 顿

halt [hɔːlt] *n./v.* 停止，暂停(stop, cease)

【例】The police ordered the thief to *halt*.

interval [ˈɪntərvl] *n.* （时间上的）间隔，间隙，间歇（the period of time between two events, activities etc. ）

【例】The *interval* between arrest and trial can be up to six months.

letup [ˈletʌp] *n.* 放松；停顿

连线题答案

customize	定制	whirl	旋转
spurious	伪造的	wiggle	摆动
duplicate	复制	occurrence	发生
paradigm	典范	originate	发源于
prototype	原型	spontaneous	自发的
repetition	重复	thrive	繁荣
replicate	复制	resurgence	复兴
supersede	替代	retrieve	重新找回
propound	提出	revitalize	使恢复元气
typify	代表	indiscriminate	不加选择的
invert	倒转	germinate	发芽
locomotion	运动	advent	出现
rotate	旋转	letup	放松

选词填空答案

undergo	fabricate	prevail	imitate	prescribe
transfer	substitute	incur	rehabilitate	generate

1. Tourism (generates) income for local communities.
2. The police were accused of (fabricating) evidence.
3. She was a splendid mimic and loved to (imitate) Winston Churchill.
4. The recipe says you can (substitute) yoghurt for the sour cream.
5. What punishment does the law (prescribe) for this crime?
6. You'll be (transferred) to the Birmingham office.
7. She wondered what she'd done to (incur) his displeasure this time.
8. I admired the creativity which (prevailed) among the young writers.
9. A lot of the older houses have now been (rehabilitated).
10. The country has (undergone) massive changes recently.

Word List 30

音频

涉他行为（一）

涉他行为(一)

吸　引

absorb [əb'sɔːrb] *vt.* 吸收；吸引(attract, allure)
【记】ab + sorb(吸)→ 吸收
【例】I used a sponge to *absorb* the spilled milk.
【派】absorbed(*adj.* 全神贯注的) absorbing(*adj.* 引人入胜的) absorption(*n.* 吸收；专注) absorptive(*adj.* 吸收的)

absorbent [əb'sɔːrbənt] *adj.* 有吸收力的(absorptive) *n.* 吸收剂

desirable [dɪ'zaɪərəbl] *adj.* 理想的，如意的(worthy of desire)
【例】I envy Jane because her job is so *desirable*.

entice [ɪn'taɪs] *vt.* 诱惑(lure, tempt)
【例】I *enticed* Mary to dinner by offering to pay for her meal.
【派】enticement(*n.* 诱惑，诱惑物)

induce [ɪn'duːs] *vt.* 导致，诱使(cause, produce)
【记】in(进入) + duce(引导)→ 导致
【例】The careless worker *induced* the fire with a cigarette butt.
【派】inducement(*n.* 引诱；刺激；鼓励)

spectacular [spek'tækjələr] *adj.* 引人入胜的，壮观的
(breathtaking, impressive, striking)
【例】The most *spectacular* thing ever happened this century would be the introduction of computer.

节　制

abstinence ['æbstɪnəns] *n.* 节制，禁欲(refraining from some action)；戒酒
【例】*Abstinence* from fatty foods and smoking can probably lengthen your life.
【派】abstinent(*n.* 禁欲者 *adj.* 饮食有度的；禁欲的)

preventive [prɪ'ventɪv] *n.* 预防措施 *adj.* 预防的，防止的
【例】While travelling abroad, take *preventive* measures to avoid illness.
【派】preventively(*adv.* 预防地)

prohibitive [prəˈhɪbətɪv] *adj.* 禁止的；价格昂贵的(forbidden；costly)

【例】*prohibitive* regulations

【派】prohibitively(*adv.* 费用过高地)

taboo [təˈbuː] *n./vt.* 禁忌；禁止(ban, prohibition)

【例】Four letter words are *taboo* words to these ladies.

tamper [ˈtæmpər] *vi.* 干预(interfere, intervene)

【例】The secretary *tampered* with the Prime Minister's schedule.

temperance [ˈtempərəns] *n.* 节制，自制(self-control, moderation)；戒酒

【例】His *temperance* couldn't be counted on, otherwise he would not have become addicted.

免　除

acquit [əˈkwɪt] *vt.* 宣告无罪(exonerate, vindicate)

【记】ac + quit(免除) → 免除罪责 → 宣告无罪

【例】The court *acquitted* Max of all charges.

【派】acquittal(*n.* 开释)

deregulate [ˌdiːˈregjuleɪt] *v.* 撤销对…的管制和限制 (to remove regulations or controls)

【例】The U.S. airline industry has been *deregulated* since 1978.

【派】deregulation(*n.* 违反规定；反常)

exempt [ɪgˈzempt] *vt.* 免除(permit not to do) *adj.* 被免除的(excused)

【例】The teacher *exempted* the smartest students from taking the quiz.

exonerate [ɪgˈzɑːnəreɪt] *vt.* 宣告无罪(acquit, vindicate)

【例】He was totally *exonerated* of any blame.

【派】exoneration(*n.* 免除责任，确定无罪)

immune [ɪˈmjuːn] *adj.* 免除的；免疫的(unaffected, unsusceptible)

【记】im(没有) + mune(责任) → 没有责任 → 免除的

【例】I am *immune* from the disease, for I had it once.

【派】immunity(*n.* 免疫性)

impunity [ɪmˈpjuːnəti] *n.* 免除处罚 (exemption or immunity from punishment)

授 权

authoritative [ə'θɔːrəteɪtɪv] *adj.* 权威性的，官方的

【例】Make sure you ask an *authoritative* source for directions.

【派】authority(*n.* 权威，官方；职权)

authorize ['ɔːθəraɪz] *vt.* 授权(empower, permit)

【例】A visa *authorizes* a person to enter and leave a country.

【派】authorization(*n.* 授权，认可)

warrant ['wɔːrənt] *n.* 授权证，许可证；依据 *vt.* 保证，担保(promise)

【例】The author hereby *warrants* that the publisher is the owner of the copyright.

【派】warranty(*n.* 保证书，保单)

拥 护

advocate ['ædvəkət] *n.* 拥护者 ['ædvəkeɪt] *v.* 提倡，主张(to support, recommend)

【例】They *advocated* state control of all public services.

【派】advocation (*n.* 拥护，支持) advocacy (*n.* 拥护；鼓吹)

align [ə'laɪn] *vt.* 使成一线(to form... into a line)；公开支持(to publicly support)

【例】The senator *aligned* himself with the critics of the proposed reforms.

【派】alignment(*n.* 排成直线)

allegiance [ə'liːdʒəns] *n.* 拥护，忠诚(devotion, loyalty, faithfulness)

bolster ['boʊlstər] *n.* 枕垫 *v.* 支持，鼓励(to support or reinforce; strengthen)

【例】New camera and film technology will *bolster* the company's market share.

espouse [ɪ'spaʊz] *v.* 支持，拥护(to support)

【例】He *espoused* a variety of scientific, social and political causes.

加 入

admittance [əd'mɪtns] *n.* 允许进入（permission to enter）

【例】Gaining *admittance* to the club was no easy matter.

affiliate [ə'fɪlɪeɪt] *v.* 加盟，入会（associate, ally）

【例】She *affiliates* herself with a new law firm.

【派】affiliation（*n.* 入会；联盟；关系）

enrollment [ɪn'roʊlmənt] *n.* 登记，注册；入伍，入会，入学

input ['ɪnpʊt] *n.* 输入；投入资源（指时间、知识、思想等）*vt.* 把…输入电脑（to put information into a computer）

【例】The information is *input* to our computer system.

installation [ˌɪnstə'leɪʃn] *n.* 安装（when someone fits a piece of equipment somewhere）；装置

【例】the *installation* and maintenance of alarm systems

intake ['ɪnteɪk] *n.* 吸入，收纳；纳入（数量）（the amount of food, drink, etc. that you take into your body）

【例】Try to reduce your *intake* of fat.

merge [mɜːrdʒ] *v.* 合并（combine, amalgamate）

【例】The two companies are going to *merge* by the end of the year.

【派】merger（*n.* 合并）

mingle ['mɪŋgl] *v.* 混合，混入（mix）

【例】Her perfume *mingled* with the smell of woodsmoke from the fire.

unionize ['juːnɪənaɪz] *v.* （使）加入工会，（使）成立工会

【例】*unionize* a firm's employees

【派】unionization（*n.* 联合，结合）unionist（*n.* 工会主义者）

integrate ['ɪntɪgreɪt] *vt.* 使结合，使并入（combine, join）

【例】Quality training was *integrated* into the newcomers' basic courses .

【派】integration（*n.* 结合，整合）

争　斗

aggressive [əˈgresɪv] *adj.* 好斗的，攻击性的（offensive, belligerent）；有进取心的（assertive, vigorous）

【例】A successful businessman has to be *aggressive*.

【派】aggression（*n.* 侵略）aggressor（*n.* 侵略者）

contend [kənˈtend] *v.* 争斗（compete, rival）

【例】The armies are *contending* for control of strategic territory.

【派】contention（*n.* 竞争，争论）

contentious [kənˈtenʃəs] *adj.* 好辩的，喜争吵的（tending to argue or quarrel）；有争议的（causing arguments）

【例】Abortion has always been a *contentious* subject.

controversial [ˌkɑːntrəˈvɜːrʃl] *adj.* 引起争论的（causing arguments）

【例】Mike wrote a very *controversial* book about the weakness of the political leaders.

【派】controversy（*n.* 争论）

opponent [əˈpoʊnənt] *n.* 敌人，对手（enemy, rival）

rival [ˈraɪvl] *vt.* 竞争，匹敌（compete, match）

【例】Edison is a genius who can't be *rivaled* by ordinary mortals.

【派】rivalry（*n.* 竞争，敌对）

scramble [ˈskræmbl] *v.* 爬行，攀登（climb）；争夺；仓促地行动（do quickly）

【例】They were *scrambling* to give the impression that the situation was in control.

strife [straɪf] *n.* 冲突，竞争（squabble, conflict）

strive [straɪv] *vi.* 努力，奋斗，力求（endeavor, struggle）

【例】The poor family *strived* to pay the rent each month.

campaign [kæmˈpeɪn] *n.* 战役；运动，竞选运动 *v.* 参加、发起运动，参加竞选

【例】Joan is *campaigning* for equal rights for women.

crusade [kruːˈseɪd] *n.* 十字军东征；改革（讨伐、肃清）运动

bombardment [bɑːmˈbɑːrdmənt] *n.* 炮轰，轰炸

聚　拢

alliance [əˈlaɪəns] *n.* 结盟(union, confederate); 同盟国

【派】ally(*v.* 结盟, 联合)

conglomerate [kənˈglɑːmərət] *n.* 集合体, 聚集物 (a thing composed of various elements); 联合大企业, 企业集团

assemble [əˈsembl] *vt.* 聚集(gather, congregate)

【例】After *assembling* the things he needed, Bob baked a beautiful cake.

【派】assembly(*n.* 集会; 装配)

glean [gliːn] *vt.* 收集(collect, gather)

【例】The scientists were delighted at these information *gleaned* from the investigation.

synthesize [ˈsɪnθəsaɪz] *vt.* 使合成, 综合(combine)

【例】DDT is a pesticide that was first *synthesized* in 1874.

【派】synthesizer(*n.* 合成器)

synthetic [sɪnˈθetɪk] *adj.* 综合的; 合成的(artificial)

coalesce [ˌkoʊəˈles] *v.* 合并, 联合, 结合(to unite, merge, fuse, blend)

【例】Gradually the different groups of people *coalesced* into one dominant racial group.

【派】coalition(*n.* 结合体, 同盟)

centralized [ˈsentrəlaɪzd] *adj.* 集中的; 中央集权的

【派】centralization(*n.* 中央集权化)

convergent [kənˈvɜːrdʒənt] *adj.* 汇合的, 汇聚的(moving towards or meeting at some common point)

【例】The member states should start to have more *convergent* policies.

【派】converge(*v.* 汇于一点)convergence(*n.* 集中, 收敛)

deposit [dɪˈpɑːzɪt] *v.* 放置, 存放(place, lay) *n.* 存款; 押金

【记】比较draw(*n.* 取款)

【例】Tom *deposited* his luggage in the hotel.

incorporate [ɪnˈkɔːrpəreɪt] *vt.* 吸收 (to include, absorb); 把…合并 (to unite, combine); 组成公司

【例】We had to *incorporate* the company for tax reasons.

bondage [ˈbɑːndɪdʒ] *n.* 奴役, 束缚

配 发

allocate [ˈæləkeɪt] *vt.* 分派，分配(to distribute, allot)

【例】They *allocated* funds for the new school.

【派】allocation(*n.* 配给，分配)

allot [əˈlɑːt] *vt.* 分配，拨给(to assign, distribute)

【例】Each passenger slept on the berth *allotted* to him.

【派】allotment(*n.* 分配)

apportion [əˈpɔːrʃn] *vt.* 分摊，分派(to divide, distribute, assign or allot)

【例】Court costs were equally *apportioned* between them.

assign [əˈsaɪn] *vt.* 分配，指派(allot, distribute)

【例】The manager *assigned* Bill to the Jones project.

【派】assignment(*n.* 分配；任务)

dispense [dɪˈspens] *vt.* 分派，分发(to give out, allot, distribute)

【例】The firm has been *dispensing* ointments.

allowance [əˈlaʊəns] *n.* 津贴，补贴；零用钱

请 求

application [ˌæplɪˈkeɪʃn] *n.* 申请，申请书；实际应用，用途

【例】This is a new discovery that had a number of industrial *applications*.

invoke [ɪnˈvoʊk] *vt.* 恳求，祈求(beg, pray)

【记】in + voke(喊)→ 恳求

【例】I *invoked* their forgiveness.

plead [pliːd] *v.* 抗辩；恳求(argue, protest; beg)

【例】"Let me out, please." The prisoner *pleaded* to the jail keeper, but in vain.

supplicant [ˈsʌplɪkənt] *n.* 乞求者，恳求者

确 定

guarantee [ˌgærənˈtiː] *vt.* 确保(secure, assure)

【例】No one can *guarantee* that you will pass the exam if you don't work hard.

ascertain [ˌæsərˈteɪn] *vt.* 确定(determine, make sure); 探知

【记】as + certain(确信)→ 确定

【例】Did the doctor *ascertain* the cause of your opinion?

assertion [əˈsɜːrʃn] *n.* 声称, 主张, 断言(declaration, affirmation, positive statement)

【例】He made an *assertion* that he was not responsible for it.

【派】assert(*v.* 声称, 断言) assertive(*adj.* 肯定的, 坚定自信的)

assure [əˈʃʊr] *vt.* 使确信, 向…保证(guarantee, pledge)

【记】as + sure(确信)→ 使确信

【例】The doctor *assured* the patient that everything would be all right.

【派】assurance(*n.* 确信; 保险) assuring(*adj.* 确信的, 给人信心的)

confirm [kənˈfɜːrm] *vt.* 证实, 确认(substantiate, verify)

【记】con + firm(坚实的)→ 证实

【例】Please *confirm* our reservations at the restaurant.

resolve [rɪˈzɑːlv] *v.* 决定(determine)

【例】He *resolved* on going out.

【派】resolved(*adj.* 下定决心的) resolution(*n.* 决心)

verdict [ˈvɜːrdɪkt] *n.* 判决, 决定(decision in court)

The tragedy of life is not so much what men suffer, but what they miss.

生活的悲剧不在于人们受到多少苦, 而在于人们错过了什么。

——英国散文家、历史学家 卡莱尔

(*Thomas Carlyle, British essayist and historian*)

练习题

连线题

absorbent	免除	aggressive	集合体
spectacular	有吸收力的	contentious	好辩的
abstinence	加盟	controversial	分配
preventative	壮观的	coalesce	好斗的
prohibitive	预防	conglomerate	攀登
deregulate	禁止的	synthesize	合并
exempt	节制	apportion	使合成
exonerate	授权	allotment	分摊
impunity	撤销管制	supplicant	确定
authorize	宣告无罪	assertion	乞求者
allegiance	免除处罚	ascertain	声称
bolster	支持	resolve	引起争论的
affiliate	拥护	scramble	决定

选词填空

induce	confirm	incorporate	strive	contend
authoritative	espouse	mingle	entice	tamper

1. Our special offers are intended to _____ people to buy.

2. Nothing would _____ me to vote for him again.

3. I don't see the point in _____ with a system that's worked fine so far.

4. He has a commanding presence and an_____ voice.

5. She _____ liberal reform.

6. Add the mint and allow the flavors to _____.

7. Three armed groups are _____ for power.

8. Research has _____ that the risk is higher for women.

9. We must continue to _____ for greater efficiency.

10. We've _____ many environmentally-friendly features into the design of the building.

练习题答案

连线题答案

absorbent	有吸收力的	aggressive	好斗的
spectacular	壮观的	contentious	好辩的
abstinence	节制	controversial	引起争论的
preventative	预防	coalesce	合并
prohibitive	禁止的	conglomerate	集合体
deregulate	撤销管制	synthesize	使合成
exempt	免除	apportion	分摊
exonerate	宣告无罪	allotment	分配
impunity	免除处罚	supplicant	乞求者
authorize	授权	assertion	声称
allegiance	拥护	ascertain	确定
bolster	支持	resolve	决定
affiliate	加盟	scramble	攀登

选词填空答案

induce	confirm	incorporate	strive	contend
authoritative	espouse	mingle	entice	tamper

1. Our special offers are intended to（entice）people to buy.
2. Nothing would（induce）me to vote for him again.
3. I don't see the point in（tampering）with a system that's worked fine so far.
4. He has a commanding presence and an（authoritative）voice.
5. She（espouses）liberal reform.
6. Add the mint and allow the flavors to（mingle）.
7. Three armed groups are（contending）for power.
8. Research has（confirmed）that the risk is higher for women.
9. We must continue to（strive）for greater efficiency.
10. We've（incorporated）many environmentally-friendly features into the design of the building.

Word List 31

音频

涉他行为（二）

涉他行为(二)

判　断

identify [aɪ'dentɪfaɪ] *vt.* 认出(recognize)
【记】iden(相同) + tify → 和(记忆中)相同 → 认出
【例】The doctor *identified* the disease that made me sick.
【派】identifiable(*adj.* 可以确认的)

identification [aɪˌdentɪfɪ'keɪʃn] *n.* 验明;认出;身份证明
【例】*Identification* Card

assess [ə'ses] *v.* 估价,评价(estimate, evaluate)
【例】It took a while to *assess* the damage from the tornado.
【派】assessment(*n.* 评估,评价)

criterion [kraɪ'tɪriən] *n.* [*pl.* criteria]标准,准则(standard)

evaluate [ɪ'væljueɪt] *vt.* 评价,估计(estimate, assess)
【记】e + valu(价值) + ate → 评价
【例】The assessor *evaluated* the plot of land before Anne sold it.
【派】evaluation(*n.* 评估,评价)

EVALUATE
· Judge
· In Your Own Words

underestimate [ˌʌndər'estɪmeɪt] *vt.* 低估(undervalue)
【例】The width of the nation has long been *underestimated* before the recent investigation.
【派】underestimation(*n.* 过低评估)

帮　助

assist [ə'sɪst] *vt.* 辅助(aid, help)
【例】A nurse *assisted* the surgeon during the operation.
【派】assistance(*n.* 帮助,援助)

endowment [ɪn'daʊmənt] *n.* 天赋,天资,才能;捐助,资助

extricate ['ekstrɪkeɪt] *vt.* 救出,使解脱(release, liberate)
【记】ex + tric(复杂) + ate → 从复杂中走出 → 使解脱
【例】Jane *extricated* herself from an unhappy relationship with her boyfriend.

facilitate [fə'sɪlɪteɪt] *vt.* 使容易(to make easier)；促进，帮助

【例】Tractors *facilitate* farming.

subscribe [səb'skraɪb] *vi.* 订阅，订购 *v.* 捐助(donate)

【例】You can *subscribe* to the magazine for as little as $32 a year.

【派】subscriber(*n.* 订购者；捐献者) subscription(*n.* 捐献；订购)

原　因

motivation [ˌməʊtɪ'veɪʃn] *n.* 动机(motive, incentive)

【记】比较motive(*n.* 动机)

【例】Unfortunately his salary is his only *motivation* for working.

ascribe [ə'skraɪb] *v.* 把…归于(accredit, attribute)

【例】The report *ascribes* the rise in childhood asthma to the increase in pollution.

attribute ['ætrɪbjuːt] *n.* 性质(characteristic, quality, trait) [ə'trɪbjuːt] *vt.* 归因于(accredit, ascribe)

【例】The discovery of electricity is *attributed* to Benjamin Franklin.

【派】attribution(*n.* 归因) attributable(*adj.* 可归因于…的)

causal ['kɔːzl] *adj.* 构成原因的

【记】caus(e)(原因) + al → 构成原因的

【例】There is a *causal* relationship between unemployment and crime.

利　用

available [ə'veɪləbl] *adj.* 可用的(obtainable, accessible)

【例】The hotel is *available* for the wedding reception next week.

【派】availability(*n.* 可用性，实用性)

feasible ['fiːzəbl] *adj.* 切实可行的(practical, possible, viable)

【记】feas(做) + ible → 能够做的 → 切实可行的

【例】Before you carry out the plan, make sure it is *feasible*.

harness ['hɑːrnɪs] *n.* 马具 *vt.* 利用(utilize)

【例】Before steam engine was *harnessed* in large machinery, the efficiency was very low.

odds [ɑːdz] *n.* 利用；可能性(probability)

【例】The *odds* are that he will commit the same crime again.

utilitarian [ˌjuːtɪlɪ'teriən] *adj.* 有效用的，实用的；功利的(useful, practical; materialistic)

【例】ugly *utilitarian* buildings

utilize [ˈjuːtəlaɪz] *vt.* 利用(use, make use of)

【例】Efficient workers *utilize* time wisely.

【派】utility(*n.* 效用) utilization(*n.* 利用)

exploit [ɪkˈsplɔɪt] *vt.* 剥削;开发(explore)

【记】ex + ploit(重叠) → 从重叠中拿出 → 开发

【例】The company *exploited* the workers by falsely promising them pay raises.

【派】exploitation(*n.* 剥削;开发利用)

overuse [ˌəʊvərˈjuːz] *vt.* 把…使用过度(to use something too much)

【例】Students tend to *overuse* certain words.

deplete [dɪˈpliːt] *vt.* 耗竭,使衰竭(to use up, reduce, exhaust)

【例】Our supplies of food are rather *depleted*.

depletion [dɪˈpliːʃn] *n.* 耗尽,弄空;【医】减液,放血

expenditure [ɪkˈspendɪtʃər] *n.* 开销,花费;(时间、精力等)耗费

【例】The new regulations will require unnecessary *expenditure* of time and money.

deploy [dɪˈplɔɪ] *v.*【军】展开,调度,部署

【例】The commander *deployed* his men along the railway.

【派】deployment(*n.* 部署,调度)

阻　碍

balk [bɔːk] *vt.* 阻碍,使受挫折(block, hinder, stall) *vi.*畏缩不前

【例】His plan was *balked*.

bar [bɑːr] *v.* 阻挡,拦住(block, hold back, obstruct);闩上

【例】A locked gate *barred* my entrance to the wood.

blockade [blɑːˈkeɪd] *n./v.* 封锁

check [tʃek] *v.* 阻止,抑制(restrain, stop)

【例】Raising interest rate is commonly used as a tool to *check* inflation.

curb [kɜːrb] *vt.* 抑制(check, control)

【例】In the 1970's, many governments' efforts to *curb* inflation were unsuccessful.

deter [dɪˈtɜːr] *v.* 制止,阻止(to discourage, hinder, prevent, prohibit)

【例】Don't let failure *deter* you.

【派】deterrent(*n.* 制止物) deterrence(*n.* 威慑;制止)

drawback ['drɔːbæk] *n.* 缺点（defect, flaw）；不利条件，障碍（disadvantage, obstacle）

【例】Everything has its *drawback*.

forestall [fɔːr'stɔːl] *v.* 先发制人，预先阻止（prevent, preempt）

【例】Bill *forestalled* a major crisis by taking care of small problems before they became worse.

hamper ['hæmpər] *vt.* 妨碍（hinder, impede）

【例】The fierce storm *hampered* our efforts to get to town by sunset.

handicap ['hændikæp] *vt.* 妨碍（hamper, impede, obstruct）；使不利 *n.* 障碍；（生理或智力上）缺陷，残疾

【例】A sore throat *handicapped* the singer.

hinder ['hɪndər] *vt.* 妨碍（hamper, impede, retard）

【例】The tall fence *hindered* the children from going to the lake.

impede [ɪm'piːd] *vt.* 阻碍，妨碍（hinder, obstruct）

【例】He was *impeded* in his work.

impediment [ɪm'pedɪmənt] *n.* 妨碍，阻碍物

stunt [stʌnt] *vt.* 阻碍（hinder, impede）

【例】The barren environment *stunt* the tree from developing into a big one.

进 攻

beset [bɪ'set] *vt.* 包围（besiege, surround）

【例】The small town was *beset* by enemy troops.

besiege [bɪ'siːdʒ] *v.* 围攻，困扰（enclose）

【记】be + siege（围攻）→ 围攻

【例】The speaker was *besieged* with questions.

charge [tʃɑːrdʒ] *v.* 猛攻（attack）

【例】Our soldiers *charged* the enemy.

incursion [ɪn'kɜːrʒn] *n.* 侵犯，入侵（a sudden invasion, attack, or raid）

【例】Enemy forces have made *incursions* into our territory.

infringe [ɪn'frɪndʒ] *vt.* 侵犯（encroach, intrude）；违反

【例】Your book *infringes* my copyright.

【派】infringement（*n.* 违反，侵犯）

interloper ['ɪntərloʊpər] *n.* 闯入者（someone who enters a place or group where they should not be）；干涉他人事务者

intrusion [ɪn'truːʒn] *n.* 闯入，侵入，打扰（when something happens that affects your private life or activities in an unwanted way）

【例】I resented this *intrusion* into my domestic affairs.

conquer ['kɑːŋkər] *vt.* 征服，克服（to overcome, defeat）

【例】I *conquered* my dislike for mathematics.

【派】conquest(*n.* 征服，克服)

capture ['kæptʃər] *v.* 俘获，占领（to take prisoner or gain control over）

【例】They *captured* this place two days ago.

captivity [kæp'tɪvəti] *n.* 监禁，被俘，束缚（the condition of being captive, imprisonment）

【派】captive(*adj.* 被俘的 *n.* 俘房)

retaliate [rɪ'tælieɪt] *vi.* 报复；反击（revenge; hit back）

【例】The British government *retaliated* by breaking off diplomatic relations.

【派】retaliation(*n.* 报复)

反　叛

betray [bɪ'treɪ] *v.* 背叛；泄漏

【记】be + tray(盘子) → 和盘托出 → 背叛

【例】The soldier *betrayed* his country and gave top secret to the enemy.

【派】betrayal(*n.* 背叛，出卖)

reverse [rɪ'vɜːrs] *vt.* 推翻；（使）反转（change to the opposite）

【例】The decision was *reversed* on appeal.

【派】reversal(*n.* 颠倒)

reversible [rɪ'vɜːrsəbl] *adj.* 可逆的（can change back）；可医治的；（衣）可两面穿的

【例】A lot of chemical reactions are *reversible*.

【派】reversibly(*adv.* 可逆地)

反　对

contradict [ˌkɑːntrə'dɪkt] *vt.* 反驳；抵触（counteract, oppose）

【记】contra(相反) + dic(言) + t → 相反之言 → 反驳

【例】I hate to *contradict* your statement, but there are many snakes in Australia.

【派】contradiction（*n.* 矛盾；否认；反驳）contradictory（*adj.* 矛盾的，抵触的）

demur [dɪˈmɜːr] *v.* 表示异议，反对（to protest, object）；迟疑，犹豫（to show reluctance）*n.* 反对，异议

【例】The workers *demur* at working on Sundays.

deprecate [ˈdeprəkeɪt] *vt.* 不赞成，反对（to disapprove, protest against）

【例】The peace-loving people *deprecate* war.

dissent [dɪˈsent] *v.* 持异议，不同意（to disagree）*n.* 意见的分歧

dissident [ˈdɪsɪdənt] *n.* 持异议者（dissenter, objector）

objection [əbˈdʒekʃn] *n.* 反对，异议（opposing or disapproving）；厌恶

【例】Normally he would have no *objection* to the whole world knowing his business.

opposition [ˌɑːpəˈzɪʃn] *n.* (强烈的)反对，对抗（strong disagreement with, or protest against something）；对手；[O-]反对党

【例】There was a great deal of *opposition* to the war.

rebut [rɪˈbʌt] *vt.* 反驳（refute）；驳回；击退

【例】He attempts to *rebut* the assertion made by the prosecution witness.

【派】rebuttal（*n.* 反驳）

refute [rɪˈfjuːt] *vt.* 驳斥，反驳，驳倒（disprove, rebut）

【记】re(反) + fute=fuse(流) → 反流 → 反驳

【例】I *refuted* him easily.

boycott [ˈbɔɪkɑːt] *n./v.* 抵制，拒绝参加（refuse to buy or take part as way of protesting）

【例】We *boycott* all products tested on animals.

confront [kənˈfrʌnt] *vt.* 面对（to face）

【例】A soldier has to *confront* danger.

【派】confrontation（*n.* 面对，对峙；对抗的事物）

resist [rɪˈzɪst] *v.* 抵抗（oppose）

【记】re(始终) + sist(坐) → 始终以静坐抵抗 → 抵抗

【例】They found a bacterium that *resisted* the antibiotic.

【派】resistance（*n.* 抵抗）

迷　惑

captivate [ˈkæptɪveɪt] *vt.* 迷惑(attract, fascinate, enamour)

　【例】The entertaining game *captivated* the children.

confuse [kənˈfjuːz] *vt.* 混淆; 把…弄糊涂(befuddle, perplex, bewilder)

　【例】His sudden change in mood completely *confused* her.

　【派】confused(*adj.* 糊涂的, 不清楚的) confusion(*n.* 困惑; 混淆)

delude [dɪˈluːd] *vt.* 欺骗, 迷惑(beguile, deceive, hoax)

　【记】de(坏) + lude(玩) → 使坏 → 欺骗

　【例】That playboy often *deludes* his girl with empty promises.

　【派】delusive(*adj.* 迷惑的, 欺骗性的) delusion(*n.* 欺骗; 错觉)

disorient [dɪsˈɔːrient] *vt.* 使迷失方位; 使迷惑(to confuse)

　【例】When he emerged into the street, he was completely *disoriented*.

stray [streɪ] *adj.* 漂泊的(wandering, random); 走失的

　【例】The *stray* dog was picked up by the dogcatcher because he had
no collar.

隐　藏

connote [kəˈnoʊt] *vt.* 隐含, 暗示(to imply or suggest)

　【例】The car's name is meant to *connote* luxury and quality.

　【派】connotation(*n.* 隐含意义)

camouflage [ˈkæməflɑːʒ] *n./v.* 伪装; 隐藏, 掩盖

　【例】I saw a truck, heavily *camouflaged* with netting and branches.

conceal [kənˈsiːl] *vt.* 把…隐藏起来(disguise, hide)

　【例】The criminal *concealed* the knife in his boot.

disguise [dɪsˈɡaɪz] *vt.* 假扮, 伪装(feign); 掩盖(cover, hide) *n.* 伪装

　【例】She *disguised* herself as a man, but she couldn't *disguise* her
voice.

练 习 题

连线题

identification	归因于	capture	可逆的
criterion	身份证明	incursion	欺骗
endowment	天赋	intrusion	迷惑
subscribe	封锁	reversible	闯入
extricate	订阅	demur	反对
attribute	标准	deprecate	俘获
depletion	救出	dissident	反驳
expenditure	阻碍物	rebut	伪装
feasible	耗尽	camouflage	隐含
balk	切实可行的	connote	不赞成
blockade	开销	captivate	伪装
forestall	阻碍	disguise	持异议者
impediment	先发制人	delude	侵犯

选词填空

underestimate	infringe	evaluate	conceal	facilitate
hamper	besiege	refute	retaliate	utilize

1. You should be able to _____ your own work.
2. Never _____ the power of the press.
3. Computers can be used to _____ language learning.
4. We must consider how best to _____ what resources we have.
5. She tried to run, but was _____ by her heavy suitcase.
6. Miller was _____ by press photographers.
7. A backup copy of a computer program does not _____ copyright.
8. The army began to _____ against the civilian population.
9. He _____ any allegations of malpractice.
10. She tried to _____ the fact that she was pregnant.

练习题答案

连线题答案

identification	身份证明	capture	俘获
criterion	标准	incursion	侵犯
endowment	天赋	intrusion	闯入
subscribe	订阅	reversible	可逆的
extricate	救出	demur	反对
attribute	归因于	deprecate	不赞成
depletion	耗尽	dissident	持异议者
expenditure	开销	rebut	反驳
feasible	切实可行的	camouflage	伪装
balk	阻碍	connote	隐含
blockade	封锁	captivate	迷惑
forestall	先发制人	disguise	伪装
impediment	阻碍物	delude	欺骗

选词填空答案

underestimate	infringe	evaluate	conceal	facilitate
hamper	besiege	refute	retaliate	utilize

1. You should be able to（evaluate）your own work.
2. Never（underestimate）the power of the press.
3. Computers can be used to（facilitate）language learning.
4. We must consider how best to（utilize）what resources we have.
5. She tried to run, but was（hampered）by her heavy suitcase.
6. Miller was（besieged）by press photographers.
7. A backup copy of a computer program does not（infringe）copyright.
8. The army began to（retaliate）against the civilian population.
9. He（refuted）any allegations of malpractice.
10. She tried to（conceal）the fact that she was pregnant.

Word List 32

音频

涉他行为(三)

涉他行为（三）

约　束

bind [baɪnd] v. 捆绑（to en circle or enclose with a band）；约束（restrict）；装订（书本）

【例】Such a slogan will *bind* our hand and foot.

binding ['baɪndɪŋ] adj. 有约束力的（restrictive, causing hindrance）n.（书籍）封面；捆绑，束缚

【例】The contract was not signed and has no *binding* force.

bound [baʊnd] adj. 被束缚的；必定的，一定的

【例】The employees are not *bound* to keep working at the factory after work.

boundary ['baʊndri] n. 边界（border, limit）

【例】A fence marked the *boundary* of the woods.

conditional [kən'dɪʃənl] adj. 有条件的（depending on other factors）；受制约的

【例】His agreement to buy our house was *conditional* on our leaving all the furniture in it.

manipulate [mə'nɪpjuleɪt] vt. 操作（handle, operate）；操纵

【例】Bob *manipulates* his friends to get what he wants.

【派】manipulative（adj. 对他人操控的）

liberalize ['lɪbrəlaɪz] vt. 使自由化（make a system, laws, or moral attitudes less strict）

【派】liberalization（n. 自由主义化）liberalized（adj. 自由的）

保　护

conserve [kən'sɜːrv] vt. 保存，贮藏（preserve, store, retain）

【例】Turning off the lights as you leave a room *conserves* energy.

protégé ['proʊtəʒeɪ] n. 被保护人，门徒（pupil）

【例】She attempted to encourage her young *protégé*.

shield [ʃiːld] *n.* 盾，庇护物 *vt.* 庇护，保护（protect）

【例】He *shielded* me by claiming that he broke the window.

shelter [ˈʃeltər] *n.* 隐蔽处，躲避处（常用来指住处）（place of protection）；庇护

合　作

coexist [ˌkoʊɪɡˈzɪst] *v.* 共存

【记】co（联合，共同）+ exist → 共存

【例】Great wealth *coexists* with extreme poverty in this country.

【派】coexistence（*n.* 共存）

collaborate [kəˈlæbəreɪt] *vi.* 合作（cooperate, work together）

【记】col（共同）+ labor（劳动）+ ate → 共同劳动 → 合作

【例】The prisoners *collaborated* to plan the escape.

cooperative [koʊˈɑːpərətɪv] *adj.* 合作的（willing to cooperate）*n.* 合作社，联合体

【例】The workmen are very *cooperative*, so the work goes on smoothly.

interdependence [ˌɪntərdɪˈpendəns] *n.* 相互依赖（a situation in which people or things depend on each other）

【例】the *interdependence* of our body's immune and nervous systems

interplay [ˈɪntərˌpleɪ] *n.* 相互作用（the way in which two people or things affect each other）

【例】the *interplay* between military and civilian populations

interrelate [ˌɪntərɪˈleɪt] *v.* 相互关联

【例】We will be discussing how the interests of state, parent and child *interrelate*.

【派】interrelated（*adj.* 相互关联的）

reciprocal [rɪˈsɪprəkl] *adj.* 相互的（mutual, exchanged）；交往的

【例】The treaty should be signed on the basis of *reciprocal* benefits.

【派】reciprocally（*adv.* 相互地）

drudgery [ˈdrʌdʒəri] *n.* 苦差事，苦工（hard, menial, and monotonous work）

信 任

credence ['kriːdns] *n.* 相信 (the acceptance of something as true)

【例】I don't give any *credence* to these rumors.

credible ['kredəbl] *adj.* 可信的，可靠的 (believable, plausible)

【例】He was unable to give a *credible* explanation for his behavior.

credit ['kredɪt] *n.* 信誉 (trust, credence)；学分

【例】I could not get a loan from the bank because my *credit* was bad.

creed [kriːd] *n.* 信仰，信条 (belief, faith)

【例】The newspaper prints its *creed* on the front page every day.

reliable [rɪ'laɪəbl] *adj.* 可靠的，可依赖的 (dependable)

【例】The subway is the most *reliable* way of getting to the airport during rush hours.

【派】reliably (*adv.* 可靠地)

reliance [rɪ'laɪəns] *n.* 依靠，依赖 (dependence)；信任

【例】the country's *reliance* on imported oil

贬 低

despise [dɪ'spaɪz] *vt.* 轻视，蔑视 (belittle, disdain, contemn)

【记】de (坏) + spi (看) + se → 用坏的眼光看 → 蔑视

【例】Mary *despised* her rude and unschooled neighbors.

disparage [dɪ'spærɪdʒ] *vt.* 毁谤；轻视 (denigrate; depreciate)

【记】dis + par (平等) + age → 不平等 → 轻视

【例】Before you *disparage* this idea, give us a better one.

【派】disparaging (*adj.* 贬抑的，轻蔑的)

debase [dɪ'beɪs] *v.* 降低；贬低 (degrade, discredit)；降低 (硬币的) 价值

【例】Such unkind action *debases* you.

depreciate [dɪ'priːʃieɪt] *v.* 贬值，跌价 (to reduce or decline in value or price)；贬低，轻视

【例】The car value will *depreciate* by 2,000 dollars in the first year.

【派】depreciation (*n.* 贬值；轻视)

descend [dɪ'send] v. 下来，降落(to fall, drop)；传下，遗传

【例】They *descended* the slope towards the town.

【派】descendant(n.子孙，后裔)

破 坏

decimate ['desɪmeɪt] vt. (较大程度地)杀死或毁灭(to destroy or kill a large proportion of)

【例】The population has been *decimated* by disease.

devastate ['devəsteɪt] vt. 使荒废；破坏(destroy, demolish)

【记】de + vast(大量) + ate → 大量弄坏 → 破坏

【例】Hurricanes often *devastate* the coffee crop.

【派】devastating(adj. 毁灭性的) devastation(n. 毁坏)

dismantle [dɪs'mæntl] vt. 脱掉…的衣服；拆除…的设备；拆开，摧毁

【记】dis(分离) + mantle(覆盖物，斗篷) → 拆开

【例】Chris *dismantled* the bike in five minutes.

spoil [spɔɪl] vt. 损坏，糟蹋(decay, ruin, rot, go bad)；宠坏

【例】Mary *spoiled* her children with expensive toys.

【派】spoiled(adj. 被宠坏的)

spoilage ['spɔɪlɪdʒ] n. (食品等的)腐败，损坏(waste)

tatter ['tætər] n. 碎步；[-s]破衣服 v. (使)破烂(break, tear)

【例】I was shocked to see him in *tatters*.

undermine [ˌʌndər'maɪn] vt. 暗中破坏，逐渐削弱(gradually weaken)

【例】The constant criticism was beginning to *undermine* her confidence.

violate ['vaɪəleɪt] vt. 违背(disobey)；侵犯；妨碍

【例】34 protesters were arrested for *violating* criminal law.

【派】violation(n. 违背；侵害) violator(n. 违反者)

sabotage ['sæbətɑːʒ] n. 阴谋破坏，颠覆活动 (deliberately spoil plans, events)

topple ['tɑːpl] vt. 倾覆，推倒

【例】This scandal could *topple* the government.

说　明

decipher ［dɪˈsaɪfər］ vt. 破译(密码)，辨认(潦草字迹)

【例】She studied the envelope, trying to *decipher* the handwriting.

【派】decipherable(*adj.* 可破译的，可辨认的)

demonstrable ［dɪˈmɑːnstrəbl］ *adj.* 可论证的，可表明的(able to be demonstrated or proved)

denote ［dɪˈnoʊt］ vt. 指示，表示(indicate, show)

【记】de(加强) + note(注意) → 加强注意 → 指示

【例】The mark"∧"*denotes* a place of omission.

exemplify ［ɪɡˈzemplɪfaɪ］ vt. 例证，例示(illustrate)

【例】Your diligence *exemplifies* the characteristics of a good employee.

explicate ［ˈeksplɪkeɪt］ vt. 解释(to explain in detail)

【例】It is essentially a simple notion, but *explicating* it is difficult.

【派】explication(*n.* 解释，说明)

expound ［ɪkˈspaʊnd］ vt. 解释(explain, interpret)

【例】The priest *expounded* his religion.

illustrate ［ˈɪləstreɪt］ vt. 给…加插图；说明(exemplify, explain)

【记】il(不断) + lustr(光明) + ate → 不断给光明 → 说明

【例】I *illustrated* my point about politics with examples from a book.

【派】illustration(*n.* 插图，图表；说明)

interpretive ［ɪnˈtɜːrprɪtɪv］ *adj.* 作为说明的，解释的(interpretative)

paraphrase ［ˈpærəfreɪz］ vt. 意译；改写(rewrite)

【记】para(旁边) + phrase(词句) → 在旁边用不同的词写 → 改写

【例】Would you please *paraphrase* the speech in colloquial English?

proclaim ［prəˈkleɪm］ vt. 宣布，声明(announce, declare)

【记】pro(前) + claim(喊) → 在前面大声喊 → 宣布

【例】The ringing bells *proclaimed* the news of the birth of the prince.

【派】proclamation(*n.* 宣布，声明)

prospectus ［prəˈspektəs］ *n.* 计划书，发起书，说明书，简介

unravel ［ʌnˈrævl］ vt. 阐明，阐释，澄清(explain, resolve)

【例】Detectives are still trying to *unravel* the mystery surrounding his death.

verify ［ˈverɪfaɪ］ vt. 验证(confirm, substantiate)

【例】Your signature here will *verify* that you understand the terms of the agreement.

【派】verification(*n.* 证实) verifiable(*adj.* 能证实的) verifiability(*n.* 可证实性)

工 作

designate [ˈdezɪɡneɪt] *vt.* 指定，指派(assign, nominate, specify)
【例】The team *designated* Sally as the captain.
【派】*designation* (*n.* 指派)

endeavor [ɪnˈdevər] *vi.* 努力(strive, struggle, try) *n.* 尽力，努力
【例】Tom *endeavored* to get better grades in college.

preside [prɪˈzaɪd] *vi.* 主持(会议等)；担任(会议)主席(be in charge of)；主管；领导

【例】The government seemed to be *presiding* over large-scale unemployment.

pragmatic [præɡˈmætɪk] *adj.* 务实的，实事求是的(dealing with problems in a sensible, practical way)
【例】Williams took a more *pragmatic* approach to management problems.
【派】pragmatically(*adv.* 实用地)

discharge [dɪsˈtʃɑːrdʒ] *v.* 放出，释放(let out, release, liberate)
【例】The patient was *discharged* from the hospital after complete recovery.

dismissal [dɪsˈmɪsl] *n.* 解雇，免职，开除(discharge from employment or service)

impeach [ɪmˈpiːtʃ] *vt.* 弹劾；控告(accuse)
【记】im(进入) + peach(告发) → 控告
【例】The Congress has the right to *impeach* a President.
【派】impeachment(*n.* 弹劾)

分 散

diffuse [dɪˈfjuːz] *vt.* 传播，扩散(scatter, spread)
【记】di(分开) + f + fuse(流) → 分流 → 传播
【例】The winds *diffused* the smoke throughout the neighborhood.

disperse [dɪˈspɜːrs] *v.* 使…散开，分散；传播(distribute, spread, disseminate)
【例】After school the children *dispersed* to their homes.

disseminate [dɪ'semɪneɪt] *vt.* 散布(disperse, distribute, spread), 传播

【记】dis + semin(种子) + ate → 散布(种子)

【例】The Public Relations Department *disseminates* information.

【派】dissemination(*n.* 分发, 散布)

diffusive [dɪ'fjuːsɪv] *adj.* 散布性的, 扩及的(spreading, scattering)

【派】diffusion(*n.* 扩散, 散布)

distribution [ˌdɪstrɪ'bjuːʃn] *n.* 分发, 分配; 散布, 分布

dilute [daɪ'luːt] *vt.* 稀释, 冲淡(thin, weaken)

【记】di(分开) + lute(冲) → 冲开 → 冲淡

【例】As the ice melted, it *diluted* my drink.

【派】dilution(*n.* 稀释)

dissolve [dɪ'zɑːlv] *v.* 溶解; 结束

【例】Water *dissolves* salt as heat *dissolves* ice.

【派】dissolution(*n.* 溶解; 解散; 消亡)

dissipate ['dɪsɪpeɪt] *v.* 驱散(dispel); 消失(disappear); 浪费(waste)

【例】The crowd *dissipated*.

evacuate [ɪ'vækjueɪt] *vt.* 疏散

【记】e + vacu(空) + ate → 使空 → 疏散

【例】The Civil Defense *evacuated* all inhabitants from the area where the storm was predicted to strike.

【派】evacuation(*n.* 撤退, 疏散)

You never know what you can do till you try.

除非你亲自尝试一下, 否则你永远不知道你能够做什么。

——英国小说家 马里亚特(*Frederick Marryat, British novelist*)

练 习 题

连线题

binding	庇护	decipher	解雇
liberalize	相互的	exemplify	阐明
shield	使自由化	interpretive	散布
protégé	依靠	prospectus	指定
drudgery	阴谋破坏	designation	破译
reciprocal	苦工	dismissal	例证
credence	降落	impeach	传播
reliance	门徒	diffuse	计划书
depreciate	倾覆	disseminate	解释的
descend	有约束力的	dilute	稀释
sabotage	贬值	evacuate	例证
decimate	相信	spoilage	弹劾
topple	杀死	unravel	疏散

选词填空

impeach	illustrate	proclaim	disparage	collaborate
manipulate	endeavor	interrelate	dismantle	conserve

1. He was one of those men who _____ people.
2. We must _____ our woodlands for future generations.
3. The two nations are _____ on several satellite projects.
4. Each part of the course_____ with all the others.
5. Matcham's theatres were widely _____ by architects.
6. They held an election to _____ the existing tax legislation.
7. She _____ her discussion with diagrams.
8. Protesters _____ that the girl was innocent.
9. The governor was _____ for using state funds improperly.
10. We always _____ to please our customers.

练习题答案

连线题答案

binding	有约束力的	decipher	破译
liberalize	使自由化	exemplify	例证
shield	庇护	interpretive	解释的
protégé	门徒	prospectus	计划书
drudgery	苦工	designation	指定
reciprocal	相互的	dismissal	解雇
credence	相信	impeach	弹劾
reliance	依靠	diffuse	传播
depreciate	贬值	disseminate	散布
descend	降落	dilute	稀释
sabotage	阴谋破坏	evacuate	疏散
decimate	杀死	spoilage	腐败
topple	倾覆	unravel	阐明

选词填空答案

impeach	illustrate	proclaim	disparage	collaborate
manipulate	endeavor	interrelate	dismantle	conserve

1. He was one of those men who (manipulated) people.
2. We must (conserve) our woodlands for future generations.
3. The two nations are (collaborating) on several satellite projects.
4. Each part of the course (interrelates) with all the others.
5. Matcham's theatres were widely (disparaged) by architects.
6. They held an election to (dismantle) the existing tax legislation.
7. She (illustrated) her discussion with diagrams.
8. Protesters (proclaimed) that the girl was innocent.
9. The governor was (impeached) for using state funds improperly.
10. We always (endeavor) to please our customers.

Word List 33

音频

涉他行为（四）

涉他行为（四）

驱　逐

dislodge [dɪsˈlɑːdʒ] *v.* 从…逐出，把…取出（to remove, displace）
【例】The coughing *dislodged* the fishbone from his throat.

evict [ɪˈvɪkt] *v.* （依法）驱逐
【例】If you don't pay your rent, you'll be *evicted*.

exile [ˈeksaɪl] *vt.* 流放（banish, deport）*n.* 放逐；被放逐者
【例】The king was *exiled* when his empire was taken over.

exorcism [ˈeksɔːrsɪzəm] *n.* 驱邪，伏魔，驱邪所用的咒语

expulsion [ɪkˈspʌlʃn] *n.* 喷出，排出；驱逐，开除
【例】the *expulsion* of sb. from school

oust [aʊst] *vt.* 驱逐（dismiss, throw out）
【例】He was *ousted* from his position as chairman.

repel [rɪˈpel] *vt.* 排斥（resist, reject）；击退
【记】re(反) + pel(推) → 排斥
【例】The soldiers *repelled* the enemy.

清　除

collapse [kəˈlæps] *n./v.* 倒塌，崩溃（crash）
【记】col(共同) + lapse(滑下) → 全都滑下来了 → 倒塌
【例】The *collapse* of the stock market in 1929 signaled the beginning of the Depression.

eliminate [ɪˈlɪmɪneɪt] *vt.* 消灭，排除（to exclude, get rid of）
【例】She went through the typescript carefully to *eliminate* all errors from it.
【派】elimination(*n.* 排除，除去)

eradicate [ɪˈrædɪkeɪt] *vt.* 根除（eliminate, get rid of, remove）
【例】One of the major goals of the government is to *eradicate* poverty in poor areas of China.

herbicide [ˈhɜːrbɪsaɪd] *n.* 灭草剂
【记】herb(草本植物) + icide(除去) → 灭草剂

revoke [rɪ'voʊk] *vt.* 取消，撤回；撤销（cancel, repeal）

【记】re(反)+voke(喊)→喊反话→取消

【例】The drunk driver had his driving licence *revoked*.

【派】revokable(*adj.* 可撤销的)

xenophobia [ˌzenə'foʊbiə] *n.* 仇外，排外（strong dislike people of other nations）

【派】xenophobic(*adj.* 恐外的)

穿　透

embed [ɪm'bed] *vt.* 把…嵌入，埋入（to put something firmly and deeply into something else）

【记】em(使入)+bed(床)→放入床里→把…嵌入

【例】Feelings of guilt are deeply *embedded* in her personality.

engrave [ɪn'greɪv] *vt.* 雕上，刻上(to carve)；深深印在(记忆或头脑中)

【例】This episode remains sharply *engraved* on my mind.

insertion [ɪn'sɜːrʃn] *n.* 插入（物）(the act of putting something inside something else)

penetrate ['penətreɪt] *vt.* 刺穿，进入(pierce)

【记】pen(全部)+etr(进入)+ate→进入

【例】The knife *penetrated* her finger and made it bleed.

【派】penetration(*n.* 穿透)

permeate ['pɜːrmieɪt] *vt.* 渗透，透过(penetrate, pervade)

【记】per(全部)+mea(通过)+te→渗透

【例】Nasty water from the flood *permeated* our carpeting.

stab [stæb] *n./v.* 刺，戳(jab, injure)

【例】He *stabbed* the woman with a knife and she died.

extract [ɪk'strækt] *vt.* 取出，榨取(remove) ['ekstrækt] *n.* 摘录；提炼物

【例】The research team undertakes the responsibility to *extract* samples from the sediments.

extraction [ɪk'strækʃn] *n.* 取出，拔出；拔牙；血统，家世

【例】The protesters are opposed to the *extraction* of minerals in the area.

incisive [ɪnˈsaɪsɪv] *adj.* 深刻的，一针见血的(profound)

【例】This is an *incisive* critique of American politics.

shatter [ˈʃætər] *n.* 碎片(fragment) *v.* 粉碎(break)

【例】The explosion *shattered* every window in the house.

包　围

encase [ɪnˈkeɪs] *vt.* 把…放入盒内，把…装箱；围住，包起

【例】His broken leg was *encased* in plaster.

enclose [ɪnˈkloʊz] *vt.* 把…围起来；把…装入信封，附上

【例】The wall *encloses* the hospital.

encompass [ɪnˈkʌmpəs] *vt.* 包围，环绕(to encircle, cover)；包含(to include)

【记】en + compass(包围) → 包围

【例】A thick fog *encompassed* the village.

entrench [ɪnˈtrentʃ] *vt.* 用壕沟围绕或保护；牢固地确立

【例】Television seems to be firmly *entrenched* as the number one medium for national advertising.

entrenched [ɪnˈtrentʃd] *adj.* 牢固确立的(strongly established and not likely to change)

【例】In the small towns racial prejudice was *entrenched*.

envelop [ɪnˈveləp] *vt.* 包围，包住(to cover or wrap)

【例】At sunset, darkness *enveloped* the town.

girdle [ˈgɜːrdl] *n.* 腰带(waistband)；环形物 *vt.* 围绕，包围(to enclose, surround)

inclusion [ɪnˈkluːʒn] *n.* 包括；内含物

mob [mɑːb] *n.* 暴徒 *vt.* 聚众包围

【例】Fans ran onto the pitch and *mobbed* the batsman.

【派】mobber(*n.* 欺负者)

occupy [ˈɑːkjupaɪ] *v.* 使从事；占领，战胜；占用(control by force; fill time, space)

【例】Football *occupies* most of my leisure time.

要　求

entail ［ɪnˈteɪl］ *vt.* 使…成为必要 (to require)
【例】The task *entailed* strict attention to procedure.

premise ［ˈpremɪs］ *vt.* 提出前提 *n.* 前提 (assumption, hypothesis)
【例】We must act on the *premise* that the worst can happen.

prerequisite ［ˌpriːˈrekwəzɪt］ *n.* 先决条件, 前提 (precondition)
【例】A reasonable proficiency in English is a *prerequisite* for the course.

requisite ［ˈrekwɪzɪt］ *adj.* 必要的, 必不可少的 (necessary, required)
【例】He lacks the *requisite* qualifications.

stipulate ［ˈstɪpjuleɪt］ *vt.* 约定, 规定 (set, specify)
【例】The workers' contract *stipulated* that they couldn't smoke on the job.
【派】stipulation (*n.* 规定)

切　割

excise ［ɪkˈsaɪz］ *vt.* 切除, 删去 (to remove, cut out)
【例】The tumor was *excised*.

intercept ［ˌɪntərˈsept］ *vt.* 中途拦截; 阻止 (hold back, stop)
【记】inter (中间) + cept (拿) → 中途拦截
【例】John threw the football to Susan, but Bob *intercepted* it.

intersect ［ˌɪntərˈsekt］ *vi.* 相交 (cross, meet)
【记】inter (中间) + sect (切, 割) → 从中间相切 → 相交
【例】These two fences *intersect* at the creek.
【派】intersection (*n.* 交叉, 十字路口)

severance ［ˈsevərəns］ *n.* 切断, 断绝, 割断 (end)
【例】the *severance* of diplomatic ties between the two countries

缠　绕

afoul [ə'faʊl] *adv.* 纠缠着；(与法律、规章等)相抵触，有冲突

implicate ['ɪmplɪkeɪt] *vt.* 牵连(involve)
【例】The mayor was *implicated* in the murder.

implication [ˌɪmplɪ'keɪʃn] *n.* 牵连(involvement)；暗示(implying)
【例】We heard of his *implication* in a conspiracy.

tangle ['tæŋgl] *vt.* 使缠结，使纠缠(knot, snarl)
【例】Her hair got all *tangled* up in the fence.

称　赞

laudable ['lɔːdəbl] *adj.* 值得赞美的(praiseworthy, commendable)
【例】a *laudable* attempt

laudatory ['lɔːdətɔːri] *adj.* 赞扬的，表扬的(expressing praise)
【例】a *laudatory* biography

tout [taʊt] *vt.* 极力赞扬(praise)
【例】Nell is being *touted* as the next big thing in Hollywood.

观　察

inspection [ɪn'spekʃn] *n.* 检查，视察(official visits to check that everything is satisfactory and that rules are being obeyed)；检验；检阅
【例】An *inspection* was carried out at the school.

observation [ˌɑːbzər'veɪʃn] *n.* 观察(watching something or someone carefully)
【派】observe(*v.* 观察，看)

perceive [pər'siːv] *vt.* 察觉到，看见(discern, see)
【记】per(全部) + ceive(拿到) → 察觉到
【例】The world we *perceived* is only a small part of the real world.

perceptive [pər'septɪv] *adj.* 感觉敏锐的，观察入微的(discerning, penetrating)
【记】per(全部) + cept(知道) + ive → 全都知道 → 感觉敏锐的
【例】A *perceptive* scholar questioned the professor's theory.
【派】perception(*n.* 察觉，发觉)

scan [skæn] *vt.* 浏览，扫描（browse）

【例】They *scanned* the picture and stored it on the disk.

screen [skriːn] *vt.* 筛选，审查（check）

【例】You can use an answerphone to *screen* your phone calls before you answer them.

scrutinize ['skruːtənaɪz] *vt.* 细察（examine, inspect）

【记】scrutin(检查) + ize → 细察

【例】The lawyer had *scrutinized* all the documents related to this case.

【派】scrutiny(*n.* 细看)

surveillance [sɜːr'veɪləns] *n.* 盯梢，监视（watch, inspect）

【例】24-hour *surveillance* of the building

镇　压

persecute ['pɜːrsɪkjuːt] *vt.* 迫害，烦扰（to treat someone cruelly or unfairly over a period of time）

【例】The Puritans left England to escape being *persecuted*.

【派】persecution(*n.* 迫害) persecutor(*n.* 迫害者) persecuted(*adj.* 被迫害的)

repress [rɪ'pres] *vt.* 抑制，约束（stop, suppress）；镇压

【例】Brenda *repressed* the urge to shout at him.

【派】repression(*n.* 压抑)

suppress [sə'pres] *vt.* 镇压，压制，抑制（stop from opposing）

【例】The police were accused of *suppressing* evidence.

【派】suppressant(*n.* 抑制物)

支　持

patron ['peɪtrən] *n.* 赞助者（someone who supports the activities of an organization, for example by giving money）

【例】a wealthy *patron*

patronage ['peɪtrənɪdʒ] *n.* 赞助，资助

【记】patron(赞助人) + age → 赞助

patronize ['peɪtrənaɪz] *vt.* 保护；支援；惠顾

【派】patronizing(*adj.* 要人领情的)

proponent [prə'poʊnənt] *n.* 支持者，建议者（supporter, advocator）

【例】Steinem has always been a strong *proponent* of women's rights.

prop [prɑːp] *n./vt.* 支持(support, mainstay)

【例】Her daughter was the only *prop* to the old lady during her illness.

protagonist [prə'tægənɪst] *n.* 提倡者, 支持者(supporter of a social or political idea)

【例】a *protagonist* of educational reform

responsive [rɪ'spɑːnsɪv] *adj.* 反应热烈的；赞同的；支持的(reacting positively)

【例】We try to be *responsive* to the needs of the customer.

【派】responsively(*adv.* 相应地) responsiveness(*n.* 响应性)

sponsor ['spɑːnsər] *n.* 赞助人, 主顾 *vt.* 赞助, 惠顾(support by paying)

【例】The competition was *sponsored* by British Airways.

supportive [sə'pɔːrtɪv] *adj.* 支持的；赞助的；鼓励的(encouraging)

【例】My family were very *supportive* throughout the divorce.

underpin [ˌʌndər'pɪn] *vt.* 在…下面加基础；[喻]巩固(strengthen)

【例】America's wealth is *underpinned* by a global system which exploits the world's poor.

【派】underpinning(*n.* 基础, 支柱)

保　留

withhold [wɪθ'hoʊld] *vt.* 扣留, 保留；拒绝给予(refuse)

【例】I *withheld* payment until they had completed the work.

preserve [prɪ'zɜːrv] *vt.* 保存(keep, save, maintain)

【记】pre(预先) + serve(保存) → 保存

【例】Max eats only good things hoping to *preserve* his health.

【派】preservation(*n.* 保存, 维护)

reservation [ˌrezər'veɪʃn] *n.* 预订(booking)；保留意见

【例】Customers are advised to make seat *reservations* well in advance.

retain [rɪ'teɪn] *vt.* 保留(hold, reserve, withhold, keep)

【例】We *retained* the original fireplace when we decorated the room.

练 习 题

连线题

dislodge	先决条件	intersect	纠缠着
exile	流放	afoul	相交
exorcism	驱邪	laudable	感觉敏锐的
expulsion	喷出	perceptive	细察
eradicate	包围	scrutinize	反应热烈的
xenophobia	切断	surveillance	深刻的
embed	把…嵌入	protagonist	提倡者
extraction	取出	responsive	值得赞美的
penetrate	刺穿	reservation	预订
encompass	必要的	herbicide	雕上
prerequisite	根除	engrave	盯梢
requisite	仇外	incisive	用壕沟围绕
severance	从…逐出	entrench	灭草剂

选词填空

persecute	repel	implicate	eliminate	sponsor
intercept	tout	stipulate	perceive	permeate

1. He knew he ought to eat, but his stomach _____.
2. The credit card _____ the need for cash or cheques.
3. Rain _____ through the ground to add to ground water levels.
4. Laws _____ the maximum interest rate that banks can charge.
5. Harker's phone calls had been _____.
6. Mary is _____ as the beauty of the year.
7. Three police officers are _____ in the cover-up.
8. Often what is _____ to be aggression is simply fear.
9. Like many celebrities, she complained of being _____ by the press.
10. The bank had offered to _____ him at university.

练习题答案

连线题答案

dislodge	从…逐出	intersect	相交
exile	流放	afoul	纠缠着
exorcism	驱邪	laudable	值得赞美的
expulsion	喷出	perceptive	感觉敏锐的
eradicate	根除	scrutinize	细察
xenophobia	仇外	surveillance	盯梢
embed	把…嵌入	protagonist	提倡者
extraction	取出	responsive	反应热烈的
penetrate	刺穿	reservation	预订
encompass	包围	herbicide	灭草剂
prerequisite	先决条件	engrave	雕上
requisite	必要的	incisive	深刻的
severance	切断	entrench	用壕沟围绕

选词填空答案

persecute	repel	implicate	eliminate	sponsor
intercept	tout	stipulate	perceive	permeate

1. He knew he ought to eat, but his stomach (repelled).
2. The credit card (eliminates) the need for cash or cheques.
3. Rain (permeates) through the ground to add to ground water levels.
4. Laws (stipulate) the maximum interest rate that banks can charge.
5. Harker's phone calls had been (intercepted).
6. Mary is (touted) as the beauty of the year.
7. Three police officers are (implicated) in the cover-up.
8. Often what is (perceived) to be aggression is simply fear.
9. Like many celebrities, she complained of being (persecuted) by the press.
10. The bank had offered to (sponsor) him at university.

Word List 34

音频

How do you handle
negative comments?

正向评价

正向评价

抱 负

ambition [æmˈbɪʃn] *n.* 抱负，雄心(strong desire for success, achievement, or distinction)
【派】ambitious(*adj.* 有抱负的，有野心的)

aspire [əˈspaɪər] *v.* 渴望，热望(crave, yearn)；抱负
【例】I *aspire* to being the president of a bank.
【派】aspiration(*n.* 渴望；抱负)

enterprise [ˈentərpraɪz] *n.* 事业，计划；事业心，进取心；公司，企业

热 情

ardent [ˈɑːrdnt] *adj.* 极热心的，热情的(passionate, enthusiastic, fervent, zealous)
【例】Jane's *ardent* admirer sent her flowers every day.

enthusiastic [ɪnˌθuːziˈæstɪk] *adj.* 极热心的，热情的(passionate, ardent, fervent, zealous)
【例】All the staff are *enthusiastic* about the project.

fanatic [fəˈnætɪk] *adj.* 狂热的；盲信的 *n.* 狂热者
【例】Alexander is a football *fanatic*.

fervent [ˈfɜːrvənt] *adj.* 炽烈的；热烈的(enthusiastic, ardent)
【记】ferv(热) + ent → 热烈的
【例】Jenny is a *fervent* supporter of the feminist movement.

慷 慨

bounty [ˈbaʊnti] *n.* 慷慨(generosity)；(政府提供的)奖金，赏金
【例】The government has placed a *bounty* on the heads of many of its opponents.
【派】bountiful(*adj.* 慷慨给予的；丰富的，充裕的)

charitable ['tʃærətəbl] *adj.* 慷慨的；慈善的(generous; benevolent)

【例】Because it was Susan's first offense, the judge was *charitable* and gave her probation.

charity ['tʃærəti] *n.* 宽厚，仁慈(benevolence)；慈善事业，救济，施舍

【例】The *charity*'s goal is to help people help themselves.

hospitable ['hɑːspɪtəbl] *adj.* 好客的(sociable, companionable)；(气候、环境)宜人的

【例】The local people were very kind and *hospitable*.

【派】hospitality(*n.* 殷勤好客)

谨　慎

conscientious [ˌkɑːnʃi'enʃəs] *adj.* 有责任心的；勤奋的(diligent)

【记】conscien(ce)(良心，道德心) + tious → 有责任心的

【例】She was a very *conscientious* student and attended all her lectures.

deliberate [dɪ'lɪbərət] *adj.* 深思熟虑的(carefully thought out in advance, planned)；故意的(intentional, purposive)

【记】de + liber(自由) + ate → 自由地行事 → 故意的

【例】It's a *deliberate* decision by the school board.

discretion [dɪ'skreʃn] *n.* 慎重(caution, prudence)

【例】The decorator showed no *discretion* in her purchases for our new house, everything costing too much money.

intent [ɪn'tent] *adj.* 专心的，专注的；意愿坚决的(to be determined to do something or achieve something) *n.* 意图，意向

【例】*Intent* upon her work, she didn't notice the time.

【派】intently(*adv.* 专心地，专注地)

meticulously [mə'tɪkjələsli] *adv.* 很仔细地(carefully, scrupulously)

【记】metic(害怕) + ulously → 害怕出错 → 很仔细地

【例】The editor kept on checking spelling mistakes *meticulously*.

modest ['mɑːdɪst] *adj.* 谦虚的(humble, unassuming)；适度的

【记】mod(方式) + est → 做事有规矩 → 谦虚的

【例】He was always *modest* about his role in the Everest expedition.

preoccupy [priˈɑːkjupaɪ] *vt.* 使专心于(concentrate on)

【例】The question of going to the Mount Tai *preoccupied* his mind.

【派】preoccupied(*adj.* 全神贯注的) preoccupation(*n.* 全神贯注)

prudent [ˈpruːdnt] *adj.* 谨慎的(cautious)

【记】prud(小心) + ent → 小心的 → 谨慎的

【例】It might be *prudent* to get a virus detector for the network.

【派】prudently(*adv.* 谨慎地)

prudery [ˈpruːdəri] *n.* 过分拘谨，装作正经(the behavior or attitude of people who are too easily shocked by things relating to sex)

scrupulous [ˈskruːpjələs] *adj.* 严谨的，讲究的(prudent, meticulous)

【例】The secretary is *scrupulous* about her dress.

【派】scrupulously(*adv.* 小心翼翼地)

vigilant [ˈvɪdʒɪlənt] *adj.* 警惕的，清醒的(watchful, alert)

【例】The President's *vigilant* bodyguard immediately noticed the man with a gun.

【派】vigilantly(*adv.* 警觉地) vigilance(*n.* 警觉)

visionary [ˈvɪʒəneri] *adj.* 梦幻的，想象的，不实际的(dreamlike, impractical)

【例】Under his *visionary* leadership, the city prospered.

quiescent [kwiˈesnt] *adj.* 静止的，沉寂的(still, quiet)；休眠的

美　丽

delicate [ˈdelɪkət] *adj.* 精巧的(dainty, elegant)；脆弱的(fragile)；微妙的(subtle)

esthetic [esˈθetɪk] *adj.* 审美的，美学的

【例】My *esthetic* standards are quite different from his.

florid [ˈflɑːrɪd] *adj.* 红润的(having a red or flushed complexion)；词藻华丽的

【例】The book is written in a very *florid* style.

【派】floridity(*n.* 艳丽；脸色好)

活　泼

animate [ˈænɪmeɪt] *vt.* 使兴奋，使活跃(to make lively, enliven)；激励(to encourage or inspire) [ˈænɪmət] *adj.* 有生命的(living, lively)

【例】Laughter *animated* his face for a moment.

【派】animation(*n.* 活跃，生气；卡通) animated(*adj.* 生气勃勃的；栩栩如生的)

dynamic [daɪ'næmɪk] *adj.* 动态的 (related to motion)；有活力的(active, energetic, lively)；不断变化的(changing)

【例】She is clearly a *dynamic* young woman with big ambitions.

lush [lʌʃ] *adj.* 草木茂盛的；多的；丰富豪华的

【例】The fields were *lush* with grass and flowers.

perk [pɜːrk] *v.* 昂首，意气洋洋；振作；活跃起来 (to become more cheerful, active, and interested in what is happening around you)

【例】She seemed kind of tired, but she *perked* up when Helen came over.

radiant ['reɪdiənt] *adj.* 绚丽的；容光焕发的(joyous, beaming)

【记】radi(光，线) + ant → 绚丽的

【例】Dozens of *radiant* candle flames lit the room.

reactive [ri'æktɪv] *adj.* 反应的；活泼的；反应灵敏的

【例】a *reactive* foreign policy

robust [roʊ'bʌst] *adj.* 强壮的(strong, sturdy)

【记】"乐百氏"的英文名称

【例】If you want to be healthy and *robust*, you need to exercise yourself routinely.

vigorous ['vɪɡərəs] *adj.* 朝气蓬勃的(dynamic)

【例】Mary stretched her muscles before an hour of *vigorous* exercise.

【派】vigorously(*adv.* 活泼地)

功　效

efficacious [ˌefɪ'keɪʃəs] *adj.* (药、措施等)有效的(effective)

【例】More *efficacious* treatments may soon be available.

efficacy ['efɪkəsi] *n.* 效力，效能(effectiveness)

efficiency [ɪ'fɪʃnsi] *n.* 效率，效能

operative ['ɑːpərətɪv] *adj.* (计划、法律等) 实施中的，起作用的(working and able to be used)

【例】the steps to be taken before the scheme can become *operative*

overwhelming [ˌoʊvər'welmɪŋ] *adj.* 势不可挡的，压倒性的 (very large or greater, more important, etc. than any other)；无法抗拒的

【例】An *overwhelming* majority of the members were against the idea.

【派】overwhelmingly(*adv.* 压倒性地)

telling ['telɪŋ] *adj.* 显著的(significant); 有效的; 生动的; 有力的

【例】a *telling* argument

【派】tellingly(*adv.* 显著地)

validate ['vælɪdeɪt] *vt.* 证实, 使有效(confirm)

【例】The Supreme Court has *validated* the lower court's interpretation of the law.

【派】validation(*n.* 确认; 批准)

valid ['vælɪd] *adj.* 有效的(soundly based)

【例】A traveler's passport is *valid* within 6 months.

【派】validity(*n.* 有效, 效力)

propitious [prə'pɪʃəs] *adj.* 吉祥的; 有利的 (likely to bring good results, favorable)

【例】Conditions after the 1905 Revolution were *propitious* for stable development.

futile ['fjuːtl] *adj.* 无益的; 徒劳的(useless; vain)

【例】It would be *futile* for you to explain it again. I just don't understand algebra.

【派】futility(*n.* 无益, 无用)

invalid [ɪn'vælɪd] *adj.* 无效的(void)

【记】in(不) + valid(有效的) → 无效的

【例】Without the right date stamped on it, your ticket will be *invalid*.

invalidate [ɪn'vælɪdeɪt] *vt.* 使作废(nullify)

null [nʌl] *adj.* 无效的(invalid, void)

【例】The contract was declared *null* and void.

优 秀

eminent ['emɪnənt] *adj.* 杰出的 (outstanding, distinguished)

【例】The *eminent* poet won numerous awards.

【派】eminence(*n.* 卓越, 著名)

exceptional [ɪk'sepʃənl] *adj.* 卓越的(extraordinary)

【例】The *exceptional* tennis player won the championship.

optimal ['ɑːptɪməl] *adj.* 最佳的，最理想的（the best or most suitable）

【例】time *optimal*

pre-eminent [prɪ'emɪnənt] *adj.* 卓越的（prominent, outstanding）

【记】pre（前）+ eminent（突出的）→ 向前突出 → 卓越的

【例】his *pre-eminent* position in society

【派】pre-eminently（*adv.* 卓越地）pre-eminency（*n.* 卓越）

preponderant [prɪ'pɑːndərənt] *adj.* 占优势的（main, most important or frequent）

【例】*preponderant* age

【派】preponderance（*n.* 压倒性优势）

prominent ['prɑːmɪnənt] *adj.* 卓越的；突出的（conspicuous, protruding）

【记】pro（前）+ minent（伸）→ 突出的

【例】The *prominent* politician made an appeal to end the war.

【派】prominently（*adv.* 显著地）

quintessential [ˌkwɪntɪ'senʃl] *adj.* 精华的；典型的（typical）

【例】"Guys and Dolls" is the *quintessential* American musical.

【派】quintessentially（*adv.* 精英地）

superb [suː'pɜːrb] *adj.* 上乘的，出色的（excellent）

【例】The food was *superb*.

【派】superbly（*adv.* 极好地）

prosper ['prɑːspər] *vi.* 繁荣，昌盛；成功（grow or develop successfully）

【例】Businesses across the state are *prospering*.

【派】prosperous（*adj.* 繁荣的）

prosperity [prɑː'sperəti] *n.* 繁荣（well-being）

【例】The *prosperity* of the society promises a rapid economic growth.

renowned [rɪ'naʊnd] *adj.* 知名的（acclaimed, distinguished, famous）

【记】re（重新）+ nown（名字）+ ed → 名字一再出现 → 知名的

【例】He's *renowned* as a brilliant speaker.

reputable ['repjətəbl] *adj.* 值得尊敬的，声誉好的（respected）

【例】If you have a burglar alarm fitted, make sure it is done by a *reputable* company.

reputation [ˌrepju'teɪʃn] *n.* 名气，名声（fame）

【例】In her last job she acquired a *reputation* as a troublemaker.

聪　颖

advisable [əd'vaɪzəbl] *adj.* 明智的，可取的(rational, sound)
【例】It is *advisable* to save part of your paycheck each month.

ingenious [ɪn'dʒiːniəs] *adj.* 机灵的，聪明的(clever, intelligent)
【记】in(内) + geni(产生) + ous → 自内心产生 → 聪明的
【例】By such *ingenious* adaptations, orchids can attract insects from afar to fertilize them.
【派】ingenuity(*n.* 巧思，聪敏)

judicious [dʒu'dɪʃəs] *adj.* 有判断力的，明智的(done in a sensible and careful way)
【例】a *judicious* choice
【派】judiciously(*adv.* 明智地)

proficient [prə'fɪʃnt] *adj.* 熟练的，精通的(skillful)
【例】There's only one way to become *proficient* at anything—practice!
【派】proficiently(*adv.* 熟练地) proficiency(*n.* 熟练)

sapience ['seɪpiəns] *n.* 智慧(wisdom)

sensible ['sensəbl] *adj.* 理智的(wise, rational)
【记】sens(感觉) + ible → 理智的
【例】His *sensible* decision greatly promoted our enterprise.
【派】sensibly(*adv.* 合理地) sensibility(*n.* 敏感性)

shrewd [ʃruːd] *adj.* 精明的(clever, smart)
【例】The *shrewd* business owner made large profits.
【派】shrewdly(*adv.* 机灵地) shrewdness(*n.* 机灵)

skillful ['skɪlfl] *adj.* 熟练的(adroit)
【例】Lisa is *skillful* at repairing lamps.
【派】skillfully(*adv.* 巧妙地)

versatile ['vɜːrsətl] *adj.* 多才多艺的(many-sided, talented, all-around)
【例】The *versatile* worker was assigned to many different jobs.
【派】versatility(*n.* 多才多艺)

trenchant ['trentʃənt] *adj.* 一针见血的，精辟的(incisive, effective)
【例】Stockman became one of the President's most *trenchant* critics.
【派】trenchantly(*adv.* 精辟地)

witty ['wɪti] *adj.* 机智的，诙谐的(clever)
【例】Laura's very *witty*.
【派】wittily(*adv.* 机智地) wittiness(*n.* 机智)

irrational [ɪˈræʃənl] *adj.* 无理性的，失去理性的；不合理的（not based on clear thought or reason, unreasonable）

【例】He's becoming increasingly *irrational*.

【派】irrationally(*adv.* 不合理地) irrationality(*n.* 不合理)

其　他

subtle [ˈsʌtl] *adj.* 微妙的，细微的，敏感的（little, sensitive, uneasy to notice）

【例】The pictures are similar, but there are *subtle* differences between them.

【派】subtly(*adv.* 隐隐约约地)

upright [ˈʌpraɪt] *adj.* 正直的

【记】up(上) + right(正的) → 正直的

【例】The *upright* witness told the truth at the trial.

【派】uprightness(*n.* 正直)

amiable [ˈeɪmiəbl] *adj.* 和蔼的，亲切的（friendly, having a pleasant or agreeable nature）

【例】The driver was an *amiable* young man.

audacious [ɔːˈdeɪʃəs] *adj.* 大胆的，勇敢的(bold, daring)

【例】He described the plan as ambitious and *audacious*.

【派】audacity(*n.* 大胆，厚颜)

erudition [ˌeruˈdɪʃn] *n.* 博学

【派】erudite(*adj.* 博学的)

frugal [ˈfruːgl] *adj.* 节约的，节俭的(thrifty, economical)

【例】She lived a careful and *frugal* life.

【派】frugality(*n.* 节俭)

imperial [ɪmˈpɪriəl] *adj.* 帝国的，帝王的（related to an empire or an emperor）

【例】History is full of attempts at *imperial* domination.

painstaking [ˈpeɪnzteɪkɪŋ] *n.* 辛劳 *adj.* 劳苦的

【记】pains(痛苦) + taking(花，费) → 付出痛苦的 → 劳苦的

【例】The work had been done with *painstaking* attention to detail.

【派】painstakingly(*adv.* 煞费苦心地)

strenuous [ˈstrenjuəs] *adj.* 辛苦的(laborious)

【例】It is really a *strenuous* job to get well prepared for a GRE test.

【派】strenuously(*adv.* 费力地)

练 习 题

连线题

enthusiastic	慎重	operative	多才多艺的
fanatic	炽热的	propitious	实施中的
fervent	慷慨	eminent	大胆的
bounty	审美的	optimal	机灵的
discretion	热情的	quintessential	吉祥的
meticulously	使作废	reputable	一针见血的
scrupulous	严谨的	ingenious	最佳的
quiescent	红润的	shrewd	精华的
esthetic	朝气蓬勃的	versatile	值得尊敬的
florid	静止的	trenchant	精明的
vigorous	有效的	audacious	辛苦的
efficacious	狂热的	erudition	博学
invalidate	很仔细地	strenuous	杰出的

选词填空

prominent	aspire	conscientious	ardent	intent
vigilant	perk	subtle	proficient	validate

1. At that time, all serious artists _____ to go to Rome.
2. Sam is an _____ supporter of free trade.
3. A _____ teacher may feel inclined to take work home.
4. She was _____ on pursuing a career in business.
5. Please remain _____ at all times and report anything suspicious.
6. The warning signs of the disease are so _____ that they are often ignored.
7. There's no doubt coffee _____ you up.
8. Many scientists plan to wait until the results of the study are _____ by future research.
9. The World Cup will have a _____ place on the agenda.
10. Martha is _____ in Swedish.

连线题答案

enthusiastic	热情的	operative	实施中的
fanatic	狂热的	propitious	吉祥的
fervent	炽热的	eminent	杰出的
bounty	慷慨	optimal	最佳的
discretion	慎重	quintessential	精华的
meticulously	很仔细地	reputable	值得尊敬的
scrupulous	严谨的	ingenious	机灵的
quiescent	静止的	shrewd	精明的
esthetic	审美的	versatile	多才多艺的
florid	红润的	trenchant	一针见血的
vigorous	朝气蓬勃的	audacious	大胆的
efficacious	有效的	erudition	博学
invalidate	使作废	strenuous	辛苦的

选词填空答案

prominent	aspire	conscientious	ardent	intent
vigilant	perk	subtle	proficient	validate

1. At that time, all serious artists（aspired）to go to Rome.
2. Sam is an（ardent）supporter of free trade.
3. A（conscientious）teacher may feel inclined to take work home.
4. She was（intent）on pursuing a career in business.
5. Please remain（vigilant）at all times and report anything suspicious.
6. The warning signs of the disease are so（subtle）that they are often ignored.
7. There's no doubt coffee（perks）you up.
8. Many scientists plan to wait until the results of the study are（validated）by future research.
9. The World Cup will have a（prominent）place on the agenda.
10.Martha is（proficient）in Swedish.

Word List 35

音频

负向评价

负向评价

贪 婪

acquisitive [əˈkwɪzətɪv] *adj.* 渴望得到的(eager to have)

【例】She boasts an *acquisitive* mind.

【派】acquisitiveness(*n.* 利欲心；求知欲)

cupidity [kjuːˈpɪdəti] *n.* 贪婪，贪心，贪欲

insatiable [ɪnˈseɪʃəbl] *adj.* 不能满足的，贪得无厌的(always wanting more and more of something)

【例】our *insatiable* thirst for knowledge

【派】insatiably(*adv.* 贪得无厌地)

voracious [vəˈreɪʃəs] *adj.* 贪吃的，贪婪的(greedy, insatiable)

【例】He is a *voracious* reader of science fiction.

【派】voracity(*n.* 贪食，贪婪)

虚 假

adulatory [ˈædʒələtɔːri] *adj.* 谄媚的，奉承的(flattering, complimentary, obsequious)

【派】adulation(*n.* 奉承，阿谀)

artificial [ˌɑːrtɪˈfɪʃl] *adj.* 人造的，假的 (man-made, false)；虚假的，不真挚的(insincere, feigned, not genuine)

【例】The new dam will form a large *artificial* lake behind it.

【派】artificially(*adv.* 人工地；虚伪地) artifact(*n.* 人造物品)

counterfeit [ˈkaʊntərfɪt] *v.* 伪造，仿造 *n.* 赝品 *adj.* 伪造的，假冒的(fake, sham)

【例】This *counterfeit* money is obviously an imitation.

deceptive [dɪˈseptɪv] *adj.* 虚伪的，骗人的(deceitful, misleading)

【例】Many customers were angered by the *deceptive* advertisements.

【派】deception(*n.* 欺骗，骗术)

fake [feɪk] *adj.* 伪造的，假冒的 (counterfeit, sham) *n.* 赝品

【例】They were selling *fake* Rolex watches on the market stall.

falsity ['fɔːlsəti] *n.* 虚伪，不真实 (the state of being false or untrue)；欺诈；谎言

fictitious [fɪk'tɪʃəs] *adj.* 虚构的 (invented, imaginary)

【记】fict(做，造) + itious → 造出的 → 虚构的

【例】She invented a *fictitious* boyfriend to put the suitor off.

fraudulent ['frɔːdʒələnt] *adj.* 欺诈的，不诚实的 (deceitful, dishonest)

【例】She entered the country using a *fraudulent* passport.

【派】fraudulence(*n.* 欺诈；欺骗性)

illusionary [ɪ'luːʒəneri] *adj.* 幻觉的，错觉的 (illusional)

【例】Don't believe in him. What he said is just an *illusionary* picture.

【派】illusion(*n.* 幻觉)

illusory [ɪ'luːsəri] *adj.* 虚幻的 (illusive, unreal)

【例】First impressions can often prove *illusory*.

mask [mæsk] *vt.* 戴面具；掩饰，伪装 (to hide or cover your feelings or the truth about a situation)

【例】Men often *mask* their true feelings with humor.

pretentious [prɪ'tenʃəs] *adj.* 装腔作势的 (showy, ostentatious)

【例】a *pretentious* film

【派】pretentiously(*adv.* 煞有介事地) pretentiousness(*n.* 狂妄)

蠢、笨、傻

dummy ['dʌmi] *n.* 哑巴；笨蛋；傀儡；人形靶

dupe [duːp] *n.* 受骗的人；傻子

gullible ['gʌləbl] *adj.* 易受骗的 (deceivable, naïve)

【记】gull(容易受骗的人) + ible → 易受骗的

【例】He's so *gullible* that he'll believe anything.

illiterate [ɪ'lɪtərət] *n./adj.* 文盲(的) (uneducated)

【派】illiteracy(*n.* 文盲，无知)

obtrusive [əb'truːsɪv] *adj.* 刺眼的 (noticeable in an unpleasant or annoying way)；冒失的；莽撞的

【例】The waiters were friendly and not *obtrusive*.

【派】obtrusively(*adv.* 冒失地)

obtuse [əb'tuːs] *adj.* 迟钝的 (slow to understand things, in a way that is annoying)；(疼痛)不剧烈的；钝角的

【例】"But why?" said Charles, being deliberately *obtuse*.

【派】obtuseness(*n.* 感觉迟钝)

trite [traɪt] *adj.* 陈腐的，陈词滥调的

【例】Her remarks sounded *trite* and ill-informed.

【派】triteness(*n.* 陈腐) tritely(*adv.* 陈腐地)

残　忍

brutal [ˈbruːtl] *adj.* 残忍的，严酷的(cruel, vicious, savage)

【例】Murder is a *brutal* crime.

inhumane [ˌɪnhjuːˈmeɪn] *adj.* 不仁慈的，无人道的，冷酷无情的(extremely cruel and causing unacceptable suffering)

【例】I was shocked by the *inhumane* conditions.

【派】inhumanely(*adv.* 残忍地)

relentless [rɪˈlentləs] *adj.* 无情的(merciless, ruthless)

【记】relent(怜悯的) + less → 无怜悯的 → 无情的

【例】The *relentless* bully beat Jimmy up.

【派】relentlessly(*adv.* 无情地)

rigorous [ˈrɪɡərəs] *adj.* 严厉的；严峻的(strict; rigid)

【记】rig(严厉的) + orous → 严厉的

【例】The trainings soldiers received were *rigorous*.

【派】rigorously(*adv.* 严厉地)

vicious [ˈvɪʃəs] *adj.* 邪恶的，狠毒的(malicious, spiteful)

【例】Abused children often grow up to abuse their own children—it's a *vicious* circle.

有　害

deleterious [ˌdeləˈtɪriəs] *adj.* (对身心)有害的，有毒的(harmful, injurious, hurtful)

【例】The cold weather had most *deleterious* consequences among the chrysanthemums.

detriment [ˈdetrɪmənt] *n.* 损害(damage, harm, loss)

【记】de + trim(修剪) + ent → 剪坏 → 损害

【例】The *detriment* caused by your thoughtless remark will never be forgotten.

detrimental [ˌdetrɪ'mentl] *adj.* 有害的，有损的

【例】The *detrimental* newspaper article may lead to a lawsuit.

lethal ['li:θl] *adj.* 致命的(fatal, deadly)

【记】leth(死) + al → 致命的

【例】These chemicals are *lethal* to fish.

noxious ['nɑːkʃəs] *adj.* 有害的；有毒的(poisonous, toxic)

【记】nox(毒) + ious → 有毒的

【例】*noxious* fumes

pernicious [pər'nɪʃəs] *adj.* 有害的，恶性的(very harmful or evil)

【例】the *pernicious* effects of poverty

【派】perniciously(*adv.* 有害地)

prejudicial [ˌpredʒu'dɪʃl] *adj.* 有害的(arousing bad effects)；引起偏见的

【例】*prejudicial* testimony

victim ['vɪktɪm] *n.* 牺牲品，受害者

toxic ['tɑːksɪk] *adj.* 有毒的，因中毒引起的(poisonous)

【例】*Toxic* chemicals were spilled into the river.

【派】toxicity(*n.* 毒性)

toxin ['tɑːksɪn] *n.* 毒素，毒质

懒　惰

disinclination [ˌdɪsˌɪnklɪ'neɪʃn] *n.* 不愿意(reluctance)

idle ['aɪdl] *adj.* 无所事事的；懒惰的 *v.* 闲逛；浪费光阴

【例】They *idled* their time away in the pub.

sloth [sloʊθ] *n.* 怠惰，懒惰(laziness)

【派】slothful(*adj.* 偷懒的)

sluggish ['slʌgɪʃ] *adj.* 怠惰的(lethargic, listless, slow)

【例】The snake was *sluggish* because of the cold weather.

【派】sluggishly(*adv.* 迟钝地)

loaf [loʊf] *vi.* 游荡，闲逛(to spend time somewhere and not do very much)；懒散地工作

【例】They spend all day *loafing* around on street corners.

恶 毒

hideous [ˈhɪdiəs] *adj.* 骇人听闻的；丑恶的；极丑的(ugly, ill-looking)

【例】Despite its low price, no one would buy the *hideous* tie.

poisonous [ˈpɔɪzənəs] *adj.* 有毒的；恶毒的 (full of bad and unfriendly feelings)

【例】She was bitten on the ankle by a *poisonous* snake.

【派】poisonously(*adv.* 有毒地)

scandal [ˈskændl] *n.* 丑闻(disgrace, defamation)

【例】The President's *scandal* was soon publicized and exaggerated.

venomous [ˈvenəməs] *adj.* 有毒的；恶毒的；充满仇恨的(poisonous; full of anger)

【例】Lisa shot him a *venomous* glance.

【派】venomously(*adv.* 恶毒地)

贫 困

monotonous [məˈnɑːtənəs] *adj.* 单调的(boring, dull)；毫无变化的

【记】mono(单个) + ton(声音) + ous → 单调的

【例】a *monotonous* diet

【派】monotonously(*adv.* 单调地)

needy [ˈniːdi] *adj.* 贫穷的(poor)

【记】need(需要) + y → 急需的 → 贫穷的

【例】Those *needy* children had to work for their keep.

paucity [ˈpɔːsəti] *n.* 少量；缺乏 (less than is needed of something)

【例】a *paucity* of information

predicament [prɪˈdɪkəmənt] *n.* 困境，穷困(a difficult or unpleasant situation)

【例】She went to the office to explain her *predicament*.

scarcity [ˈskersəti] *n.* 缺乏，稀缺(lack)

【例】the *scarcity* of employment opportunities

sparse [spɑːrs] *adj.* 稀少的(existing only in small amounts)；零落的，分散的

【例】rural areas with *sparse* population

【派】sparsely(*adv.* 稀疏地) sparseness(*n.* 稀疏)

傲 慢

complacent [kəmˈpleɪsnt] *adj.* 自满的，自鸣得意的（extremely self-satisfied, contented）

【例】The winner's *complacent* smile annoyed some people.

【派】complacency（*n.* 自满，得意）

narcissism [ˈnɑːrsɪsɪzəm] *n.* 自我陶醉，自恋

【例】He went to the gym every day, driven purely by *narcissism*.

【派】narcissist（*n.* 自我陶醉者）narcissistic（*adj.* 自我陶醉的）

ostentation [ˌɑːstenˈteɪʃn] *n.* 夸示，炫耀（deliberately show for admiration）

【例】Her lifestyle was remarkably free from *ostentation*.

overweening [ˌoʊvərˈwiːnɪŋ] *adj.* 自负的，过于自信的（too proud and confident）

【例】*overweening* ambition

【派】overweeningly（*adv.* 自负地）

pompous [ˈpɑːmpəs] *adj.* 自大的，浮夸的（boastful）

【例】He seems rather *pompous*.

【派】pompously（*adv.* 傲慢地）pomposity（*n.* 浮华）

superior [suːˈpɪriər] *adj.* 较高的；较好的（better）；高傲的

【例】Your computer is far *superior* to mine.

【派】superiority（*n.* 优势）

vanity [ˈvænəti] *n.* 虚荣心（self-conceit, pride）

【记】van（空）+ ity → 虚荣心

冗 长

profusion [prəˈfjuːʒn] *n.* 丰富，大量，充沛（large amount）

【例】The house was overflowing with a *profusion* of strange ornaments.

redundant [rɪˈdʌndənt] *adj.* 过多的，冗长的（unnecessary, superfluous）

【例】As the economy weakens, more and more jobs will be made *redundant*.

tedious [ˈtiːdiəs] *adj.* 冗长乏味的，沉闷的（tiresome, boring）

【例】John's job at the factory is trivial and *tedious*.

【派】tediously（*adv.* 沉闷地）

voluminous [vəˈluːmɪnəs] *adj.* 宽松的，肥大的（large, loose）；著作多的

【例】a *voluminous* cloak

【派】voluminously（*adv.* 庞大地）

其他

adamant [ˈædəmənt] *adj.* 坚定的（determined）
【例】We are *adamant* on the building of a well-off society.

apathetic [ˌæpəˈθetɪk] *adj.* 无兴趣的，冷淡的；无动于衷的（having or showing little or no emotion; indifferent）
【例】I realized I was becoming increasingly depressed and *apathetic*.
【派】apathy（*n.* 漠然，冷淡）

bleak [bliːk] *adj.* 荒凉的；暗淡的，没有希望的（desolate; gloomy）
【例】High Andes are *bleak*, treeless regions.

crude [kruːd] *adj.* 天然的，未加工的（raw, unpolished, unprocessed）；粗俗的，粗野的（vulgar）
【例】Last night a cargo ship collided with a tanker carrying *crude* oil.

envious [ˈenviəs] *adj.* 妒忌的，羡慕的（jealous）
【例】Colleagues were *envious* of her success.
【派】envy（*v.* 羡慕，妒忌）

sapless [ˈsæpləs] *adj.* 枯萎的；无精神的；无价值的
【例】Her body looked *sapless*.

The ideals which have lighted my way, and time after time have given me new courage to face life cheerfully have been kindness, beauty and truth.
有些理想曾为我指引过道路，并不断给我新的勇气以欣然面对人生，那些理想就是——真、善、美。
——美国科学家　爱因斯坦（*Albert Einstein, American scientist*）

练 习 题

连线题

acquisitive	贪得无厌的	detrimental	恶毒的
insatiable	易受骗的	pernicious	恶性的
voracious	渴望得到的	disinclination	丰富
adulatory	谄媚的	sluggish	怠惰的
counterfeit	伪造	hideous	有害的
fictitious	虚构的	venomous	骇人听闻的
fraudulent	幻觉的	monotonous	困境
illusionary	无情的	predicament	自大的
gullible	冒失的	paucity	单调的
obtrusive	贪吃的	profusion	宽松的
obtuse	(对身心)有害的	voluminous	缺乏
relentless	欺诈的	sapless	不愿意
deleterious	迟钝的	pompous	枯萎的

选词填空

redundant	artificial	complacent	vicious	rigorous
lethal	idle	deceptive	superior	apathetic

1. There are _____ barriers of gender and race.
2. Gwen's students may look angelic, but appearances can be _____.
3. There's a danger of becoming _____ if you win a few games.
4. It is a _____ analysis of defence need.
5. She was shocked by the _____ tone in his voice.
6. Higher taxes and higher inflation were a _____ combination.
7. Seventy factory workers were made _____ in the resulting cuts.
8. I cannot afford to leave the land lying _____.
9. Your computer is far _____ to mine.
10. How can you be so _____ about the world and its problems?

练习题答案

连线题答案

acquisitive	渴望得到的	detrimental	有害的
insatiable	贪得无厌的	pernicious	恶性的
voracious	贪吃的	disinclination	不愿意
adulatory	谄媚的	sluggish	怠惰的
counterfeit	伪造	hideous	骇人听闻的
fictitious	虚构的	venomous	恶毒的
fraudulent	欺诈的	monotonous	单调的
illusionary	幻觉的	predicament	困境
gullible	易受骗的	paucity	缺乏
obtrusive	冒失的	profusion	丰富
obtuse	迟钝的	voluminous	宽松的
relentless	无情的	sapless	枯萎的
deleterious	（对身心）有害的	pompous	自大的

选词填空答案

redundant	artificial	complacent	vicious	rigorous
lethal	idle	deceptive	superior	apathetic

1. There are（artificial）barriers of gender and race.
2. Gwen's students may look angelic, but appearances can be（deceptive）.
3. There's a danger of becoming（complacent）if you win a few games.
4. It is a（rigorous）analysis of defence need.
5. She was shocked by the（vicious）tone in his voice.
6. Higher taxes and higher inflation were a（lethal）combination.
7. Seventy factory workers were made（redundant）in the resulting cuts.
8. I cannot afford to leave the land lying（idle）.
9. Your computer is far（superior）to mine.
10. How can you be so（apathetic）about the world and its problems?

Word List 36

负向行为
人及相关动作

负向行为

痛　苦

afflict [ə'flɪkt] *vt.* 使痛苦，折磨(torture)
　【记】af(一再) + flict(打击) → 一再打击 → 折磨
　【例】He was *afflicted* with arthritis.
　【派】affliction(*n.* 苦恼，折磨)

grueling ['gru:əlɪŋ] *adj.* 艰难的，痛苦的(very difficult and tiring)
　【例】The cast took a break from their *grueling* schedule.

pang [pæŋ] *n.* 剧痛；痛苦(a sudden feeling of pain, sadness etc.)
　【例】She felt a sudden *pang* of guilt.

犯　罪

convict [kən'vɪkt] *vt.* 判罪 (to pronounce guilty; penalize)；证明(prove)
　['kɑ:nvɪkt] *n.* 囚犯
　【例】The defendant was *convicted* of murder.
　【派】conviction(*n.* 定罪；确信)

criminology [ˌkrɪmɪ'nɑ:lədʒi] *n.* 犯罪学

guilty ['gɪlti] *adj.* 内疚的；有罪的(blameworthy; culpable)
　【例】The jury found her *guilty* of murder.

homicide ['hɑ:mɪsaɪd] *n.* (法律上的)杀人行为(slaughter)；杀人犯

illicit [ɪ'lɪsɪt] *adj.* 违法的(unlawful, illegal)
　【例】They were prosecuted for *illicit* liquor selling.

incriminate [ɪn'krɪmɪneɪt] *vt.* 控告；显示…有罪；连累某人；归罪于
　【例】He had been forced to *incriminate* himself in cross-examinations.

inmate ['ɪnmeɪt] *n.* (监狱或精神病院等处的)同住者；同狱犯人(someone who is being kept in a prison)

reprisal [rɪ'praɪzl] *n.* 报复性暴力(retaliation)
　【例】They didn't tell the police for fear of *reprisal*.

shoplift ['ʃɑ:plɪft] *vi.* 入店行窃(take without paying)
　【派】shoplifting(*n.* 冒充顾客进商店行窃) shoplifter(*n.* 商店窃贼)

smuggle [ˈsmʌgl] *vt.* 偷运, 私运, 走私

【例】The guns were *smuggled* across the border.

【派】smuggling(*n.* 走私)

solicit [səˈlɪsɪt] *v.* 拉客

【例】Bob was almost arrested for *soliciting* in an apartment building.

【派】solicitation(*n.* 拉客)

掠 夺

abduct [æbˈdʌkt] *vt.* 绑架, 拐走(to kidnap)

【记】ab + duct(引导)→ 把人带走 → 绑架

【例】The police think the boy has been *abducted*.

【派】abduction(*n.* 绑架)

kidnap [ˈkɪdnæp] *vt.* 绑架(abduct)

【记】kid(小孩) + nap(睡)→(小孩睡时被)绑架

【例】Two businessmen have been *kidnapped*.

bereft [bɪˈreft] *adj.* 丧失了的, 被剥夺了的(deprived of, parted from); 绝望的(feeling very sad, hopeless)

【例】The team now seems *bereft* of hope.

denude [dɪˈnuːd] *vt.* 使赤裸, 剥光覆盖物(to make bare, uncover, strip)

【例】The fact that people have left farm work has *denuded* many villages of their working populations.

deprive [dɪˈpraɪv] *v.* 剥夺, 夺去(to take away)

【例】This law will *deprive* us of our most basic rights.

【派】deprivation(*n.* 剥夺; 丧失) deprived(*adj.* 丧失的; 贫困的)

encroach [ɪnˈkroʊtʃ] *vi.* 侵犯, 侵占(intrude, trespass)

【例】The reporter *encroached* on my privacy.

【派】encroachment(*n.* 侵蚀; 侵犯)

engulf [ɪnˈgʌlf] *vt.* 吞没, 吞食(devour, swallow)

【记】en + gulf(沟)→ 使入沟 → 吞没

【例】Huge waves *engulfed* the small boat.

fade [feɪd] *v.* 褪色；消退

【例】Will the color in this material *fade*?

inalienable [ɪn'eɪliənəbl] *adj.* 不可分割的；不可剥夺的；不能转让的

【例】Life, liberty, and the pursuit of happiness have been called the *inalienable* rights of man.

monopoly [mə'nɑːpəli] *n.* 垄断；专卖

【例】For years Bell Telephone had a *monopoly* on telephone services in the U.S.

undercut ['ʌndərkʌt] *n.* 底切 [ˌʌndər'kʌt] *vt.* 从下部切开；与…抢生意（undersell）

【例】Online bookstores can *undercut* retailers by up to 30%.

counteract [ˌkaʊntər'ækt] *v.* 对抗；抵消（to oppose, neutralize, or mitigate）

【例】They gave him drugs to *counteract* his withdrawal symptoms.

人及相关动作

视　听

acoustic [ə'kuːstɪk] *adj.* 声音的，听觉的（relating to sound and hearing）

【例】Animals use *acoustic,* visual and chemical signals to communicate.

【派】acoustical（*adj.* 听觉的，声学的）acoustics（*n.* 声学）

chirp [tʃɜːrp] *vi.* 喳喳（虫和鸟的叫声）

【例】The injured bird did not move or *chirp*.

monitor ['mɑːnɪtər] *v.* 监视，监听 *n.* 班长

【例】The president can *monitor* the whole campus through advanced computer system.

pry [praɪ] *v.* 刺探，打听（try to find out）；撬开

【例】If you want to know his name, you have to *pry* it out of her.

browse [braʊz] *n./v.* 吃嫩叶或草；浏览（to look through）

【例】John was *browsing* through the photographs.

detect [dɪ'tekt] *vt.* 探测，发觉（explore, discover）

【例】I *detected* Bob's lie because he wouldn't look at me directly.

【派】detection（*n.* 察觉，发觉）

detectable [dɪ'tektəbl] *adj.* 可发觉的，可看穿的（noticeable, perceptible）

【例】*detectable* error

discern [dɪˈsɜːrn] *vt.* 看见，辨明 (detect, distinguish)

【例】I can't *discern* the difference between the twins.

discernible [dɪˈsɜːrnəbl] *adj.* 可辨别的 (perceptible, evident, observable)

【例】Her face was barely *discernible* in the gloom.

invisible [ɪnˈvɪzəbl] *adj.* 看不见的 (invisible or cannot be seen)；暗藏的

【例】The house was surrounded by trees and *invisible* from the road.

【派】invisibly (*adv.* 看不见地) invisibility (*n.* 看不见的东西)

tangible [ˈtændʒəbl] *adj.* 可见的；确实的 (touchable, substantial)

【记】tang (接触) + ible → 接触得到的 → 确实的

【例】One *tangible* benefit of my new job is a company car.

【派】tangibility (*n.* 确切性)

visual [ˈvɪʒuəl] *adj.* 看的，视力的 (relating to seeing)；栩栩如生的

【例】Artists translate their ideas into *visual* images.

short-sighted [ˌʃɔːrt ˈsaɪtɪd] *adj.* 没有远见的 (not considering future)

【例】a *short-sighted* policy of reducing investment in training

【派】short-sightedly (*adv.* 目光短浅地) short-sightedness (*n.* 近视)

spectator [ˈspekteɪtər] *n.* 观众，旁观者 (audience)

【例】The match attracted over 40,000 *spectators*.

interrogate [ɪnˈterəgeɪt] *vt.* 审问；询问

【记】inter (中间) + rog (问) + ate → 拉到中间问 → 审问

【例】The police *interrogated* Sally about the robbery.

【派】interrogation (*n.* 询问，质问)

身体行为

adolescent [ˌædəˈlesnt] *adj.* 青春期的，青少年的 (juvenile, young) *n.* 青少年

【派】adolescence (*n.* 青春期)

elevate [ˈelɪveɪt] *vt.* 抬起，使升高 (to raise, lift)；提高 (思想)；振奋

【例】The marchers *elevated* the flag as they passed the President. / A child should be given books which *elevate* his mind.

embrace [ɪmˈbreɪs] *vt.* 拥抱 (hug, cuddle)；接受 (accept)

【例】The students tearfully *embraced* each other on their last day of school. / She *embraced* my offer to go to the hospital.

excrete [ɪk'skriːt] *vt.* 排泄，分泌（to get rid of waste material from your body）

【派】secrete（*v.* 分泌）excretion（*n.* 排泄；排泄物）

excursion [ɪk'skɜːrʒn] *n.* 远足，短途旅行

expedition [ˌekspə'dɪʃn] *n.* 远征（exploration）

【记】ex + ped（脚）+ ition → 脚出动 → 远征

【例】The explorers started on a year-long *expedition* down the Nile.

hum [hʌm] *n.* 嗡嗡声 *v.* 哼（歌）；忙碌；充满活力

【例】The bees were *humming* in the garden.

impact ['ɪmpækt] *n.* 冲击，影响 [ɪm'pækt] *v.* 冲击（affect, influence）

【例】The Revolution greatly *impacted* many families.

indulge [ɪn'dʌldʒ] *vt.* 使自己沉迷，放纵；允许某人延期付款

【例】Women do not *indulge* in crime to the same extent as men.

【派】indulgence（*n.* 纵容，放纵）

intangible [ɪn'tændʒəbl] *adj.* 难以捉摸的，难以理解的；无法确定的

【例】The island has an *intangible* quality of holiness.

【派】intangibly（*adv.* 无形地；模糊地）

posture ['pɑːstʃər] *n.* 人体的姿势（pose, bearing）

raid [reɪd] *n./v.* 袭击（attack, foray）

【例】Air *raids* involved in the war destroyed many families.

rally ['ræli] *n./v.* 召集（gathering, assemblage）

【记】比较ally（*n.* 联盟）

【例】We *rallied* together to save our leader from prison.

sedentary ['sedntəri] *adj.* 案头的；不爱活动的

【例】health problems caused by our *sedentary* lifestyles

siege [siːdʒ] *n./vt.* 围困，围攻（besiege, encircle）

【例】During the enemy's *siege*, no one could leave or enter the city.

stamp [stæmp] *n.* 邮票；印章 *v.* 顿足（put foot down loudly）

【例】The audience *stamped* and shouted.

stance [stæns] *n.* 站姿；立场（stand）

【例】What is your *stance* on environmental issues?

stroke [stroʊk] *n.* 一击；中风 *vt.* 轻抚，抚摸（touch gently）

【例】He reached out and *stroked* her cheek tenderly.

vulnerable ['vʌlnərəbl] *adj.* 易受伤的，脆弱的，敏感的（easily hurt or harmed）

【例】He took advantage of me when I was at my most *vulnerable*.

【派】vulnerably（*adv.* 易损地）vulnerability（*n.* 弱点）

barrack [ˈbærək] *v.* 大叫；喝倒彩（to criticize loudly or shout against）

【例】They *barracked* throughout the meeting.

behavioral [bɪˈheɪvjərəl] *adj.* 行为上的（relating to behavior）

【例】*behavioral* abnormality

startle [ˈstɑːrtl] *vt.* 使大吃一惊（amaze, surprise）*n.* 吃惊

【派】startling（*adj.* 惊人的）

能　力

afford [əˈfɔːrd] *v.* 买得起，负担得起（be able to pay or do）

【例】She cannot *afford* a new dress.

【派】affordable（*adj.* 付得起的）

aptitude [ˈæptɪtuːd] *n.* （学习方面的）才能，资质

【例】I have no musical *aptitude* and I can't even sing a simple tune.

competent [ˈkɑːmpɪtənt] *adj.* 能胜任的（capable, qualified）

【例】Mike did a *competent* job fixing my car.

【派】competence（*n.* 能力，技能）

omnipotent [ɑːmˈnɪpətənt] *adj.* 全能的，万能的（able to do everything, all-powerful）

【派】omnipotence（*n.* 全能，万能）

potent [ˈpoʊtnt] *adj.* 强有力的（cogent, powerful）；有全权的

【记】poten（力量）+ t → 强有力的

【例】His *potent* speech impressed all the people present.

【派】potently（*adv.* 强有力地）

viable [ˈvaɪəbl] *adj.* 可行的（feasible, workable）；能活下去的

【例】The committee came forward with one *viable* solution.

【派】viably（*adv.* 可行地）viability（*n.* 可行性）

inability [ˌɪnəˈbɪləti] *n.* 无能，无力（lack of ability, incapability）

嗅　觉

aromatic [ˌærəˈmætɪk] *adj.* 芳香的（fragrant）*n.* 芳香植物；【化】芳香族

【派】aroma（*n.* 芳香，香味）

aura [ˈɔːrə] *n.* （人或物发出的）气味，香味；【电】辉光；【医】预感，先兆

foul [faʊl] *adj.* 恶臭的；邪恶的；下流的 *n.*【体育】犯规

【例】The house was filled with *foul* odor.

fragrance ['freɪɡrəns] *n.* 芳香

【派】fragrant(*adj.* 芳香的)

身体特征

idiosyncrasy [ˌɪdɪə'sɪŋkrəsi] *n.* (某人特有的)气质，习性，癖好

【例】I adjusted to my husband's many *idiosyncrasies*.

【派】idiosyncratic(*adj.* 特殊的，异质的)

personality [ˌpɜːrsə'næləti] *n.* 人格；个性，魅力（character, the qualities of character）

【例】He was an ambitious man with a strong *personality*.

gender ['dʒendər] *n.* 性别

masculinity [ˌmæskju'lɪnəti] *n.* 男性(气概)

【例】Children's ideas of *masculinity* tend to come from their fathers.

hardy ['hɑːrdi] *adj.* 强壮的（tough, rugged）；吃苦耐劳的

【例】Those *hardy* and stocky Eskimos have been living in this frozen world for centuries.

viscous ['vɪskəs] *adj.* 黏的，黏性的(thick, sticky)

【例】As the liquid cools, it becomes *viscous*.

【派】viscosity(*n.* 黏度)

练 习 题

连线题

grueling	犯罪学	excursion	拉客
criminology	侵犯	intangible	难以捉摸的
homicide	归罪于	sedentary	远足
incriminate	可发觉的	aptitude	不爱活动的
reprisal	报复性暴力	vulnerable	才能
bereft	杀人行为	aromatic	脆弱的
encroach	丧失了的	foul	芳香的
engulf	不可分割的	idiosyncrasy	男性(气概)
inalienable	可辨别的	masculinity	黏的
acoustic	青春期的	viscous	强有力的
detectable	听觉的	potent	恶臭的
discernible	吞食	startle	气质
adolescent	艰难的	solicit	使大吃一惊

选词填空

siege	smuggle	elevate	deprive	abduct
detect	interrogate	rally	indulge	competent

1. Illegal immigrants are _____ into the country by boat.
2. She was _____ late last night.
3. A lot of these children have been _____ of a normal home life.
4. Dan _____ a change in her mood.
5. The police _____ the suspect for several hours.
6. Language has _____ humans above the other animals.
7. A _____ mechanic should be able to fix the problem.
8. Surely the local business community could have_____ to raise the cash.
9. In June 1176 King Richard laid _____ to Limoges.
10. Most of us were too busy to _____ in heavy lunchtime drinking.

练习题答案

连线题答案

grueling	艰难的	excursion	远足
criminology	犯罪学	intangible	难以捉摸的
homicide	杀人行为	sedentary	不爱活动的
incriminate	归罪于	aptitude	才能
reprisal	报复性暴力	vulnerable	脆弱的
bereft	丧失了的	aromatic	芳香的
encroach	侵犯	foul	恶臭的
engulf	吞食	idiosyncrasy	气质
inalienable	不可分割的	masculinity	男性(气概)
acoustic	听觉的	viscous	黏的
detectable	可发觉的	potent	强有力的
discernible	可辨别的	startle	使大吃一惊
adolescent	青春期的	solicit	拉客

选词填空答案

siege	smuggle	elevate	deprive	abduct
detect	interrogate	rally	indulge	competent

1. Illegal immigrants are (smuggled) into the country by boat.
2. She was (abducted) late last night.
3. A lot of these children have been (deprived) of a normal home life.
4. Dan (detected) a change in her mood.
5. The police (interrogated) the suspect for several hours.
6. Language has (elevated) humans above the other animals.
7. A (competent) mechanic should be able to fix the problem.
8. Surely the local business community could have (rallied) to raise the cash.
9. In June 1176 King Richard laid (siege) to Limoges.
10. Most of us were too busy to (indulge) in heavy lunchtime drinking.

Word List 37

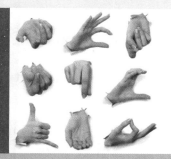

语言
其他（一）

语言&其他(一)

尖酸讽刺

absurd [əb'sɜːrd] *adj.* 荒谬的(ridiculous)
【例】Wearing a swimming suit during a snowstorm is *absurd*.
【派】absurdity(*n.* 荒谬)

acid ['æsɪd] *adj.* 酸的(sour in taste);尖酸的(bitter in speech or manner)
【例】Nobody likes to hear the *acid* remarks. / *acid* rain
【派】acidity(*n.* 酸度;尖刻)

cynical ['sɪnɪkl] *adj.* 愤世嫉俗的

ironic [aɪ'rɑːnɪk] *adj.* 冷嘲的,挖苦的 (using words that are the opposite of what you really mean);出乎意料的
【例】When I told Lucy I loved her book, she thought I was being *ironic*.
【派】ironically(*adv.* 挖苦地;出乎意料地)

poke [poʊk] *vt.* 刺,戳(stick with a finger);嘲弄
【例】*poke* and pry

tease [tiːz] *vt.* 逗乐,戏弄(taunt, jeer);强求
【例】The girl was *teasing* her mother for more candy.

批 评

accuse [ə'kjuːz] *vt.* 控告(to charge);指责
【例】We *accused* him of taking bribes.
【派】accusation(*n.* 指责;控告) accused(*n.* 被告) accuser (*n.* 原告)

censure ['senʃər] *n./v.* 责难,非难(reproach, blame)
【例】Bill received a *censure* from his boss for the failure of the project. / The warden *censured* the guard for letting the prisoner escape.

critique [krɪ'tiːk] *n.* (文艺等的)批评,评论

denounce [dɪ'naʊns] *vt.* 公开谴责,声讨(to censure, condemn openly)
【记】de(坏) + nounce(讲话) → 讲坏话 → 声讨
【例】He *denounced* the election as a farce.

denunciation [dɪˌnʌnsiˈeɪʃn] *n.* 公开谴责，指责

【派】denunciative / denunciatory(*adj.* 指责的，谴责的)

reproach [rɪˈproʊtʃ] *v.* 责备

【记】比较approach(*v.*接近)

【例】Do not *reproach* yourself. It was not your fault.

repudiate [rɪˈpjuːdieɪt] *vt.* 批判(reject, renounce)

【例】The scientist *repudiated* the results of the shoddy experiment.

【派】repudiation(*n.* 拒绝)

stigmatize [ˈstɪɡmətaɪz] *vt.* 指责，污辱(humiliate)

【例】Single mothers often feel that they are *stigmatized* by society.

【派】stigmatization(*n.* 侮辱)

victimize [ˈvɪktɪmaɪz] *vt.* 责怪或处罚某人不当；欺负某人(pick on)

【例】The men claim they have been *victimized* because of their political activity.

【派】victimized(*adj.* 受害的) victimization(*n.* 牺牲，欺负)

aspersions [əˈspɜːrʒnz] *n.* 诽谤，中伤(slander, defamation)

complaint [kəmˈpleɪnt] *n.* 抱怨，怨言；投诉，控告

【例】The boss had a *complaint* about Bill's tardiness. / Our neighbors lodged a *complaint* against us with the police.

grievance [ˈɡriːvəns] *n.* 委屈，抱怨，不满(dissatisfaction)

【记】griev(悲伤) + ance → 说悲伤的话 → 抱怨

【例】The committee has many *grievances* against the school board.

口　才

articulate [ɑːrˈtɪkjuleɪt] *v.*清楚说话(to speak or enunciate clearly and distinctly)；接合，连接(to be jointed or form a joint) [ɑːrˈtɪkjələt] *adj.* 口齿清楚的，表达能力强的

【例】*Articulate* speech is very important.

eloquence [ˈeləkwəns] *n.* 雄辩

【例】Because of her *eloquence*, Anne made an excellent lobbyist.

eloquent [ˈeləkwənt] *adj.* 雄辩的，有口才的；有说服力的(persuasive, fluent)

【例】The *eloquent* lecture was interesting to listen to.

其 他

abruptly [əˈbrʌptli] *adv.* 突然地(suddenly); 无礼地
【例】He closed his speech *abruptly*.

afterlife [ˈæftərlaɪf] *n.* 来生, 来世

alleged [əˈledʒd] *adj.* 声称的, 所谓的(so-called, presumed)
【例】The *alleged* victim made the complaint at a police station in York.
【派】allege(v. 断言, 宣称) allegedly(adv. 据称, 据说)

alumni [əˈlʌmnaɪ] *n.* [alumnus的复数] 校友

burrow [ˈbɜːroʊ] *n.* 地洞 *v.* 挖洞; 翻寻
【例】What are you *burrowing* around in my drawer for?

cellular [ˈseljələr] *adj.* 多孔的, 有网眼的; 由许多小单元组成的(relating to, resembling, or composed of cells)
【例】The organization has a *cellular* structure.

cure-all [ˈkjʊrɔːl] *n.* 万灵药

deluxe [dəˈlʌks] *adj.* 奢华的(luxurious, sumptuous, opulent)
【例】This book will be published in an *deluxe* edition in autumn.

despite [dɪˈspaɪt] *prep.* 不管, 尽管(in spite of)
【例】*Despite* the fact that she is short, she is an excellent basketball player.

encode [ɪeˈkoʊd] *vt.* 把(电文等)译成电码(或密码)

evolutionary [ˌevəˈluːʃəneri] *adj.* 进化的; 逐渐的(gradual)
【例】*evolutionary* theory

excavate [ˈekskəveɪt] *vt.* 挖掘(dig, delve)
【记】ex + cav(洞) + ate → 挖出洞 → 挖掘
【例】They *excavated* a huge hole for the foundation of the building.

excavation [ˌekskəˈveɪʃn] *n.* 挖掘, 发掘; 挖掘成的洞; 出土文物

extant [ekˈstænt] *adj.* 现存的, 仍然存在的(existing)
【例】Few of the manuscripts are still *extant*.

feat [fiːt] *n.* 功绩, 壮举(achievement, accomplishment)

feudal [ˈfjuːdl] *adj.* 封建的

【例】The *feudal* system lasted for two thousand years in China.

granular [ˈɡrænjələr] *adj.* 粒状的，含颗粒的

【派】granule(*n.* 小颗粒)

hallmark [ˈhɔːlmɑːrk] *n.* (伦敦金业公会证明金银纯度的)检验标记；品质证明；标志，特点

hegemony [hɪˈdʒemoʊni] *n.* 霸权；领导权

heritage [ˈherɪtɪdʒ] *n.* 遗产

hierarchy [ˈhaɪərɑːrki] *n.* 等级制度

【派】hierarchical(*adj.* 分等级的)

highlight [ˈhaɪlaɪt] *vt.* 突出显示；强调（underline, underscore, stress）*n.* 最精彩的部分(climax)

【例】A beam of light was cast onto the dancer, *highlighting* her vivid imitating action of a peacock.

ice-polished [ˈaɪs ˈpɑːlɪʃt] *adj.* 冰蚀的

idealize [aɪˈdiːəlaɪz] *v.* 使理想化(to consider or represent something as ideal)

【派】idealization(*n.* 理想化)

immediacy [ɪˈmiːdiəsi] *n.* 直接，直接性

【例】Television brings a new *immediacy* to world events.

immobilize [ɪˈmoʊbəlaɪz] *vt.* 使不动，使固定(to make or become immobile)

【例】The broken limb must be *immobilized* immediately.

improvise [ˈɪmprəvaɪz] *vt.* 即席创作(extemporize)

【记】im(不) + pro(前) + vise(看) → 没有预先看过 → 即席创作

【例】The actors *improvised* a scene based on an audience's suggestion.

【派】improvisation(*n.* 即席创作，即兴作品)

incomplete [ˌɪnkəmˈpliːt] *adj.* 不完全的，未完成的(not complete)

【例】*incomplete* combustion

inconclusive [ˌɪnkənˈkluːsɪv] *adj.* 非决定性的；无结果的(not conclusive)

【例】The jury found the evidence against the prisoner *inconclusive* and acquitted him.

incumbent [ɪnˈkʌmbənt] *adj.* 在职的；义不容辞的(obligatory)

【例】He defeated the *incumbent* governor by a large plurality.

indigenous [ɪnˈdɪdʒənəs] *adj.* 土产的，当地的(native)

【例】The *indigenous* people of the area know which plants are safe to eat and which are poisonous.

aquatic [əˈkwætɪk] *adj.* 水产的，水栖的，水中的（growing, living, or happening in water）

【例】*Aquatic* sports include swimming and rowing.

embalm [ɪmˈbɑːm] *vt.* 以香油（或药料）涂；保存（尸体）不腐

offshoot [ˈɔːfʃuːt] *n.* 分支；支脉，支流；旁系的一员（a new stem or branch on a plant or organization）

【例】The company was originally an *offshoot* of Bell Telephones.

particular [pərˈtɪkjələr] *n.* 细节；[*pl.*] 详细情况（the facts and details about a job, property, legal case, etc.）

【例】You may be required to give *particulars* of the change in your financial position.

【派】particularly（*adv.* 特别，尤其）

predicate [ˈpredɪkeɪt] *vt.* 使基于（be based on）

【例】The company's expansion was *predicated* on the assumption that sales would rise.

【派】predication（*n.* 论断）

register [ˈredʒɪstər] *vt.* 登记，记录（enroll, enlist）

【例】It is for the historian to discover and *register* what actually happened.

【派】registration（*n.* 登记，注册）

reign [reɪn] *n.* 王朝 *vt.* 统治（govern, rule）

【例】The old King has been *reigning* the nation for 30 years.

scapegoat [ˈskeɪpɡoʊt] *n.* 替罪羊

【例】She believed she had been made a *scapegoat* for what happened.

seniority [ˌsiːniˈɔːrəti] *n.* 年长，资历深，职位高

【例】I had fifteen years *seniority*, and they couldn't fire me.

specialize [ˈspeʃəlaɪz] *vi.* 专门从事，专攻，专门研究（major）

【例】Simmons *specialized* in contract law.

【派】specialized（*adj.* 专门的）specialization（*n.* 专门化）

stitch [stɪtʃ] *n.* 缝法，（缝纫中的）一针 *v.* 缝，缝补，缝合（sew）

【例】Mary is *stitching* a bedspread.

tenure [ˈtenjər] *n.* 保有权；任期（the period of time when someone has an important job）

【派】tenured（*adj.* 在任的）

tickle	['tɪkl] *v.* 使有痒感；逗乐

【例】Mazie's fur collar was *tickling* her neck.

trait	[treɪt] *n.* 特点，特性（characteristic, attribute）
virgin	['vɜːrdʒɪn] *n.* 处女，贞女 *adj.* 处女的；未开采的

【例】*virgin* territory

virtually	['vɜːrtʃuəli] *adv.* 几乎（almost, practically, actually）

【例】He was *virtually* unknown before running for office.

wingspan	['wɪŋspæn] *n.* 翼展（wingspread）
zing	[zɪŋ] *n.* （子弹等的）尖啸声；精力，活力（energy）

【例】Lemon juice adds *zing* to drinks.

【派】zingy（*adj.* 吸引人的）

Histories make men wise; poems witty; the mathematics subtle; natural philosophy deep; moral grave; logic and rhetoric able to contend.

历史使人明智；诗词使人灵秀；数学使人周密；自然哲学使人深刻；伦理使人庄重；逻辑修辞学使人善辩。

——英国哲学家 培根（*Francis Bacon, British philosopher*）

练 习 题

连线题

cynical	责难	hegemony	当地的
censure	愤世嫉俗的	hierarchy	霸权
victimize	诽谤	immobilize	义不容辞的
repudiate	多孔的	improvise	即席创作
aspersions	委屈	inconclusive	非决定性的
grievance	雄辩	incumbent	水产的
complaint	突然地	aquatic	以香油涂
eloquence	抱怨	embalm	任期
abruptly	挖洞	indigenous	尖啸声
burrow	批判	scapegoat	使固定
cellular	粒状的	zing	替罪羊
encode	译成电码	tenure	专门研究
granular	责怪某人不当	specialization	等级制度

选词填空

stigmatize	absurd	articulate	denounce	excavate
alleged	idealize	highlight	predicate	reign

1. It seems an _____ idea.
2. Amnesty International _____ the failure by the authorities to take action.
3. The indigenous people often feel _____ by society.
4. He was so drunk that he could barely _____ his words.
5. Their _____ involvement in international terrorism is absurd.
6. Schliemann _____ the ancient city of Troy.
7. Your resume should _____ your skills and achievements.
8. Society continues to _____ the two-parent family.
9. The company's expansion was _____ on the assumption that sales would rise.
10.Pharaohs _____ over Egypt for centuries.

练 习 题 答 案

连线题答案

cynical	愤世嫉俗的	hegemony	霸权
censure	责难	hierarchy	等级制度
victimize	责怪某人不当	immobilize	使固定
repudiate	批判	improvise	即席创作
aspersions	诽谤	inconclusive	非决定性的
grievance	委屈	incumbent	义不容辞的
complaint	抱怨	aquatic	水产的
eloquence	雄辩	embalm	以香油涂
abruptly	突然地	indigenous	当地的
burrow	挖洞	scapegoat	替罪羊
cellular	多孔的	zing	尖啸声
encode	译成电码	tenure	任期
granular	粒状的	specialization	专门研究

选词填空答案

stigmatize	absurd	articulate	denounce	excavate
alleged	idealize	highlight	predicate	reign

1. It seems an（absurd）idea.
2. Amnesty International（denounced）the failure by the authorities to take action.
3. The indigenous people often feel（stigmatized）by society.
4. He was so drunk that he could barely（articulate）his words.
5. Their（alleged）involvement in international terrorism is absurd.
6. Schliemann（excavated）the ancient city of Troy.
7. Your resume should（highlight）your skills and achievements.
8. Society continues to（idealize）the two-parent family.
9. The company's expansion was（predicated）on the assumption that sales would rise.
10.Pharaohs（reigned）over Egypt for centuries.

Word List 38

音频

其他（二）

其他(二)

首 尾

entrée [ˈɑːntreɪ] *n.* 入场权；[美]主菜；(歌剧等)开始的乐章

initial [ɪˈnɪʃl] *adj.* 初始的 (original, beginning, early, oldest)
【记】in(进入) + it(走) + ial → 走进 → 初始的
【例】His *initial* step to start a small business is to do a market research. 【派】initially (*adv.* 开始，最初)

preface [ˈprefəs] *n.* 开端；序言 (an introduction at the beginning of a book or speech)

intermediary [ˌɪntərˈmiːdieri] *adj.* 媒介的 *n.* 媒介物；居间者(mediator)
【记】inter(中间) + medi(中间) + ary → 媒介物
【例】I always play *intermediary* when my sisters quarrel with each other.

intermediate [ˌɪntərˈmiːdiət] *adj.* 中级的，中间的，中等的 *n.* 中级学生 (a student, sports player, etc. who has reached a level of knowledge or skill that is between the basic level and the advanced level)
【例】This book aims at students at the *intermediate* level and above.

medium [ˈmiːdiəm] *n.* 媒介；中间 *adj.* 中等的
【记】medi(中间) + um → 中间；媒介
【例】Advertising is a powerful *medium*.

conclusive [kənˈkluːsɪv] *adj.* 决定性的；最后的(decisive; definitive, final)
【例】The committee didn't reach any *conclusive* decision.

demise [dɪˈmaɪz] *n.* 死亡，终止(death, end)

denouement [ˌdeɪnuːˈmɑːŋ] *n.* (小说的)结尾，结局

destination [ˌdestɪˈneɪʃn] *n.* 目的地，终点

ramification [ˌræmɪfɪˈkeɪʃn] *n.* 结果，后果(result)
【例】an agreement which was to have significant *ramifications* for British politics

repercussion [ˌriːpərˈkʌʃn] *n.* 后果，反响（consequence）

【例】There were serious *repercussions* on his career.

stagnant [ˈstæɡnənt] *adj.* 停滞的，不流动的（not changing or developing）；呆笨的

【例】a government plan to revive the *stagnant* economy

stagnate [ˈstæɡneɪt] *vi.* 停滞，不发展（stop developing）

【例】Growth is expected to *stagnate* next year.

【派】stagnation（*n.* 停滞）

terminate [ˈtɜːrmɪneɪt] *vt.* 终止（end, finish, conclude, stop）

【记】termin（结束）+ ate → 终止

【例】The author *terminated* his contract with the publisher.

【派】termination（*n.* 终止）

sequel [ˈsiːkwəl] *n.* 续集，续篇；继续；结局

terminal [ˈtɜːrmɪnl] *n.* 终点站，终端，航空站 *adj.* 末端的；无可救药的，晚期的（hopeless）

【例】The once great industry is now in *terminal* decline.

【派】terminally（*adv.* 末尾）

物　质

cobble [ˈkɑːbl] *n.* 鹅卵石

emerald [ˈemərəld] *n.* 祖母绿；绿宝石

entity [ˈentəti] *n.* 实际存在物，实体

immaterial [ˌɪməˈtɪriəl] *adj.* 无关紧要的（unimportant）；非实体的，无形的

【例】The body is material but the soul is *immaterial*.

memento [məˈmentoʊ] *n.* 纪念品（souvenir）

milepost [ˈmaɪlpoʊst] *n.* 里程碑，里程标（milestone）

mosaic [moʊˈzeɪɪk] *n.* 镶嵌细工，马赛克

mote [moʊt] *n.* 斑点，尘埃（a very small piece of dust）

notch [nɑːtʃ] *n.* 槽口，凹口，切口

wig [wɪɡ] *n.* 假发（fake hair）

逻　辑

deduce　[dɪ'duːs] *v.* 演绎，推断(to infer, reason out)

【例】On the basis of evidence we *deduced* that he was guilty.

generalize　['dʒenərəlaɪz] *v.* 归纳，概括(summarize, outline)

【例】He *generalized* from the President's speech that the nation is not going to involve in the war.

【派】generalization(*n.* 归纳；一般化，普通化)

inference　['ɪnfərəns] *n.* 推论

【例】What *inferences* have you drawn from this evidence?

【派】inferable(*adj.* 能推理的，能推论的) inferential(*adj.* 据推理得出的)

methodical　[mə'θɑːdɪkl] *adj.* 有条理的(systematic)

【记】method(方法) + ical → 有方法的 → 有条理的

【例】He always checked every detail in a *methodical* way.

【派】methodically(*adv.* 有条不紊地)

plausible　['plɔːzəbl] *adj.* 貌似合理的(reasonable)

【例】Susie's story about how she lost her books sounded *plausible*, but it wasn't actually true.

【派】plausibility[*n.* (论点等)貌似有理]

rational　['ræʃnəl] *adj.* 合理的(reasonable)

【例】Parents need to be fully informed so they can make a *rational* decision.

【派】rationally(*adv.* 理性地) rationality(*n.* 合理性)

rationale　[ˌræʃə'næl] *n.* 理由，逻辑依据，基本原理(reasons)

【例】The *rationale* behind the changes is not at all evident.

unwarranted　[ʌn'wɔːrəntɪd] *adj.* 未经保证的；无根据的(without good reasons)

【例】*unwarranted* interference

主 义

altruism [ˈæltruɪzəm] *n.* 利他主义
【派】altruistic(*adj.* 无私的，利他的) altruist(*n.* 利他主义者)

chauvinism [ˈʃoʊvɪnɪzəm] *n.* 沙文主义

femininity [ˌfeməˈnɪnəti] *n.* 女性特质，柔弱性，温柔

feminist [ˈfemənɪst] *n.* 女权主义者（a person who advocates equal rights for women）

hedonist [ˈhiːdənɪst] *n.* 享乐主义者
【派】hedonism(*n.* 享乐主义)

humanitarian [hjuːˌmænɪˈteriən] *n./adj.* 人道主义者(的)，博爱主义者(的)，慈善家(的)
【例】He was released from prison on *humanitarian* grounds.
【派】humanitarianism(*n.* 人道主义，博爱主义)

Activity is the only road to knowledge.
行动是通往知识的唯一道路。
——英国剧作家 肖伯纳(*George Bernard Shaw, British dramatist*)

练 习 题

连线题

denouement	纪念品	mosaic	终止
destination	续集	inference	推论
entrée	媒介的	plausible	槽口
intermediary	终点站	unwarranted	貌似合理的
intermediate	入场权	altruism	沙文主义
ramification	反响	chauvinism	女性特质
repercussion	停滞的	femininity	利他主义
stagnant	结果	hedonist	未经保证的
sequel	鹅卵石	milepost	享乐主义者
cobble	目的地	notch	里程碑
terminal	祖母绿	mote	马赛克
emerald	中级的	preface	斑点
memento	(小说的)结尾	demise	序言

选词填空

immaterial	rational	methodical	stagnate	deduce
humanitarian	generalize	initial	terminate	conclusive

1. The investigation failed to provide any _____ evidence.
2. His career had _____.
3. The court ruled that the contract must be _____.
4. From her son's age, I _____ that her husband must be at least 60.
5. She has a tendency to _____ from her husband to all men.
6. I'm sure there's a _____ explanation for all this.
7. _____ aid is being sent to the refugees.
8. She's a very _____ person.
9. These are the _____ stages of the disease.
10. If you sign a document, it is wholly _____ whether you have read it carefully or not.

练习题答案

连线题答案

denouement	（小说的）结尾	mosaic	马赛克
destination	目的地	inference	推论
entrée	入场权	plausible	貌似合理的
intermediary	媒介的	unwarranted	未经保证的
intermediate	中级的	altruism	利他主义
ramification	结果	chauvinism	沙文主义
repercussion	反响	femininity	女性特质
stagnant	停滞的	hedonist	享乐主义者
sequel	续集	milepost	里程碑
cobble	鹅卵石	notch	槽口
terminal	终点站	mote	斑点
emerald	祖母绿	preface	序言
memento	纪念品	demise	终止

选词填空答案

immaterial	rational	methodical	stagnate	deduce
humanitarian	generalize	initial	terminate	conclusive

1. The investigation failed to provide any（conclusive）evidence.
2. His career had（stagnated）.
3. The court ruled that the contract must be（terminated）.
4. From her son's age, I（deduced）that her husband must be at least 60.
5. She has a tendency to（generalize）from her husband to all men.
6. I'm sure there's a（rational）explanation for all this.
7. （Humanitarian）aid is being sent to the refugees.
8. She's a very（methodical）person.
9. These are the（initial）stages of the disease.
10. If you sign a document, it is wholly（immaterial）whether you have read it carefully or not.

Word List 39

音频

词　组

词 组

account for 指出…的用途；解释…的原因

【例】He could not *account for* his foolish mistake.

allow for 考虑到，体谅；留出（时间等）

【例】You'd better *allow for* the members voting against you. / *Allow for* time to complete the task.

assembly line 装配线（生产上一环接一环的）

at one stroke 一笔；一举

【例】They intended to devastate the town *at one stroke*.

at stake 存亡攸关，在危险中

be at issue 在争论中，不和的；待裁决的

【例】Her ability *is* not *at issue*—it's her character I'm worried about.

price out of （价格太高而）被排挤出

【例】The photographer *priced* himself *out of* the market and had to change his job.

better off 境况（尤指经济境况）较好的

bring about 产生，导致（lead to, result in）

【例】Gambling had *brought about* his ruin.

call for 要求

【例】The letter *calls for* an investigation of the facts.

center on 集中于，以…为中心

【例】All his attention has *centered on* that experiment.

cling to 坚持，忠于；紧抓，紧附

【例】She *clung to* the hope that her son was not dead.

daylight saving time 夏时制

delve into 深入探究，钻研（to explore, search deeply）

【例】He *delved into* the family archives looking for the facts.

detract from 毁损，贬低，减损（lessen, derogate）

【例】One mistake is not going to *detract from* your achievement.

die out 灭绝，绝种

【例】He is the last of the family; after his death the name of the family will *die out*.

dote on 溺爱，过分喜爱

【例】She *dotes on* her youngest son.

draw in 收(网);(车)靠站;天近黄昏;紧缩开支

【例】The fishermen *drew in* their nets full of fish. / I'm getting short of money. I have to *draw in* my expenditure.

draw on 戴上,穿上;渐渐来临;鼓励,鼓动

【例】Winter is *drawing on*. / Her refusal only *drew* her lover *on*.

embark on 从事,开始做

【例】He is about to *embark on* a new business venture.

fall into a rut 陷入陈规,落入俗套

field study 实地考察

fool around 闲荡;干蠢事(或无用、琐碎的事)

【例】If you go to college, you must work hard, not *fool around*.

gear to 调整(某物)使其适合…

【例】We have to *gear* our lives *to* the new changes.

get by 通过,走过;勉强混过

【例】She never works but somehow she *gets by*.

get through 到达;办完,花光;通过;打通(电话)

give rise to 引起;发生

【例】Unclean conditions *give rise to* disease.

give way to 让位于

【例】We refused to *give way to* their demands.

government intervention 政府干预

hit show 风行一时的演出

in full bloom 花盛开;全盛时期

【例】The flowers in the garden are now *in full bloom*.

in kind 以货代款;以实物(援助等)偿付

【例】Farmers often like to pay their bills *in kind*.

insofar as 在…的限度内,在…的范围内(to the degree that)

【例】The research suggests that the drug will be successful, *insofar as* one can draw conclusions from such a small sample size.

lay off 解雇;关闭;停止活动

【例】The factory has *laid off* workers because of the drop in sales.

live show 现场表演

look to 指望

make(both)ends meet 使收支相抵,量入为出;靠微薄收入为生

more often than not 经常,时常(often)

more than ever 更有甚者；比以往任何时候都…

at odds 争执（disagree）

【例】Briggs found himself *at odds* with his colleagues.

on pain of death （违者）以死论处

other than 除了（except）

【例】The truth was known to no one *other than* herself.

prime-time ratings 黄金时间收视率

prior to 在…之前

prone to 易于…的

pull away 脱身，离开，脱出

【例】She tried to *pull* her hand *away*, but it was held fast.

put away 把…收起来，放好；储存（save）

【例】He *put* his toys *away* every night.

resort to 求助；凭借，诉诸（use）

【例】Officials fear that extremists may *resort to* violence.

rule of thumb 单凭经验来做的方法，比较粗糙的方法

shut off 关掉（煤气等）；切断，使隔绝，脱离

【例】The iron *shuts off* automatically if it gets too hot.

side effect 副作用

【例】*side effect* of the medicine

speak out 大胆地说；清楚并响亮地说

【例】Five people who had *spoken out* against the regime were arrested.

take issue 就某事与某人争论

【例】It is difficult to *take issue* with his analysis.

take issue with somebody 与…争论

【例】I must *take issue with* you over what you said yesterday.

take over 接收，接管，接任

【例】His only reason for investing in the company was to *take* it *over*.

take precedence over 优先于…；地位在…之上

【例】Do we want a society where appearance *takes precedence over* skill or virtue?

the Bering Sea 白令海

the Federal Reserve 美国联邦储备银行（系美国的中央银行）

the Great Lakes 北美五大湖（在美国与加拿大交界处）

the Parthenon （希腊）巴特农神庙

the Warsaw Pact 华沙条约

| Wall Street | 华尔街(美金融业集中之地) |

trade off 交替换位；通过交换抛掉

【例】Companies are under pressure to *trade off* price stability for short-term gains.

trade...in for 以…对换；购买

【例】He *traded* his old car *in for* a new model.

turn down 拒绝，摒弃；把(音量)调低

【例】They offered her the job but she *turned it down*.

bona fides [拉]诚意，真诚(good faith, honest intention)

If you shed tears when you miss the sun, you also miss the stars.

如果你因错过太阳而流泪，那么你也将错过群星。

——印度诗人 泰戈尔(*Ranbindranath Tagore, Indian poet*)

Word List 40

音频

MBA 词汇

MBA词汇

business model [ˈbɪznɪs ˈmɑːdl] 商业模型(一笔生意是否有价值投资、是否能持续赢利,重要的在于商业模型,这几乎是创业课程每天必用的词汇)

【例】In this Internet era, many new *business models* appear. Somehow some of them are not feasible, hence unable to arouse investors' attention. 在互联网时代,出现了很多新的商业模型,但其中一些并不可行,所以不能引起投资者的关注。

core competency [kɔːr ˈkɑːmpɪtənsi] 核心竞争力

competitive advantage [kəmˈpetətɪv ədˈvæntɪdʒ] 竞争优势

【派】competitive edge(竞争优势)

SWOT analysis [swɑːt əˈnæləsɪs] SWOT分析,包含对strength(优势)、weakness(弱点)、opportunity(机会)、threat(挑战)四个方面的分析

cash cow [kæʃ kaʊ] 摇钱树

segment [ˈsegmənt] *n.* 部分 [segˈment] *v.* 分割(segment the market: 这是做市场战略分析常用的一步,就是要分割市场,比如分成高端、低端,等等)

【例】The company dominates this *segment* of the market.

sector [ˈsektər] *n.* 产业;行业(比泛泛地说 industry 要更细一些)

【例】 "Hi, David, which *sector* you would like to work for after this MBA?" "Well, to tell the truth, I will go non-profit. It turned out I am not meant for profit." "嗨,戴维,你拿到MBA后想干哪行啊?" "说实话吧,我想进非营利组织,搞半天我原本就不是赚钱的料。"

subdivision [ˌsʌbdɪˈvɪʒn] *n.* 市场细分(例如:最初人们说计算机市场,后来已经细分到台式机市场、笔记本市场,有时创造一个细分市场能够成全企业的竞争力)

marketing mix [ˈmɑːrkɪtɪŋ mɪks] 销售组合〔常见的销售组合有4P理论,即影响销售的主要有 product(产品)、price(价格)、place(地点)、promotion(促销)〕

direct marketing [dəˈrekt ˈmɑːrkɪtɪŋ] 直接营销(直接将产品销售给使用客户而不通过分销商的市场手段)

Good Friday [ɡʊd ˈfraɪdeɪ] 受难节(纪念耶稣受难的节日,复活节前的星期五)

Easter Sunday [ˈiːstər ˈsʌndeɪ] 复活节(Resurrection Day, 纪念耶稣基督复活

的节日）

Ascension [ə'senʃn] *n.* 升天节（耶稣复活后第四十天升天的节日）

Whit Monday [wɪt 'mʌndeɪ] 圣灵降临节，亦称五旬节（据《圣经·新约全书》载：耶稣复活后第五十天差遣圣灵降临，门徒领受圣灵后开始向世界各地传布福音。教会规定每年复活节后第五十天为圣灵降临节。基督教多数教派不守此节）

Thanksgiving Day [ˌθæŋks'gɪvɪŋ deɪ] 感恩节（4th Thursday in November 十一月的第四个星期四）

Advent ['ædvent] *n.* 降临节（基督耶稣降临的圣诞节当天及包括前四个礼拜天的一段时间）

leverage ['levərɪdʒ] *v.* 利用（to describe how a resource can be applied to a particular environment or situation）

【例】We intend to *leverage* our investment in IT infrastructure across our business units to drive profits.

paradigm ['pærədaɪm] *n.* 范例，样式（an extra fancy word for "model"）

scalable ['skeɪləbl] *adj.* 可攀登的；可升级的（describing how flexible a system is in response to increases in scale）

value proposition ['væljuː ˌprɑːpə'zɪʃn] 价值主张；价值定位（the unique set of benefits that you offer to customers to suck them into buying your products or services）

corporate finance ['kɔːrpərət 'faɪnæns] 公司财务

financial economics [faɪ'nænʃl ˌiːkə'nɑːmɪks] 金融经济学

liquidity [lɪ'kwɪdəti] *n.* 资产折现力，资产流动性

venture capital ['ventʃər 'kæpɪtl] 风险资本

exit ['eksɪt] *n.* 退出（资本一般有指定期限，为了获取风险投资资金所创造的利润，必须出售一部分股票或以某种方式减少持有的股权，这一过程称为"退出"）

Initial Public Offering(IPO) [ɪ'nɪʃl 'pʌblɪk 'ɔːfərɪŋ] 首次发行股票，上市

harvest ['hɑːrvɪst] *n.* 收获（某些风险投资家用这个词来表示"退出"阶段）

institutional investor [ˌɪnstɪ'tuːʃnl ɪn'vestər] 机构投资者（符合法律法规规定可以投资证券投资基金的注册登记或经政府有关部门批准设立的机构）

multiple ['mʌltɪpl] *n.* 倍数（指收益达到投资组合公司售价所翻的倍数）

Portfolio Company [pɔːrt'foʊlioʊ 'kʌmpəni] 投资组合公司

upside ['ʌpsaɪd] *n.* 资本升值（投资组合公司在资本清算时比资本投入时价值的增加）

acquisition [ˌækwɪˈzɪʃn] *n.* 收购

Advisory Board [ədˈvaɪzəri bɔːrd] 咨询部；顾问委员会

benchmark [ˈbentʃmɑːrk] *n.* 基准 (a standard measure used to assess the performance of a company)

burn rate [bɜːrn reɪt] 资金消耗率 (the rate at which a start-up uses its venture capital funding before it begins earning any revenue)

debt financing [det faɪˈnænsɪŋ] 债权融资 (是有偿使用企业外部资金的一种融资方式，包括银行贷款、银行短期融资、企业短期融资券、企业债券等等)

due diligence [duː ˈdɪlɪdʒəns] 尽职调查，审慎调查 (指投资人在与目标企业达成初步合作意向后，经协商一致，投资人对目标企业一切与本次投资有关的事项进行现场调查、资料分析的一系列活动)

equity financing [ˈekwəti faɪˈnænsɪŋ] 股权融资 (一种融资方式，包括发行股票、配股、债转股等)

holding period [ˈhoʊldɪŋ ˈpɪriəd] 持有期 (持有股票的期间)

incubator [ˈɪŋkjubeitər] *n.* 孵化器 (an entity designed to nurture business ideas or new technologies to the point that they become attractive to venture capitalists)

internal rate of return (IRR) [ɪnˈtɜːrnl reɪt əv rɪˈtɜːrn] 内涵报酬率 (指能够使未来现金流入量现值等于未来现金流出量现值的折现率，或者说是使投资方案净现值为零的折现率)

leveraged buy-out (LBO) [ˈlevərɪdʒd ˈbaɪaʊt] 杠杆收购 (指公司或个体利用自己的资产作为债务抵押，收购另一家公司的策略)

management buy-in (MBI) [ˈmænɪdʒmənt ˈbaɪɪn] 外部管理层收购 (当管理团队从外部收购一家公司并拥有多数股时，很可能需要私募股权融资。如果内部管理层缺乏从内部"收购"公司的经验或资金，就可能出现外部管理团队收购。有时也可能是因为继承问题，比如家族企业中可能没有人能接管公司。外部管理团队收购要比管理层收购多担一点风险，因为新的管理团队对公司的运作方式不熟悉)

management buy-out (MBO) [ˈmænɪdʒmənt ˈbaɪaʊt] 管理层收购 (公司的经理层利用借贷所融资本或股权交易收购本公司的一种行为，从而引起公司所有权、控制权、剩余索取权、资产等变化，以改变公司所有制结构)

private equity [ˈpraɪvət ˈekwəti] 私募股本；非上市股本 (the holding of stock in unlisted companies)

term sheet [tɜːrm ʃiːt] 条款书 (a summary sheet detailing the terms and conditions of an investment opportunity)

turnaround ['tɜːrnəraʊnd] *n.* 重振（Turnaround finance is provided to a company that is experiencing severe financial difficulties. The aim is to provide enough capital to bring a company back from the brink of collapse.）

entrepreneurship [ˌɑːntrəprə'nɜːrʃɪp] *n.* 创业；工商企业家的身份等
【派】entrepreneur(*n.* 企业家)

human resources management ['hjuːmən 'riːsɔːrsəs 'mænɪdʒmənt] 人力资源管理

marketing management ['mɑːrkɪtɪŋ 'mænɪdʒmənt] 市场管理

strategic marketing [strə'tiːdʒɪk 'mɑːrkɪtɪŋ] 战略营销

manufacturing and production [ˌmænju'fæktʃərɪŋ ənd prə'dʌkʃn] 生产与制造

operations management [ˌɑːpə'reɪʃns 'mænɪdʒmənt] 运营管理

statistics [stə'tɪstɪks] *n.* 统计学

technology and information systems [tek'nɑːlədʒi ənd ˌɪnfər'meɪʃn 'sɪstəmz] 技术与信息系统

management information system(MIS) ['mænɪdʒmənt ˌɪnfər'meɪʃn 'sɪstəm] 管理信息系统

microeconomics [ˌmaɪkroʊˌekə'nɑːmɪks] *n.* 微观经济学

macroeconomics [ˌmækroʊˌekə'nɑːmɪks] *n.* 宏观经济学

promotion [prə'moʊʃn] *n.* 届，期，入学、晋级的年度；同届学生；同年升级者

intake ['ɪnteɪk] *n.* 届；(学校等人员)收纳容量
【例】an *intake* of around 120 students each year

track [træk] *vt.* [美] 把学生按能力分组(to put schoolchildren in groups according to their ability)

curriculum [kə'rɪkjələm] *n.* 课程(subjects)
【例】Languages are an essential part of the school *curriculum*.

obligatory [ə'blɪgətɔːri] *adj.* 必修的(compulsory)
【例】Attendance is *obligatory*.

mandatory ['mændətɔːri] *adj.* 必修的；强制的(compulsory)
【例】The Council has made it *mandatory* for all nurses to attend a refresher course every three years.

optional ['ɑːpʃənl] *adj.* 选修的(selectable)
【例】three *optional* courses

elective [ɪ'lektɪv] *n.* 选修(course that students can choose to take)

lecture ['lektʃər] *n.* 讲座(speech)

workshop ['wɜːrkʃɑːp] *n.* 工作室(studio)

seminar ['seminɑːr] *n.* 研讨会 (class on a particular subject)

【例】Publishers and writers from 13 countries attended the *seminar*.

economic value added (EVA) [ˌekə'nɑːmɪk 'vælju: 'ædɪd] 经济价值增值 (又称经济利润、经济增加值，是一定时期的企业税后营业净利润与投入资本的资金成本的差额)

return on investment (ROI) [rɪ'tɜːrn ɑːn ɪn'vestmənt] 投资回报率 (是指通过投资而应返回的价值，企业从一项投资性商业活动的投资中得到的经济回报)

price to equity (PE) [praɪs tu 'ekwəti] 资产

balance sheet ['bæləns ʃiːt] 平衡表 (又称资产负债表、财产状况表，表示企业在一定日期的财务状况的主要会计报表)

profit and loss ['prɑːfɪt ənd lɑːs] 损益表 (表示公司经营业绩和各项交易与事项产生的损益)

cash flow chart [kæʃ floʊ tʃɑːrt] 现金流量表 (表示各现金流入、流出与相应时间的对应关系)

working capital ['wɜːrkɪŋ 'kæpɪtl] 运营资本 (又称运营资金，是指流动资产与流动负债的净额)

sustainable development [sə'steɪnəbl dɪ'veləpmənt] 可持续发展

【例】environmentally *sustainable development*

mergers and acquisitions ['mɜːrdʒərz ənd ˌækwɪ'zɪʃns] 兼并与收购

【例】jobs losses as a result of *mergers and acquisitions*

small and medium enterprise (SME) [smɔːl ənd 'miːdiəm 'entərpraɪz] 中小型企业

shareholder ['ʃerhoʊldər] *n.* 股东 (someone who owns shares in a company or business)

【例】*Shareholders* have been told to expect an even lower result next year.

stakeholder ['steɪkhoʊldər] *n.* 利益相关者 (ones affected)

【例】Citizens should be *stakeholders* in the society they live in.

orientation [ˌɔːriən'teɪʃn] *n.* 适应期 (a period of time during which people are trained and prepared for a new job or course of study)

【例】This is *orientation* week for all the new students.

social security number ['soʊʃl sə'kjʊrəti 'nʌmbər] 社会保障号

【例】You need a *social security number* to get a job, collect social security benefits and receive some other government services.

insurance [ɪn'ʃʊrəns] *n.* 保险

【例】Do you have *insurance* on your house and its contents?

medical care [ˈmedɪkl ker] 医疗保险

【例】welfare system of *medical care*

lease a car 长租一辆车(短租常用 rent, 长期, 如一年, 一般用lease)

babyfoot [ˈbeɪbɪfʊt] *n.* 桌面迷你足球(很多老外乐此不疲)

tournament [ˈtʊrnəmənt] *n.* 大赛(competition)

【例】I feel I can win this *tournament*.

barrier to entry [ˈbæriər tu ˈentri] 进入壁垒(是影响市场结构的重要因素, 指产业内既存企业对于潜在进入企业和刚刚进入这个产业的新企业所具有的某种优势的程度)

capital stock [ˈkæpɪtl stɑːk] 股本(股东在公司中所占的权益, 多用于指股票。股本=股票面值*股份总额)

demand curve [dɪ ˈmænd kɜːrv] 需求曲线(是显示价格与需求量关系的曲线, 是指其他条件相同时, 在每一价格水平上买主愿意购买的商品量的表或曲线)

division of labor [dɪ ˈvɪʒn əv ˈleɪbər] 劳动分工(是指人们社会经济活动的划分和独立化、专门化, 又称specialization of labor)

economic agent [ˌekə ˈnɑːmɪk ˈeɪdʒənt] 经济主体(指在市场经济活动中能够自主设计行为目标、自由选择行为方式、独立负责行为后果并获得经济利益的能动的经济有机体)

economic efficiency [ˌekə ˈnɑːmɪk ɪ ˈfɪʃnsi] 经济效率(situation in which it is impossible to generate a larger welfare total from the available resources)

economies of scale [ɪ ˈkɑːnəmɪs əv skeɪl] 规模经济(是指在一定的产量范围内, 随着产量的增加, 平均成本不断降低的事实)

exclusion principle [ɪk ˈskluːʒn ˈprɪnsəpl] 排他性原则

equilibrium [ˌiːkwɪ ˈlɪbriəm] *n.* 平衡

【例】The government is anxious not to upset the economic *equilibrium*.

game theory [geɪm ˈθiːəri] 对策论, 博弈论(又称赛局理论, 是研究具有斗争或竞争性质现象的理论和方法)

government regulation [ˈɡʌvərnmənt ˌreɡju ˈleɪʃn] 政府调控

invisible hand [ɪn ˈvɪzəbl hænd] 看不见的手(资本主义完全竞争模式的形象用语)

marginal benefit [ˈmɑːrdʒɪnl ˈbenɪfɪt] 边际收益(increase or decrease in an activity's overall benefit caused by a unit increase or decrease in the level of that activity, all other factors remaining constant)

marginal cost(MC) [ˈmɑːrdʒɪnl kɔːst] 边际成本(是指厂商每增加一单位产量所增加的成本)

marginal social benefit(MSB) ['mɑːrdʒɪnl 'souʃl 'benɪfɪt] 社会边际收益(指人们对某种物品或服务的消费量每增加一个单位所增加的满意程度)

market economy ['mɑːrkɪt ɪ'kɑːnəmi] 市场经济(又称为自由市场经济或自由企业经济。是一种经济体系,在这种体系下产品和服务的生产及销售完全由自由市场的自由价格机制所引导)

market mechanism ['mɑːrkɪt 'mekənɪzəm] 市场机制(即市场运行的实现机制。作为一种经济运行机制,是指市场机制体内的供求、价格、竞争、风险等要素之间互相联系及作用机理)

market share ['mɑːrkɪt ʃer] 市场份额(指一个企业的销售量或销售额在市场同类产品中所占的比重)

natural monopoly ['nætʃrəl mə'nɑːpəli] 自然垄断(经济学中的一个传统概念。早期的自然垄断概念与资源条件的集中有关,主要是指由于资源条件的分布集中而无法竞争或不适宜竞争所形成的垄断。现在已经不多见)

necessity [nə'sesəti] *n.* 必需品
【例】She saw books as a *necessity*, not a luxury.

oligopoly [ˌɑːlɪ'gɑːpəli] *n.* 寡头垄断(又称寡头、寡占,一种由少数卖方主导市场的市场状态)

oligopoly market [ˌɑːlɪ'gɑːpəli 'mɑːrkɪt] 寡头市场(是介于垄断竞争与完全垄断之间的一种比较现实的混合市场,是指少数几个企业控制整个市场的生产和销售的市场结构)

optimal resource allocation ['ɑːptɪməl 'riːsɔːrs ˌælə'keɪʃn] 最佳资源配置

perfect competition ['pɜːrfɪkt ˌkɑːmpə'tɪʃn] 完全竞争(是一种不受任何阻碍和干扰的市场结构,指那些不存在足以影响价格的企业或消费者的市场。是经济学中理想的市场竞争状态,也是几个典型的市场形式之一)

perfect monopoly ['pɜːrfɪkt mə'nɑːpəli] 完全垄断(又称独家垄断,是整个行业的市场供给完全为独家企业所控制的状态。可分为完全政府垄断和完全私人垄断)

present value ['preznt 'væljuː] 现值(又称未来现金流转贴现值)

property rights ['prɑːpərti raɪts] 产权(财产所有权及与财产所有权有关的财产权)

profit maximization ['prɑːfɪt ˌmæksɪmə'zeɪʃn] 利润最大化

subsidize ['sʌbsɪdaɪz] *vt.* 给…补贴
【例】Farming is heavily *subsidized* by the government.
【派】subsidy(*n.* 补贴) subsidization(*n.* 补助)

symmetry of information [ˈsɪmətri əv ˌɪnfərˈmeɪʃn] 信息对称（指在某种相互对应的经济关系中，对应的双方都掌握有对方所具备的信息，了解对方所具有的知识和所处的环境）

technical constraints [ˈteknɪkl kənˈstreɪnts] 技术限制

transaction costs [trænˈzækʃn kɔːsts] 交易成本（又称交易费用）

value judge [ˈvæljuː dʒʌdʒ] 价值判断（subjective assessment that a behavior, object, person, principle, etc., is good or bad or something is ought to or not ought to happen）

welfare maximization [ˈwelfer ˌmæksɪməˈzeɪʃn] 福利最大化

The people who get on in this world are the people who get up and look for circumstances they want, and if they cannot find them, they make them.

在这个世界上，取得成功的人是那些努力寻找他们想要机会的人，如果找不到机会，他们就去创造机会。

——英国剧作家 肖伯纳（*George Bernard Shaw, British dramatist*）

索 引

check / 288
chef / 94
chemical / 35
chirp / 340
chisel / 92
chocolate / 103
cholesterol / 35
chord / 5
chordate / 74
choreography / 82
chromosome / 74
chronic / 168
chronicle / 108
chronology / 108
cinder / 37
circulation / 266
circumscribe / 242
circumvent / 208
civic / 109
civil / 109
civilization / 110
clam / 103
clan / 116
clarify / 131
classify / 243
clause / 68
clavicle / 74
clay / 59
clerical / 94
cliché / 166
climatology / 84
cling to / 366
clinical / 26
cluster / 168
coalesce / 279
cobble / 359
cocaine / 35
cocoa / 35
coefficient / 5
coexist / 297
cogent / 141
coherent / 168
coincide / 136
collaborate / 297
collapse / 306
collar / 254
collateral / 22
collide / 137
colorize / 190

combustible / 223
comedian / 94
comet / 82
commercial / 18
commission / 110
commitment / 245
committee / 110
common divisor / 5
commonplace / 127
commuter / 102
compact / 170
comparable / 160
comparative / 160
compatible / 160
compatriot / 110
compendium / 108
compensate / 243
competent / 343
competitive advantage / 372
compile / 211
complacent / 333
complaint / 349
complement / 160
complementary / 160
complex / 171
complexity / 171
comply / 240
component / 92
composite number / 5
composition / 70
compound / 35
compound interest / 18
comprehend / 251
compress / 211
compromise / 240
compulsory / 244
conceal / 292
concede / 245
conceive / 245
concentric / 5
concentric circle / 5
conceptual / 85
concert / 83
concerto / 83
conclusive / 358
concrete / 85
concurrent / 160
condense / 212
conditional / 296

condor / 42
conductive / 50
cone / 5
confer / 241
configuration / 178
confine / 242
confirm / 281
conform / 240
confront / 291
confuse / 292
congested / 100
conglomerate / 279
congregation / 110
congress / 110
congruent / 5
conjunction / 68
connive / 230
connote / 292
conquer / 290
conscientious / 317
conscious / 250
consecutive integer / 5
consensus / 136
consequence / 176
conserve / 296
consistent / 136
consolidate / 201
consortium / 18
conspire / 251
constant / 169
constituent / 92
constitute / 192
constraint / 242
consultant / 94
consume / 22
contagious / 257
container / 102
contaminate / 148
contemplate / 252
contemporary / 111
contend / 278
contentious / 278
context / 108
contiguous / 159
contingent / 129
continuation / 169
continuous / 169
contour / 178
contraction / 108

386

ethnocentric / 112
ethnographic / 112
ethnology / 112
ethnomusicology / 83
ethylene / 35
etymology / 68
euphoria / 146
Eurasian / 59
evacuate / 302
evaluate / 286
evaporate / 221
even number / 5
eventual / 179
evict / 306
evolutionary / 350
exacerbate / 201
exaggerate / 182
excavate / 350
excavation / 350
exceed / 256
exception / 189
exceptional / 320
excerpt / 219
excessive / 182
excise / 309
exclusion principle / 377
exclusionary / 130
excrete / 342
excursion / 342
executioner / 94
exemplify / 300
exempt / 275
exhale / 222
exhaust / 150
exhaustive / 182
exile / 306
exit / 373
exodus / 156
exonerate / 275
exorbitant / 182
exorcism / 306
exotic / 127
expand / 202
expatriate / 234
expectation / 210
expedient / 137
expedite / 202
expedition / 342
expenditure / 288

experimental / 231
expertise / 231
explicate / 300
explicit / 131
exploit / 288
exposure / 255
expound / 300
expressly / 131
expulsion / 306
extant / 350
extensive / 188
extent / 188
exterior / 178
exterminate / 140
external / 189
extinct / 140
extinction / 140
extinguish / 141
extract / 307
extraction / 307
extracurricular / 230
extrapolate / 211
extraterrestrial / 127
extremely / 182
extricate / 286
extrinsic / 189
fabricate / 262
facilitate / 287
faction / 111
factor / 5
factorial / 6
factual / 167
fade / 340
fake / 329
fall into a rut / 367
fallacy / 219
falsity / 329
familiarity / 229
familiarize / 229
famine / 138
fanatic / 316
far-reaching / 176
fatal / 176
fatality / 176
fatigue / 150
fault / 219
fauna / 42
feasible / 287
feat / 350

fecundity / 157
federal / 111
femininity / 361
feminist / 361
fertile / 157
fertilizer / 53
fervent / 316
fetal / 74
feudal / 351
fiberglass / 102
fiction / 70
fictitious / 329
field study / 367
figurative / 68
filtration / 252
finale / 83
financial crash / 18
financial economics / 373
fiscal / 19
fissure / 213
flawed / 219
fledgling / 42
flexible / 51
flora / 58
florid / 318
fluctuate / 203
fluorescent / 222
foe / 130
foliage / 58
fool around / 367
forage / 58
forebear / 116
forecast / 210
foresee / 210
foreshorten / 83
forestall / 289
forge / 262
formaldehyde / 35
formation / 192
formidable / 149
formula / 6
fortify / 201
fortress / 75
fossil / 74
foster / 245
foul / 344
fraction / 6
fracture / 212
fragile / 214

388

insecticide / 35
insertion / 307
insight / 118
insofar as / 367
insomnia / 27
inspection / 310
inspiration / 210
installation / 277
instantaneous / 180
instill / 220
institutional investor / 373
instrument / 83
insulate / 234
insulin / 27
insurance / 102
insurance / 376
intact / 183
intake / 277
intake / 375
intangible / 342
integer / 6
integral / 162
integrate / 277
intense / 141
intensify / 201
intent / 317
intention / 119
intercept / 309
interdependence / 297
interest rate / 19
interfere / 242
interior / 189
interloper / 290
intermediary / 358
intermediate / 358
intermingled / 136
intermittent / 170
internal rate of return(IRR) / 374
interplay / 297
interpretive / 300
interracial / 112
interrelate / 297
interrogate / 341
intersect / 309
intersperse / 253
interstate / 190
interval / 268
intervene / 243
intestine / 27

intimate / 181
intolerable / 269
intracellular / 58
intricate / 171
intrigue / 251
intrinsic / 158
intrusion / 290
intuition / 250
inundate / 220
invalid / 320
invalidate / 320
invariable / 204
invariant / 6
inventory / 19
inverse / 128
invert / 264
invertebrate / 42
investigate / 66
investment / 19
invigorate / 19
invisible / 341
invisible hand / 377
invoke / 280
ion / 51
irate / 150
ironic / 348
irradiate / 223
irrational / 323
irreconcilable / 138
irrelevant / 162
irrigate / 220
irritant / 27
Islam / 76
isolation / 235
isosceles / 6
isosceles triangle / 6
isotope / 51
jar / 265
jeopardize / 140
jettison / 254
jog / 118
jolt / 118
judgment / 66
judicious / 322
jumbo / 190
jurisdiction / 66
justify / 66
juvenile / 111
keynesian / 19

kidnap / 339
kidney / 27
kinship / 116
lactation / 42
laissez-faire capitalism / 19
lamellar / 193
landfill / 148
larva / 42
laser / 51
latch / 92
lateral / 189
latitude / 59
laudable / 310
laudatory / 310
launder / 221
laurel / 58
lawsuit / 66
lay off / 367
leakage / 221
lease / 170
lease a car / 377
leaven / 42
lecture / 375
leeway / 59
leg / 6
legacy / 66
legislature / 66
legitimate / 66
length / 6
lepidopter / 42
lethal / 331
letup / 268
leverage / 51
leverage / 373
leveraged buy-out(LBO) / 374
levy / 75
liability / 66
liberalize / 296
lien / 66
liken / 137
limestone / 59
lineage / 116
lingo / 69
linguistics / 69
linkage / 162
lionize / 256
liquidation / 243
liquidity / 373
list price / 19

390